145 Things to Be When You Grow Up

145 THINGS TO BE
WHEN YOU GROW UP

JODI WEISS AND RUSSELL KAHN

RANDOM HOUSE, INC.

NEW YORK

WWW.PRINCETONREVIEW.COM

Princeton Review Publishing, L. L. C.
2315 Broadway
New York, NY 10024
Email: bookeditor@review.com

ISBN 0-375-76369-4
ISSN 1015-8675

Editorial Director: Robert Franek
Editor: Erica Magrey
Designer: Scott Harris
Production Editor: Vivian Gomez
Production Coordinator: Scott Harris

2004 Edition

ACKNOWLEDGMENTS

The authors would like to thank the talented and dedicated staff of The Princeton Review, including their indefatigable editor, Erica Magrey. Thanks also to Erik Olson, Lisa Marie Rovito, Scott Harris, and Vivian Gomez for their terrific editorial and production work on the project. Their devotion to this book was apparent on every late night.

As we wrote this book, we had the pleasure of meeting and talking to a great many creative, interesting, and inspiring people. Our warmest thanks go out to each of you for taking time out of your busy schedules to fill us in on what you do.

Russell Kahn would like to thank his brother, Jordan, for explaining the ins and outs (and ups and downs) of being a lawyer *and* an environmentalist. His thanks also go to Beth Cornwell (soon to be Beth Kahn) for her inspired view of teaching—and everything else.

Russell would like to acknowledge Mayor Natalie Rogers for providing an eye-opening look at the wild world of politics. Thanks to Adam Weintraub, Justin Riservato, Max Cascone, Orf, Jill Sherman, Kenneth de Anda, David Plevan, J.P. and Chad Harries, Justin Bass, Gabe Miller, D. Marcus Arm, Mike Thomas, Sam Globus, and Robert Elstein for sharing the passions of their respective professions and for being such incredible friends.

Further thanks go to the fabulous filmmakers Andy and Arlene Sidaris, hip historian Kai Bird, professional paleontologist Sunny Hwang, amazing archaeologist Sarah Jackson, very cool video game producer Daniel Suarez, super ski instructor Matt Gorman, and awesome auctioneer Jamie Krass.

Finally, his thanks go to Mom and Dad, for giving their sons the chance to be whatever they wanted to be . . .

Jodi Weiss would like to send special thanks to Andrew Weiss, Arthur Flatto, Aviva Kamander, Barrie Huberman, Christiane Bennet, Daniel McBride, David Linker, Donna Puzio, Evan Slamka, Gina Brooke, Julie Dahlen, Max Peters, Michele Arcand, Michele Toth, Nicole Brooke, Dr. Paul Friedman, Rita Comisky, Rocco Seccafico, and Rosemary Vargas for always being there to answer her career-related questions (or point her in the right direction), and for being such great friends.

Her thanks also go to Alyssa Zahorcak, Brother Wayne, Gary Goldsneider, Dr. George L. Cameron, Gladys Kartin, Dr. Ivan Damjanov, James Flatto, John Devito, Dr. Kenny Dobbins, Professor Lee K. Abbott, Luis Berrios, Pamela Shannon, Pastor Demetrius, Paul Nison, Pauline Raiff, and Tony Traguado for sharing insights into their careers. Jodi's sincere thanks also go to Russell Kahn for inspiring her to come on board with this project.

Finally, Jodi would like to extend her warmest thanks to Mom & Dad Weiss and to Art Flatto for reminding her daily that the most challenging yet most beneficial job in life is that of being true to oneself.

CONTENTS

INTRODUCTION

So you want to be a rock star . . . or a dancer, or a doctor, or a scientist, or a magician. But what exactly do these people really do all day anyway? For example, did you know that crocodile hunting is a real career? It's true. And it doesn't involve killing crocs or hosting your own TV show, either.

The goal of this book is to give you some information about what each job requires, what you can expect, and how to get there. The career profiles include everything from accountant to zookeeper and explain what people in these fields do, why their work is important, and whether they'll be rich. Oh, and being *rich* doesn't always refer to making a lot of money.

Think of this book as your career bible, your private advisor, or just a cool book to browse through. Use it as a resource when you meet someone who has a job you never heard of—an *Ayurvedic what*?—or if you think you might know what you want to be. The sooner you know what to expect down the road, the sooner you can get started in the right direction. And since it's important to have fun along the way, the book contains interesting facts about each career. Did you know, for instance, that you *and* your pet can be taste testers?

Is It Behind Door #1 or Door #2?

There are tons of different careers to choose from. It seems that as soon as you're able to talk, people ask, "What do you want to be when you grow up?" It's a question that can follow you around like a shadow. While some people have a quick response, others haven't got a clue. It doesn't matter which type of person you are. This book can help you figure out what to do—and how to do it— whether you are totally clueless or have your whole future already planned out.

We're going to help you figure out what might be best for you. But first, there's something important that you should know: *You don't have to pick one career and stick with it for the rest of your life.*

You can actually have many careers in your lifetime. It's never too late to learn something new. You can even go back to school and get another degree. You can learn something in one career that will be helpful in another career later on. It's all about being open to new possibilities every step of the way. So if what you're looking for isn't behind door #1 or door #2, try door #3 (or #4 or #5 or #6 . . .).

Okay, But Do I Have to Decide on a Career *Now*?

Not at all. Many people don't know what their major will be when they start college. And a lot of students who thought they knew what they wanted to do end up changing their majors—sometimes more than once. That's totally okay. The purpose of this book is to open your eyes to many of the possibilities that exist and give you an idea of what to expect down each career path. There's no pressure to make a decision, so you can just relax and explore.

Of course, there are some advantages to thinking about this stuff early on. You can use your time in the classroom, in extracurricular activities, and outside of school to develop more knowledge in the areas that interest you most. If you're really passionate about a certain career, you can get a head start by joining clubs and getting some real hands-on experience through part-time jobs, volunteer work, or internships. And if you decide that you don't enjoy it, well—it's better that you find out sooner than later. So try on some different hats, and see what fits.

I Like to Do Lots of Stuff. How Do I Figure Out What I Want to Do?

It's not easy to know what you want to do in life, let alone know how to actually reach your goal. While you're reading through the career profiles in this book, consider your answers to the following questions:

- *What job will help me be myself?*

- *What job will enable me to incorporate my interests, values, and skills?*

First, consider your **interests.** What do you like to do? How do you like to spend your time away from school? What types of books do you like to read? Do you like to build things, draw pictures, or work with numbers? Do you love to act in school plays or have debates with your friends? Only you know what really interests you!

Next, consider what you **value** in life. Do you like to be in charge, or do you prefer to have someone else guide you? Do you like to be creative? Do you like to take it easy, or work really hard? Do you like a lot of variety in your life, or do you like routines? What's more important to you: the amount of money you make or the amount of joy your work brings to others? There's no right or wrong answer, so be honest with yourself.

What about your **skills?** What are you really great at? Are you a math whiz or a super athlete? Do you get good grades in science? Do you put puzzles and models together faster than most people can get them out of a box? When you talk in front of a group, does the audience hang on your every word?

Whenever you come across a career profile that interests you, ask yourself if it fits in with your interests, values, and skills. Is it a job that you would enjoy doing all day? Is it a job that suits your values? Will you have the chance to use your strongest talents and skills on the job?

Check out some of the lists below for a sample of how your interests, skills, and values can lead you to a career. And keep an open mind!

Jobs for People Who . . .

. . . like adventure: Astronaut, cowboy/cowgirl, race car driver, detective, FBI agent, special agent, police officer, firefighter, athlete, paramedic, pilot, stunt double, rock star

. . . like to work with their hands: Artist, athlete, massage therapist, auto mechanic, carpenter, construction worker, doctor, chef, hairdresser, makeup artist, florist, costume designer, music conductor, plumber

. . . are superorganized: Wedding planner, publicist, historian, librarian, administrative assistant, homemaker, lawyer, postal worker, travel agent, stockbroker, banker

. . . like to lead: Politician, college president, college dean, military personnel, clergy member, principal, professor, teacher

. . . don't want to work in an office: Rock star, musician, dancer, choreographer, actor, artist, cowboy/cowgirl, florist, makeup artist, sailor, tour guide, waiter/waitress, professor, military personnel, filmmaker, ski or snowboard instructor, athlete

. . . like to work with numbers: Accountant, auctioneer, banker, financial analyst, mathematician, stock broker, test developer, computer programmer, professional gambler

. . . like animals and nature: Environmentalist, scientist, zookeeper, park ranger, veterinarian, crocodile hunter, farmer, fisherman, ski or snowboard instructor, cowboy/cowgirl

. . . like to help other people: Teacher, professor, special education teacher, social worker, occupational therapist, speech therapist, guidance counselor, clergy member, firefighter, police officer, doctor, nurse, paramedic, nutritionist

. . . like to gaze up into the sky: Pilot, flight attendant, astronaut, scientist, astrologer

Something For Everyone

No matter what you like to do or what you're good at, there's a job out there for you. You just have to know where to find it. There will be many chances along the road to challenge you and give you the chance to develop your skills. For more information about how to get the most out of your experiences, read on.

RIGHT HERE, RIGHT NOW

You're still quite a few years away from working full-time. So take a look at where you are right now—in school, looking toward the future. Before you get to your dream job, you may have a number of hurdles ahead of you, from technical school to college or graduate school. But there are things you can do at this very moment that can get the ball rolling. Earlier, we mentioned that in high school, you'll have the opportunity to join clubs, work part-time, or volunteer to learn more about a career.

I'm Already Superbusy. Now I Have to Join a Club, Get a Job, or Volunteer?

Absolutely not. And if you're already busy, you're probably gaining skills that will help you for your future. But if you do have some free time after school and you're really passionate about a subject, consider joining a club or organization. You will meet other folks who share your interests. You may participate in activities that you wouldn't normally get to do during the school day. There are all sorts of clubs, so check out what your school and your community have to offer. If your school doesn't offer a club that suits your interests, consider starting up a club. A teacher can usually help you make it happen.

Volunteering can help you decide if a career is right for you. If you want to be a nurse or a doctor, for example, volunteering at a health care facility or a hospital can help you discover what it's like to work with sick patients. While you won't earn any money as a volunteer, you will learn a great deal.

A part-time job after school or in the summer is a great way to earn money, gain confidence, and experience what it's like to hold a job. If you can get a job that's related to your career goals, great! If not, that's okay. You'll learn a lot from any job—whether you get a part-time job selling popcorn at a movie theater or delivering newspapers. Being responsible, working well with others, and taking pride in what you do are traits that people in every career need. You can work from one hour to over twenty hours per week, depending on how old you are and what your state allows. Just make sure that your part-time job doesn't take away from your full-time job—school.

Will I use anything I learn in high school when I'm working?

Believe it or not, what you will do in your job has a lot in common with what you learn in high school. For instance, you will need to be on time to your job, just as you need to be on time to class. Many jobs require you to communicate by speaking and writing, just like you do in front of the class and in your reports. In fact, spelling, grammar, reading comprehension, and basic math skills are necessary for succeeding in almost any job. In addition, turning in papers on time, taking tests, and interacting with fellow students will prepare you to meet deadlines, remain calm under pressure, and work well with others.

THE ROAD AHEAD

After high school graduation, your path may split off from the paths of your classmates. If you have a career in mind at this point, it will help you decide what direction to head off in; if not, college may help you decide what you'd like to do. Along the way, you'll pick up the knowledge and skills you need from your education and experience. This may include college, graduate or professional school, vocational school, and/or internships.

College—More School?

Sure, college means more school, and more school means studying and tests and papers. But college is also a great opportunity to try new things, meet new people, and explore different routes. Most colleges require you to take core (or foundation) classes. Core classes introduce you to subjects that you may not have even known you were interested in. You will also need to choose a major in college. You'll take many classes that relate to your major, so you'll know a lot about the subject when you graduate. You may also choose a minor to learn a lot about another specific subject.

The more you put into college, the more you will get out of it. Join clubs, get a part-time job, and find out what internships are available from your college career office or your dean. College is a great place to network or meet like-minded people who share your interests and goals. You can also use your time in college to prepare for life after college. If you want to be a writer, write for your college newspaper or literary journal. To become a disc jockey, work for your college radio station. And if you want to be an actor, perform in college plays.

Graduate and Professional School

Graduate school allows you to focus on the stuff you're really interested in. This means that if you are in graduate school for chemistry, all your classes will revolve around chemistry. There are different types of graduate and professional schools, including law school, medical school, and business school. Degrees from graduate and professional schools are required to pursue some careers; doctors and lawyers, for instance, need graduate degrees in order to work. You may need to go to school for an additional two to seven years, depending on the degree you want to pursue and on whether you attend school part- or full-time.

Vocational and Technical Schools—What Are Those All About?

Technical and vocational schools offer training for many different careers. Auto mechanics, computer technicians, chefs, massage therapists, and yoga teachers are just some of the people who go to vocational and technical schools to learn how to do their jobs. Some people go to vocational and technical schools straight out of high school; others go after college or when they decide to switch from one career to another. Vocational and technical schools usually supply classroom training as well as hands-on training, and the programs can last anywhere from a few weeks to over a year.

I've Heard of Internships, but I'm Not Sure What They're All About.

An internship is a chance to test-drive a career. You work for a company (usually for no pay) and have a chance to gain experience in the field. Most internships are offered to college students or college graduates, and you can often earn college credits for participating in an internship program. If you do a good job, your internship may even lead to a full-time job offer. Check with the career center at your school for more information about internships.

HIRED

So now you know about the different ways you can prepare to work as a professional in your chosen career. But what's going to happen when you get there? It seems pretty foggy from here, right? Allow us to provide a little glimpse into the world of careers.

First of All, What Exactly *Is* a Career?

A career is a profession, a calling, a job, a way of life, or a way to earn a living—depending on whom you ask. The truth is that a career is all of those things and usually more, too. For some people, a career is both their greatest challenge and their utmost passion; for others, it is simply a way to support themselves and their families. In an ideal situation, you will truly enjoy the work you do on a daily basis. Your feelings toward a career may even evolve over time—the right career for you at one point in your life may not be right for you at another time. And if you outgrow one career, you can always pursue a new one.

What's Working Life Like?

It all depends on what you do. If you're a doctor, for instance, you will spend a lot of your time meeting with patients, examining them, and updating medical charts. If you are a chef, you will spend a lot of your time in a kitchen preparing meals. You can work in your home, a nightclub, an office building, a school, or on a playing field. You can work for a huge company, a tiny company, a government agency, or your living room. You may need to wear a suit to work each day, or you may get to go to work in jeans and a T-shirt. Heck, you might even be able to do your work in your pajamas. The possibilities are endless, and there are pros and cons to each and every work situation.

On average, a full-time job requires you to work about forty hours per week. If you work in an office, your schedule will probably be along the lines of nine-to-five. But once again, your schedule and the amount of hours you work will entirely depend on your career. Big actors may work super long shifts while they are filming a movie but have plenty of time off between films. Police officers may work totally odd shifts, patrolling the streets while most people are asleep.

Job Lingo: Mini Glossary

In order to get a job, you'll have to prepare a resume and cover letter and go on an interview with a potential employer. Now back up a minute. You may be wondering . . . a cover letter? A resume? What exactly are those things?

The professional world of jobs and careers has its own vocabulary. Below is a list of some of the common terms you will encounter in this book:

- A **candidate** is a person that is being considered for a job by a potential boss or employer.

- A **client,** or customer, is a person that uses your (or your company's) services.

- A **cover letter** is a letter that explains who you are and why you are qualified for a certain job. It's your chance to explain in your own words why someone should hire you over other candidates. A cover letter generally accompanies your resume.

- An **employee** is what you become when you are hired to work for a person or a company.

- An **employer,** or boss, is the person or company that hires you.

- An **interview** is an appointment where you sit down and speak with an potential employer. You may be asked questions about why you want to work for the company and why you are qualified for the job. During an interview, you will also have the chance to ask any questions you may have about a specific job or company.

- The **interviewer** is the person who asks the questions during an interview.

- **A portfolio** is a book or folder that contains a collection of your work. If you create a portfolio in high school, it may contain writing samples or artwork. A portfolio is a way for you to share your accomplishments and talents with employers and to show what you can do. Photographers, for instance, keep samples of their photographs in portfolios, while models keep in their portfolios samples of photographs in which they appear.

- **References** are people who know you well enough to vouch for your character and your work qualifications. Potential employers generally ask for references to learn a little bit more about you. Some colleges and technical schools ask for references, too. References may be teachers, family friends, or past or present employers.

- A **resume** provides a positive and accurate summary of your education, experience, job skills, extracurricular activities, honors, and interests. When you apply for a job, you will have to provide a resume. Over time, as your list of accomplishments and job experiences grows, you will update your resume.

Check out The Princeton Review's career books for more information at www.PrincetonReview.com/cte/bookstore.asp.

TURN THE PAGE ALREADY!

Now you're ready to explore some career options. As you read through our career profiles, remember to keep an open mind. Relax, have fun, and enjoy.

How to Use This Book

The career profiles in this book are listed in alphabetical order. If you don't see a career listed, check for other possible names of the career. For example, if you want to know what an attorney does, check under lawyer. For a list of careers according to what field they're in, check out the index on page 327.

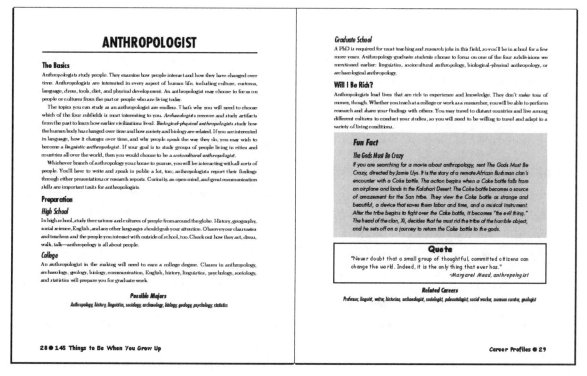

Most of the profiles are two pages long and cover everything from how you can prepare for the career while in high school to quotes from professionals. A small number of profiles (eight, to be exact) had so much information that we decided to make them a bit longer and explain some of the different jobs available in each respective field.

Here is what each section of the profile tells you:

The Basics

This section gives you an overall explanation of each career. Some of the topics covered include: daily responsibilities, work environment, significance of the career, professionals in other careers that you'll interact with, and personality traits that help people excel in the career.

Preparation

This section offers helpful tips about what you can do while in high school, college, or graduate school to prepare for your career. We'll tell you what you need to do to be eligible for the job, whether that's earning a bachelor or master's degree, completing a training program, obtaining certification, or anything else.

High School

Everyone has to take the same basic classes in high school, but some classes may be especially important, depending on your career choice. We encourage you to check out any related elective courses and pursue opportunities outside of the classroom—like clubs, school plays, and even your own experiments—that will give you a chance to explore your interests.

College

You can find out whether a college degree is necessary for obtaining a job in your career choice. While some jobs don't require a degree, it almost always helps if you have one. In addition, we give some suggestions about what else you can do during college to learn more about your future career and gain some useful hands-on experience. Although we don't mention it in every single profile, an internship is one of the best ways to gain experience in almost any field.

Possible Majors

Some careers require a specific major; for others, it doesn't matter what you major in. You can find out more about most of these majors in our book *Guide to College Majors* or on our website, www.PrincetonReview.com.

Graduate and Professional School

To get a job in some professions, you will need to earn an advanced degree in graduate or professional school (law school, business school, or medical school). You may need a master's degree, which usually takes two or three years if you attend school full time. You may even need to earn a PhD, which will tack on a few more years.

In most professions, earning a master's degree will help you move up the ranks or earn more pay; since this is standard, we did not discuss it in each profile.

Additional Training

If there is anything else specific you need to do to get started in your career, here's where you'll find it. You'll find out whether you need to take training classes or tests to become licensed or certified.

Will I Be Rich?

There are pros and cons to every job out there. While you can earn a large amount of money, you may have to work really long shifts at odd hours. On the other hand, it's possible to be perfectly happy at a job that will never make you a millionaire. There are other types of riches that have nothing to do with how much you earn. Your career may be rich in friendships, creativity, or fulfillment. You just have to decide what's most important to you and weigh your options.

Fun Facts

This section lists historical facts, trivia, and related books, movies, and TV shows.

Related Careers

These are careers that are in the same field, use the same skills, are good for the same personality type, or have something else in common with the career being profiled. If a professional in a certain career interacts with tons of different people on the job, you'll see their careers here.

Some career profiles may also have one or more of the following:

Myth v. Reality

You have heard rumors about some of these careers through the grapevine—some true and some not so true. Find out what really goes on in this job.

Quote

Professionals from the profiled careers offer insight and advice based on their personal experiences.

CAREER PROFILES

ACCOUNTANT

The Basics

When a person or company (a client) needs someone to keep track of the money they spend, earn, and invest, they hire an accountant. Basically, each client submits financial information to the accountant. The accountant then studies and checks the figures and reports the results to the client. When tax season comes in April, accountants prepare and submit paperwork to federal and state governments that details how much money a person or company has earned that year.

If you're an accountant, you will need to love numbers! You'll use math to analyze, compare, and interpret facts and figures. As an accountant, you can specialize in auditing, taxes, or consulting. An *auditor* examines and reviews a person's or company's records; a *tax accountant* computes and submits tax payments to the government for the client; and a *consultant* offers financial advice and helps people develop a budget and plan ahead.

Accountants spend a lot of time doing paperwork and working on the computer, so good organizational and computer skills are a must. Communication skills are vital because accountants interact with clients on a daily basis. You will also need to be honest, trustworthy, and reliable. Clients trust you to mind their money honestly and efficiently.

Preparation

High School

Take as many math and AP math classes as you can! Computer classes will prepare you for a job in accounting, too. In addition, you could start up an accounting club in which you and fellow members keep track of where all of your money goes. It's never too early to start keeping track of how you spend your money!

College

You'll need to go to college for accounting or a related field if you plan to be an accountant. Sign up for classes such as accounting, business ethics, calculus, communications, computers, economics, statistics, taxation, finance, and marketing. Job experience is a great way to break into the field, so a summer internship is highly recommended.

Possible Majors
Accounting, business, finance

The CPA Exam

You will need to take the two-day, four-part CPA exam to become a U.S. Certified Public Accountant. In most states, you will need to have a bachelor degree and thirty additional college credits before you even take the test. If possible, take additional classes while you are still in college so you don't have to return to school to take them later on. Once you graduate, studying for the difficult CPA exam will be enough of a challenge!

Will I Be Rich?

You can earn a comfortable living as an accountant. Whether you are self-employed or work for a company, you will most likely travel often to meet with your clients. During tax season, you can expect to work long hours. But if you love numbers and like to help people become more efficient with their money, you will enjoy being an accountant.

Fun Facts

Want to talk like an accountant? Check out the terms below!

- An investment *is a purchase that you expect to make a profit from over time. You might consider the collection of old valuable items, such as baseball cards, to be an investment.*

- An acquisition *is the term used when a company takes over another company. You may want to try to acquire your older sister's double bed when she goes off to college!*

- Bankruptcy *is the legal state in which a company or a person is unable to pay back money that is owed. So if you can't repay the five bucks you owe your friend until the end of the week, you're broke at the moment, but you're not bankrupt!*

[Source: www.ventureline.com/glossary.asp]

Related Careers

Actuary, financial analyst, financial planner, loan officer, bookkeeper, insurance agent, investment banker, stock broker/banker

ACTOR

The Basics

An actor entertains and inspires an audience, bringing scripts to life. Actors perform in theater, movies, television, children's theater groups, commercials, and on the radio. People of all ages and backgrounds are actors. Passion is generally the driving force that leads a person to acting, but persistence is necessary to cope with rejection and fierce competition for roles. Great communication skills, commitment, creativity, and patience are also important traits for actors. The ability to sing and dance is a plus, too.

As an actor, you will spend your days going on auditions and waiting to hear back from agents, directors, and managers. You'll probably have to go on a few callbacks and then wait until the powers that be make their final decisions before landing a role. Although the life of an actor is unpredictable and often stressful, it's also exciting, fun, and challenging. According to one New York actor, "Getting a role is like hitting the lottery!"

While the hot spots for acting are New York City and Los Angeles, you don't need to move to one of those locations in order to act. Every state and town has performances in which you can participate and gain experience.

Preparation

High School

Starring in high school plays is the perfect way to launch your acting career. You will have four years to get over stage fright and learn firsthand what it's like to be an actor. Performing in community theater productions is great preparation, too. Check your local paper to find out what plays community theaters are planning, and audition for a role. Art and English classes will also be helpful.

College

A college degree is a great way to round out your acting career, but it's not required. Classes in communications, film, drama, dance, art, and theater will give you a greater knowledge of the visual and performing arts. English or writing courses will deepen your knowledge of the scripts you read. In addition, many colleges put on a number of plays each year; this is your chance to get lots of stage experience and work with a wide variety of performers. While talent is vital for actors, experience and some formal training will strengthen your skills.

Possible Majors

Theater, art, music, dance, musical theater, communications, English, psychology

Will I Be Rich?

Be prepared to ride a financial roller coaster! Most actors need to take on part-time jobs to make a living so that they can continue to act. Stress, rejection, and working long hours are part of an actor's life. When you are shooting a film or in a play, expect to work nights and weekends and spend lots of time rehearsing. "If your passion is to act, it's all worth it!" a New York actor told us.

Fun Facts

Crossing Over

Celebrities often use their fame to cross over into other areas of entertainment. Here are some singers who tried their luck at acting, for better or for worse: Eminem, Will Smith, Britney Spears, Madonna, Cyndi Lauper, Busta Rhymes, LL Cool J, Eve, Joey Fatone, Lance Bass, Nas, Snoop Dogg, Dr. Dre, Ice T, Mick Jagger, Elvis, Prince, Cher, Barbra Streisand, Queen Latifah, David Bowie, Vanilla Ice, Courtney Love, Björk, Meat Loaf, Mandy Moore, and Dwight Yoakam.

A smaller crowd of actors took a chance in the music industry, including William Shatner, Bruce Willis, Jennifer Love Hewitt, Joey Lawrence, David Hasselhoff, Patrick Swayze, and Keanu Reeves.

And who's to say that TV and movie roles are off-limits to sports stars? Athletes Shaquille O'Neal, Rick Fox, Dennis Rodman, David Beckham, and Bob Uecker didn't think so.

Bedtime for Bonzo

Q: Who is the only actor-turned-president?

A: Ronald Reagan, fortieth president of the United States.

Related Careers

Artist, dancer, choreographer, director, fashion designer, model, musician, producer, publicist, writer

ADMINISTRATIVE ASSISTANT

The Basics

An administrative assistant, formerly referred to as a secretary, keeps an office running smoothly. He or she may schedule appointments, keep computer databases and paper files up to date, perform research, handle payroll and bookkeeping, and pay bills on behalf of the company. In addition to assisting other people with their daily tasks, administrative assistants may have some projects to complete entirely on their own.

As an administrative assistant, you will need to act as a representative of your company. You'll also need to know some basics about the company's history, practices, and products. In specialized offices, such as medical or law offices, you may need to have more in-depth knowledge of the field. To best communicate with your coworkers, managers, and customers, you will need to act friendly and be patient, with a positive attitude.

You'll be responsible for a wide range of tasks and projects in this position, so you'll need to be prepared for anything. Of course, you will need basic office skills: typing, using word processing and accounting programs, handling complex email and phone systems, faxing, and photocoping. But the most important trait you can bring to this position is the ability to organize. You may be responsible for important company records and transactions, so it's your duty to keep everything in its place. In addition, knowing how to prioritize and work well under pressure is vital to this career.

Preparation

High School

A part-time job as an administrative assistant (or any type of assistant) will give you a taste of what this career is like. Do you work well with others? Can you get the job done quickly and effectively? Are you okay with taking orders? In high school, computer classes, as well as those in English and math, will be most relevant to this career.

College

You don't need a college degree to be an administrative assistant, but you can acquire a lot of additional skills in college. You'll have access to more advanced computer courses, as well as business courses, such as those in accounting and finance. If you want to work in a particular type of company, you can learn more about the industry while still in school. In addition, you can probably find some more hands-on experience right on campus.

Business administration, communications, data processing

Will I Be Rich?

You will be rich in office supplies as an administrative assistant, and you can generally make enough money to pay your bills, too. The more experience and the more skills you have, such as bookkeeping experience, the more money you can earn. Some people use this position as a stepping-stone to other positions within a company; others remain administrative assistants or go on to become executive assistants, who earn more money. You may not survive in this career, though, unless you truly love working with people.

Fun Facts

Giving Thanks

Administrative Professionals Week occurs each year during the last full week in April. The event began back in 1952 to recognize and celebrate all the great work that administrative assistants perform for offices and to attract newcomers to the profession. It was originally called Professional Secretaries Week, but its name was changed in 2001 to reflect the evolving role of the administrative professional.

Did You Know?

The U.S. Department of Labor statistics report that there are 3.9 million secretaries and administrative assistants working in all types of offices across the United States.

[Source: www.iaap-hq.org]

Related Careers

Librarian, postal worker, steward, waiter, hotel manager, homemaker, accountant, bookkeeper

ADVERTISING EXECUTIVE

The Basics

Every company needs customers to buy its products and services in order to stay afloat. But people need to actually *know* about a company's products and services before they can purchase them. And that's where the advertising executive comes in. An advertising agency creates ads for companies; the advertising executive is the link between the client, or company, and the ad agency.

As an advertising executive, you will work with many different people to create a suitable ad or ad campaign (a series of ads). You'll use your knowledge of the company and its target audience to come up with some creative ways to present the product. Market researchers, media experts, and employees in the creative department will all help with the production of the ad. You can create ads that will appear in magazines or newspapers, on the radio or television, or in public places, such as buses or subways. You could be working on an ad for any number of different product types, from food to toys to office supplies to vacation cruises to prescription medicines.

You will be responsible for the ads that your team creates, and in most cases, you will present your team's work to your client. In addition to keeping existing clients happy, it's your job to find new clients. Because of the close contact you'll have with team members and clients, you'll have to communicate and work well with others. You'll also have to be very organized and detail-oriented. Your career as an advertising executive will be fast paced, exciting, and creative.

Preparation

High School

English, graphic art, and statistics classes will give you a great head start to becoming an advertising executive. Outside of school, you can also do some research of your own. Check out some magazine and commercial ads and consider how they make you feel about the product. If an ad has ever made you hungry, happy, or intrigued, it was no coincidence! That was the work of the advertising executive and his or her team.

College

College is a must if you want to be an advertising executive. Sprinkle your schedule with courses in advertising, copywriting, communication, English, graphic design, art, marketing, psychology, and statistics. In addition, an internship can help you get your break in an advertising firm.

Possible Majors

Advertising, journalism, communications, marketing, English, psychology, graphic design

Will I Be Rich?

As an advertising executive, you can make a lot of money; however, you have to pay your dues and gain experience first. Expect to work long hours, including nights and weekends, to meet deadlines. Although the job can be stressful, the excitement of creating ads and working with intelligent, creative people makes it worthwhile for many.

Fun Facts

Got milk?

That simple question was the slogan for an advertising campaign that made it stylish to have a milk mustache! Check out a sampling of celebrities who were spokespersons for the famous Got milk? campaign:

- Austin Powers
- Backstreet Boys
- Britney Spears
- Buffy the Vampire Slayer
- Serena and Venus Williams
- Carson Daly
- LeAnn Rimes
- Mandy Moore
- Nelly

- The Hulk
- Jackie Chan
- Pikachu
- Mario (from Super Mario Bros.)
- Hanson
- Tony Hawk
- Freddie Prinze Jr.

[Source: www.whymilk.com]

That's One Big Audience

The Super Bowl attracts huge crowds each year. It's not just football fanatics who are glued to the tube, though—people also watch the annual game for the commercials. The airtime is considered so valuable that a thirty-second spot in Super Bowl XXXVI in 2002 cost $2,200,000!

[Source: www.nielsenmedia.com]

Related Careers

Market researcher, agent, graphic designer, artist, editor, marketing executive, sales person, media specialist

AGENT

The Basics

There are many different types of agents, and each has a wide range of responsibilities. But there is one theme to the job that is constant: Whether you're a *sports agent,* a *literary agent,* or a *booking/ talent agent,* you have to work to help your client's career. A client can be anyone from a young actor trying to "make it" to a popular sports superstar.

Part of the agent's job involves looking for work, such as movie roles for actors, book deals for writers, or contracts and endorsements for athletes. The other part of the job is keeping the clients motivated. Agents need to be in touch with their clients, helping them understand their roles and keeping them focused. Depending on the client, this level of day-to-day hand-holding can vary. Sometimes it's easy; sometimes it's tough.

Some agents work for full-service firms. These firms may provide investment or tax counseling, whereas agents aren't usually responsible for what their client does with his or her money. One firm can employ more than one hundred agents, and others may only have a few. The size of a firm or the number of clients it has doesn't always translate into success.

To be a successful agent, you'll need to be a smooth talker so you can convince clients that you will do a good job (whether it's true or not). A good agent also needs to negotiate and have a solid understanding of the economics of the field. You have to multitask—in other words, juggle a handful of important jobs and handle a crisis without panicking.

Preparation

High School

Read trade publications to get a grip on the industry (players, actors, writers, etc.). Pay special attention to the people behind the scenes, like general managers, directors, and other agents. If you can, get a job or internship with a current agent to learn the ropes. You can try to get in touch with an association in the business, but it's tough to break in. If you happen to know a talented actor or a stud quarterback, you can become his or her agent. If you begin your career with a client, you'll have a head start.

College

It is possible to be a successful agent without a college degree. The experience certainly helps, though. What you learn in college is how to be more mature and how to interact with people. A negotiation or speech class can help you hone your skills, and writing classes will help you put pen to paper. But the key to being an agent is timing and the rare combination of connection and experience.

Graduate School

Attending graduate school is a new approach for agents. Lawyer skills are used a lot by agents in the field. For example, a lawyer needs to look over the contracts that an agent negotiates. The agent is usually more qualified if he or she can review contracts and consider legal issues. A law degree, therefore, can give you an edge in a crowded market.

Will I Be Rich?

It's very possible. But the range is from making no money (because you have no clients) to living like you're a superstar yourself. Through hard work, luck, and timing, immense wealth is attainable. But there are people who can't catch a break, and they don't make a lot of money. There are a lot of cool perks, however. Agents get to rub elbows with the stars, and they get tickets to many fun events.

Fun Fact

Help Wanted: Need Clients!

There are more registered agents in every sport than there are athletes. That means there are a lot of agents who have no clients!

Quote

"The most important qualities for an agent are integrity and honor. Without your reputation, you don't have a whole lot. And that's what separates the good agents from the bad agents. The shady, smooth-talking agents are a dime a dozen and come and go."

— *Justin Bass*

Related Careers

Writer, editor, athlete, actor, musician, comedian, rock star, publicist

ANTHROPOLOGIST

The Basics

Anthropologists study people. They examine how people interact and how they have changed over time. Anthropologists are interested in every aspect of human life, including culture, customs, language, dress, tools, diet, and physical development. An anthropologist may choose to focus on people or cultures from the past or people who are living today.

The topics you can study as an anthropologist are endless. That's why you will need to choose which of the four subfields is most interesting to you. *Archaeologists* recover and study artifacts from the past to learn how earlier civilizations lived. *Biological-physical anthropologists* study how the human body has changed over time and how society and biology are related. If you are interested in language, how it changes over time, and why people speak the way they do, you may wish to become a *linguistic anthropologist*. If your goal is to study groups of people living in cities and countries all over the world, then you would choose to be a *sociocultural anthropologist*.

Whichever branch of anthropology you choose to pursue, you will be interacting with all sorts of people. You'll have to write and speak in public a lot, too; anthropologists report their findings through either presentations or research reports. Curiosity, an open mind, and great communication skills are important traits for anthropologists.

Preparation

High School

In high school, study the customs and cultures of people from around the globe. History, geography, social science, English, and any other languages should grab your attention. Observe your classmates and teachers and the people you interact with outside of school, too. Check out how they act, dress, walk, talk—anthropology is all about people.

College

An anthropologist in the making will need to earn a college degree. Classes in anthropology, archaeology, geology, biology, communication, English, history, linguistics, psychology, sociology, and statistics will prepare you for graduate work.

Possible Majors

Anthropology, history, linguistics, sociology, archaeology, biology, geology, psychology, statistics

Graduate School

A PhD is required for most teaching and research jobs in this field, so you'll be in school for a few more years. Anthropology graduate students choose to focus on one of the four subdivisions we mentioned earlier: linguistics, sociocultural anthropology, biological-physical anthropology, or archaeological anthropology.

Will I Be Rich?

Anthropologists lead lives that are rich in experience and knowledge. They don't make tons of money, though. Whether you teach at a college or work as a researcher, you will be able to perform research and share your findings with others. You may travel to distant countries and live among different cultures to conduct your studies, so you will need to be willing to travel and adapt to a variety of living conditions.

Fun Fact

The Gods Must Be Crazy

If you are searching for a movie about anthropology, rent The Gods Must Be Crazy, directed by Jamie Uys. It is the story of a remote African Bushman clan's encounter with a Coke bottle. The action begins when a Coke bottle falls from an airplane and lands in the Kalahari Desert. The Coke bottle becomes a source of amazement for the San tribe. They view the Coke bottle as strange and beautiful, a device that saves them labor and time, and a musical instrument. After the tribe begins to fight over the Coke bottle, it becomes "the evil thing." The head of the clan, Xi, decides that he must rid the tribe of the horrible object, and he sets off on a journey to return the Coke bottle to the gods.

Quote

"Never doubt that a small group of thoughtful, committed citizens can change the world. Indeed, it is the only thing that ever has."

–Margaret Mead, anthropologist

Related Careers

Professor, linguist, writer, historian, archaeologist, sociologist, paleontologist, social worker, museum curator, geologist

ARCHAEOLOGIST

The Basics

An archaeologist is a person who studies past human cultures. He or she looks for clues by uncovering (excavating) items left by past societies. An excavated item could be a piece of pottery or an early tool, for example. Archaeologists use these clues to improve our understanding of how people lived in the past. Most archaeologists have a specialty, such as Egyptian hieroglyphics. Archaeologists also work all over the world. Thus, many archaeologists travel quite a bit, and they sometimes live in tents or experience other primitive living conditions.

It's true that archaeologists strive to find thrilling discoveries and expose secrets, but their work isn't always exciting. Much of the work involves painfully slow digging, mapping, and labeling. (You have to be careful when you dig not to break anything!) It can require hard, grueling manual labor. Each tiny bit of history that you dig up is a clue to our past. You need to put those clues together and analyze them to gain some new knowledge.

Because archaeologists work to learn and discover, it makes sense that most work for colleges or museums. You can teach what you've learned to museum visitors or university students. And you will have time to go on digs that can last for several months. That can be fun, but it's only a small fraction of the actual work. You'll spend a great deal of time trying to understand what you find— and trying to explain your theories to an interested audience.

Preparation

High School

You'll need a lot of formal education to be an archaeologist. So buckle down, get good grades, and pay special attention in your history and social studies classes. Spend some quality time in museums, and you'll see how the discoveries from archaeological digs help people understand history. You'll need to create reports, so sharpen your writing skills. Dig in your backyard, if your parents don't mind. Maybe you'll find an arrowhead or a buffalo nickel.

College

There are many fields you can study in college to prepare you for a job as an archaeologist. Ancient history or anthropology will give you a strong base of useful knowledge. Some colleges even offer an archaeology degree. A study of ancient or foreign languages, geography, or even English will be practical, too. It's very useful to attend a field school, where students learn hands-on field methods at a real archaeology site.

Graduate School

An advanced degree is essential for a career in archaeology. Without one you can be an assistant or aide, but nothing more. You'll likely need a PhD to teach in a college, so get the best degree you can at the best institution possible. Remember that there are a lot of people who want to be archaeologists, and there are few positions available. If you can write archaeology-related articles for magazines or journals, you can begin to make yourself known.

Will I Be Rich?

Archaeology is not a career that will make you rich. If your passion is trying to understand the history of our society, however, there may be no greater job. The lifestyle is adventurous and interesting, and the pay is pretty reasonable.

Fun Fact

Burried Civilization

One of the greatest archaeological discoveries in history was the unearthing of the ancient town of Pompeii, in southern Italy. Pompeii was a thriving city for many centuries until a volcano destroyed it. Mount Vesuvius erupted in AD 79, burying the entire city in twenty feet of ash. Pompeii was not discovered again for at least 1,500 years! When archaeologists finally started to dig out the ash, they found the city nearly completely intact. The findings have taught us much about the Holy Roman Empire.

Related Careers

Anthropologist, historian, paleontologist, researcher, scientist, professor, museum curator, detective

ARCHITECT

The Basics

Architects are responsible for designing and overseeing the construction of buildings. Those buildings can be anything from churches or houses to 110-story skyscrapers. An architect plans the way a building looks and works. He or she also has to ensure that the structure is safe, and that it won't cost too much money. Architecture is a blend of art and science, and it has the power to change landscapes.

An architect is a jack-of-all-trades. He or she has to take a vision from a client and turn it into working documents, so the builders know how to build it. A building requires electrical, mechanical, and structural engineers, as well as scores of other contractors. It's the architect's job to manage this—as well as everything from the materials on the roof to the placement of a light fixture in the basement. So architects have to supervise and communicate, as well as draw and plan.

Besides organizing the people involved in a project, you will have a lot of other responsibilities as an architect. You have to research and follow zoning laws and building codes. You should make sure your project is environmentally friendly. You have to visit the site to ensure the work being done is up to par. You may even have to sell your abilities to a prospective client, which can be stressful. Stress is just part of the job, but there aren't many other occupations where you can creatively craft a skyline.

Preparation

High School

Get the best grades you can so you can get into a good architecture school. Focus on your math courses, because geometry and trigonometry are crucial in architecture. Drafting is important, too. Try to work at an architectural firm or for a carpenter—even if you have to volunteer. You can go to construction sites and watch how a building is constructed. It can be fascinating and educational to witness a project come together.

College

Most architectural firms prefer their employees to have a degree in architecture. At an accredited institution, that is a five-year program. If you don't get a bachelor degree in architecture, you might have to go to graduate school. (Otherwise, graduate school is largely unnecessary.) While you're in college, learn about the construction industry; it's important background for going into architecture.

Architecture, architectural history, interior architecture, architectural engineering

Academic experience will only teach you so much, so try to get some real-world experience—even if it's just working for a summer as an apprentice. College teaches you about form and function, but not how to handle the frequent crises that arise in actual practice. You'll have to take the theories you learned and apply them to real situations.

Getting Your License

Even after five years in an architectural program, you still need to jump through a few other hoops to be a licensed architect. You'll need three years of practice in the field. You also need to pass a difficult test: the Architect Registration Exam (ARE). Each state has its own licensing procedures.

Will I Be Rich?

Considering all the hard work architects do, it's not a very high-paying job. You can strike it rich, however, if you're extremely talented and get in with the right people.

Fun Fact

Organic Architecture

Frank Lloyd Wright is one of the most famous American architects of all time. He designed the Guggenheim Museum in New York City, as well as hundreds of other structures. His style was often called "organic architecture" because it combined buildings with their natural surroundings.

Quote

"As an architect, you spend a lot of time in front of a computer and a lot of time drawing. It's great to see something you've spent hours drawing being built into reality. But a single project can take up to five years from conception to the end; you put in the hours."

— *Chad Harries, architect intern*

Related Careers

Carpenter, engineer, real estate developer, artist, city planner, construction worker, plumber, interior designer, electrician

ART AND ANTIQUE RESTORER

The Basics

Ever wonder why a painting in a museum doesn't seem to age, or why the furniture in an antique shop doesn't have any chipped edges? These works of art and antique items are restored, preserved, and maintained by art and antique restorers. Antique restorers work on items like books, clocks, furniture, jewelry, lamps, leather, radios, and rugs; art restorers dedicate most of their time to paintings and sculptures. Certain objects are considered to be antiques *and* works of art, so it's no surprise that some restorers work on items in both categories. Art and antique restorers may work for museums, antique shops, or for private customers. The process is often laborious and time-consuming, but art enthusiasts and antique collectors agree that the results are well worthwhile.

As a restorer, you will begin your work by assessing the object that you are to work on. You try to determine what time period the piece is from and what it's made of. If you can't determine what materials were used, you may take X-rays and use microscopes or other lab equipment to find out. Then you will gather the materials you need to do the job and get to work restoring the item. Depending on the scope of the project, it can take anywhere from a week to a few months to complete the assignment.

If you are detail-oriented and have a passion for works of the past, a career in art or antique restoration may appeal to you. You may work on projects on your own for long stretches of time, so you'll need to be patient, persistent, and self-motivated.

Preparation

High School

Trips to local museums and antique shops are great opportunities to take a closer look at art and antiques. Ask someone who works at the museum or antique shop to fill you in on the piece's history, or do your own research in a library or online. Art, art history, chemistry, and wood or metal shop classes will help boost your restoration skills.

College

An internship with an antique restorer or with a museum's art conservation department will help to immerse you in this career. Experience is your best teacher, but classes in archaeology, art history, chemistry, history, and studio art will also expand your knowledge of the subject.

Graduate School

If you plan to restore works of art for a museum, you'll need to earn an art conservation degree. These programs are competitive, since they're few and far between. You will need a strong background in chemistry, archaeology, studio art, and art history to qualify for a graduate program. Graduate programs in art conservation are offered at Buffalo State College, New York University, Queen's University, and University of Delaware.

Coursework

If you plan to restore antiques, classes and workshops in antique restoration will be a great help. You can take courses that teach you about materials, methods, and techniques to restore and touch up wood, ceramic, and metal antiques.

Will I Be Rich?

You can earn a decent living if you specialize in restoration, but you will work hard for your money. The job involves a certain amount of stress, considering that you will be working on important pieces of art and antiques. One antique restorer shared with us the fears and joys of restoring art: "One wrong move and the whole house tumbles. Once you complete a project, though, the satisfaction you feel when you look at the artwork is priceless!"

Fun Fact

Help!

Art conservation can be costly, so some important projects are sometimes put off due to lack of funding. As of 2004, Yosemite Park's Cemetery needs $28,500 in funding for restoration. The grounds are currently in poor shape and the entrance sign needs fixing. The park's oldest covered bridge, Wawona Covered Bridge, needs $33,000 in funding to restore its support structure.

[Source: www.yosemitefund.org]

Related Careers

Anthropologist, archaeologist, artist, museum curator, art historian

ART DEALER

The Basics

An art dealer earns a living by selling art or representing an artist to sell his or her art. Because the job deals heavily with the art world, art dealers need to have a trained eye for high-quality artwork. That means they must be able to recognize art that might be undervalued or has good potential to increase in value. It also means having a good sense of what types of art people want to buy. Art dealing is a cross between the art world and the business world. For some folks who love to surround themselves with art, being an art dealer is an ideal occupation.

Being a successful art dealer takes more than just a good knowledge of what art is marketable. An art dealer needs to be a social person because making contacts is a big part of the business. A dealer needs to know many artists and private collectors, so the dealer can try to work deals between them. He or she also needs to know owners of art galleries and museum curators because art needs to be on display to attract a buyer.

Most art dealers focus on a particular type of art or period. For example, you might have a passion for Portuguese paintings. If that's the case, you should use your knowledge to find and facilitate deals. Just remember that tastes always change, and you have to stay on top of the most current trend. Being able to anticipate the "next hot thing" will be your ticket to success.

Preparation

High School

Immerse yourself in the art world. Visit every art institution you can find, from national museums down to local galleries. Compare prices to get a sense of the business side of art, and study the financial history of art.

College

Because most art dealers work for themselves, there are no formal requirements for the job. However, to know your stuff, you should study art or art history in college. While you're in college, work at a gallery. That will teach you what types of art sell, for how much, and to what kind of people. More importantly, it will teach you how to sell a piece of art. Simply watching experienced art dealers market their wares can teach you a lot about the business. You might even develop a client or two.

Possible Majors

Art, art history, museum studies, history, business administration, public relations

Graduate School

Many art dealers are also museum curators, so a graduate degree in art history or museum studies can give you an edge in that direction. But you should also do everything you can to learn business and sales. Therefore, a business degree might be a big boost to the dealing aspect of the job.

Will I Be Rich?

Art is a fickle business. There can be swings in the market when people simply aren't spending money on art. But most of the time high-quality art sells for a good price. Art dealers can get a percentage of that business, making some dealers very rich.

Fun Fact

Solo!

Vincent van Gogh's brother, Theo, was a professional art dealer. Theo worked in Holland and France in the 1880s. His specialty was landscape portraits and impressionist paintings. Unfortunately, Theo was not very good at selling his talented brother's works. Vincent van Gogh sold only one painting during his lifetime!

[Source: www.absolutearts.com]

Related Careers

Artist, agent, museum curator, tour guide, publicist, art historian

ARTIST

Scultptor • ceramicist • illustrator • painter • photographer • video artist

The Basics

Have you ever seen a work of art in a museum, gallery, book, or school that inspired you or made you feel awestruck? You may have already created drawings, paintings, sculptures, and photographs of your own in art class or at home. Art can mean different things to different people, but the main gist is this: Art is a way to express oneself. And artists are the creative and talented people who excel in art making. The term *art* can cover a wide range of expressive pursuits, including dancing, filmmaking, writing, theater, and music. Here, we have chosen to focus on artists who create visual art.

So, how do artists do what they do? What makes someone a successful artist? Although that depends on what art form you pursue, successful artists generally create art that is beautiful, curious, thought-provoking, inspiring, and original. Of course, everyone has his or her own idea of what's beautiful and that can include a work of art that someone else finds horribly ugly. As they say, beauty is in the eye of the beholder. No matter what the end result, artists work with shapes, forms, colors, light, perspective, composition, and other design elements to come up with their own personal style. Artistic styles can range from being totally realistic to completely abstract and include everything in between.

Artists can make a living in a number of different ways: They can work independently, showing their work at galleries and museums and relying upon the sale of their artwork and grants. They can teach courses at colleges and art schools, as well as workshops. Artists can also use their skills for commercial purposes. This includes photographing products for graphic design firms, creating advertisements, and illustrating textbooks or billboards.

There are many different art forms you can practice as an artist; below is a sampling:

- *Sculptors* create three-dimensional art. They mold, carve, and build sculptures out of clay, glass, wood, metal, plastic, wax, cloth, and just about any other material you can think of.

- *Ceramicists* sculpt objects out of clay. They may create plates, vases, bowls, and other objects for practical use; they may sculpt artistic figures, objects, or shapes; or they can make decorative pieces of pottery.

- *Illustrators* draw pictures for comic books, books, magazines, newspapers, ads, and CD covers, to name a few. Some illustrators use pencil, while some use pen and ink or even paint; some also use a computer to enhance their drawings.

- *Painters* use paint, including oils, acrylics, and watercolors, to create works of art. They usually use a series of paintbrushes to apply paint to canvas, wood, or other surfaces. In addition to painting with rags, palette knives, and their own hands, some artists have even thrown paint onto the canvas straight from the can.

- *Photographers* take pictures of popular subjects such as landscapes, portraiture, still lifes, and street scenes, but the possibilities are endless. Some photographers choose to capture their subjects without posing them or changing anything around; these are documentary photographers. Others choose to set up a scene and make it seem like it's totally natural. A portrait photographer takes pictures of people commercially; a photojournalist takes pictures for newspapers, magazines, or other media; and a fashion photographer takes pictures of models.

- *Video artists* create artistic videos using a video camera. A relatively new art form—artists have only been creating videos for about thirty years—video art is similar in some ways to filmmaking and photography. Some videos are documentaries and are about real people and events, some are abstract or conceptual, and some are just plain funny.

Preparation

High School

In school, sign up for general art courses, as well as specialized classes like ceramics, photography, and computer graphic design, to find out where your interests lie. Keep a sketchbook to record your thoughts, ideas, and images. Art history will give you an understanding and appreciation for different artists and art movements, including those of ancient civilizations. Visit nearby museums and art galleries, take notes, and start building a portfolio of your work—you'll need it to get into art school.

College

A college degree is not a requirement for an artist, but going to an art school or an art program at a college or university is highly recommended. There, you can learn advanced techniques in your chosen art field, and you can develop your own artwork in a constructive artistic community of peers and professors. There are some courses that all art students must take, like art history and theory, but each art major has its own unique set of class requirements.

Possible Majors

Art, painting, photography, sculpture, ceramics, graphic art, video art

Will I Be Rich?

It can be very difficult to make a living as an artist, so you will need to be passionate and motivated to give it a go. Some artists make enough money selling their work to get by, but they are the minority. If you choose to be an artist, you may have to accept freelance jobs to help pay the bills. Still, if you love what you do (which most artists do!), no financial reward can compare.

Fun Facts

Now That's Dedication

Did you know that Rembrandt completed close to 2,900 artworks in his lifetime? He created 600 paintings, roughly 300 etchings, and about 2,000 drawings.

Man's Best Friend

William Wegman is most famous for his photographs and videos, but he also draws, paints, and writes. Wegman's videos and his photographs, which are collected in a number of books, feature his dogs Man Ray and Fay Ray in humorous situations.

Myth v. Reality

Myth: Making art is a breeze!
Reality: Many artists are incredibly focused and intense. Most art forms require enormous attention to detail, a tremendous amount of dedication, and a deep-rooted sense of discipline, not to mention talent and a rich, creative mind!

Quote

"When I finish a painting and see the colors and images on the canvas the way that I see them in my mind's eye, it's all worthwhile. Every minute of fear and frustration is worthwhile for that one moment of recognition."
—Pamela Shannon, a New York painter

Related Careers

Painter, photographer, sculptor, ceramicist, video artist, illustrator, animator, art dealer, critic, art director, art critic, museum curator, graphic designer, Web designer, creative director, fashion designer, dancer, musician

ASTROLOGER

The Basics

Astrologers predict the future based on the positions and movements of the planets, the sun, and the moon. They believe that there is a direct link between the universe and our behavior on Earth. You've probably read a fair share of horoscopes in newspapers and magazines; now is your chance to find out how they're determined.

Let's review some astrology basics. There are twelve different birth signs, or signs of the zodiac. Each sign is associated with certain elements (fire, earth, air, and water) and qualities (cardinal, fixed, or mutable), as well as other characteristics. A reading or prediction based on a birth sign is called a horoscope. A birth chart marks the positions of the stars and planets at the moment of birth, taking into account the day and year in addition to the zodiac sign. Astrologers claim to predict important life events and opportunities by studying a birth chart.

As an astrologer, you will use your understanding of the universe and different birth signs to create birth charts for customers. This will require a lot of reading and research, so a love of learning is necessary. You will then make educated guesses about what they can expect in the days, weeks, and years ahead. People will rely on you to provide honest advice about relationships, jobs, and other topics. Therefore, you must be trustworthy and possess strong analytical and communication skills.

Preparation

High School

Why not start an astrology club? You could read horoscopes from a newspaper or other source and discuss whether or not they are valid. Or you could take a stab at writing your own horoscopes just for fun. Classes in history, English, mythology, astronomy, psychology, and physics will be helpful.

College

You don't need a college degree to become an astrologer, but it can't hurt. Try some classes in astronomy, communication, mythology, psychology, and sociology. You could also join the newspaper staff as official astrologer. Maybe you could ask an astrologer for advice about your own astrology career!

Possible Majors

Psychology, sociology, history, ancient studies

Will I Be Rich?

If you earn a good reputation, you can make a lot of money. It really depends on how much you charge for your services. Your working conditions will vary. You can work in a shop or out of your home, and you may counsel people in person, online, or over the phone. Many astrologers write books or create yearly calendars full of astrological information to supplement the money they earn doing consultations.

Fun Facts

Walking Backward

Mercury is the planet that rules communication and transportation. When it's in retrograde (moving backward), communication and transportation slow down! If your computer is breaking down or you're having trouble communicating with someone, look to the stars! Check out an astrology book or website to find out when Mercury is in retrograde.

[Source: www.writerinthewindow.com]

Birth Signs of the Stars

- Mariah Carey: 3/27—Aries
- Willie Mays: 5/6—Taurus
- Prince: 6/7—Gemini
- Kevin Bacon: 7/8—Cancer
- Ben Affleck: 8/15—Leo
- Michael Jackson: 8/29—Virgo

- Neve Campbell: 10/3—Libra
- Julia Roberts: 10/28—Scorpio
- Brad Pitt: 12/1—Sagittarius
- Jim Carey: 1/17—Capricorn
- Jennifer Aniston: 2/11—Aquarius
- Liza Minnelli: 3/12—Pisces

Myth v. Reality

Myth: Astrologers are all fakes.

Reality: Many astrologers have formal training in science and other subjects before they venture into astrology. For example, Gary Goldschneider, astrologer and best-selling author of *The Secret Language of Birthdays*, *The Secret Language of Relationships*, and *The Secret Language of Destiny,* studied psychiatry and medicine at Yale University and English literature at the University of Pennsylvania.

[Source: www.goldschneider.com]

Quote

"Helping people to understand themselves and their relationships better is the greatest job in the world!"

—Arthur G. Flatto, astrologer

Related Careers

Psychologist, sociologist, consultant, astronomer

ASTRONAUT

The Basics

Do you dream of being the first person to land on Mars, exploring its canals and canyons and looking for signs of life? Do you want to work on the International Space Station (ISS), floating in space miles above Earth's atmosphere? These are the dreams of an astronaut, one of the most adventurous occupations in the world—and beyond!

If you want to be an astronaut, your best bet is to join NASA, the National Aeronautics and Space Administration. That's the government-run organization that has managed the American space program since 1958. There are other international space agencies, but NASA is the best funded, and most astronauts in the world travel through it.

There are three different astronaut jobs for NASA: *Commanders or pilots* fly the spacecraft and are responsible for the safety of the crew; *mission specialists* work to achieve the goal of each mission, performing experiments or other activities such as space walks; and *payload specialists* have a special job, providing their unique talents for specific missions.

NASA is always accepting applications for new astronauts. To be considered, you must be smart and extremely brave. You'll have to be a hard worker, too; astronauts often work for months at a time, rarely seeing family or friends. You'll need to be a team player with good communication skills because every person involved in a mission is crucial for success. There are also some physical requirements to being an astronaut. You need to have very good vision, low blood pressure, and a height of no more than six feet four. Pilots and commanders must be between five feet four and six feet four.

Preparation

High School

Your science and math classes are going to lay the foundation for your astronaut training—study hard! Students between the ages of twelve and fourteen who are interested in the space program can attend the U.S. Space Academy in Alabama. An advanced program is also available for students between the ages of fifteen and eighteen.

College

To become an astronaut, you will need a degree in mathematics, engineering, biology, chemistry, physics, or a related field. A degree in astrophysics, for example, could help you get on a good track. It's also crucial that you get some related experience, whether through a paying job or an internship.

Possible Majors

Astrophysics, aerospace engineering, aviation, planetary science

Graduate School

NASA does not require their astronauts to have a graduate degree, but it does *prefer* its applicants to have one. The more you can learn about your specialized field, the better your chances will be.

Required Training

If you want to become a NASA pilot, you will need experience flying a jet aircraft. (See PILOT.) Mission specialists will need several years of experience that relates to their specialization.

Will I Be Rich?

Although astronauts are highly skilled, they are not paid very well. If you're looking to get wealthy, try another job. But if you want to have a life rich with adventure, it doesn't get much better than this!

Fun Facts

Fat Chance?

You may think the odds of becoming an astronaut are one in a million. Well, they're not that bad. Every few years about 20 astronaut jobs open up, and about 3,500 people apply. That makes the odds about one in 175.

[Source: http://usgovinfo.about.com]

Soggy Drawers

Astronauts in training must learn how to adapt to new environments, new tasks, and even new clothes. For example, they are required to pass a swimming test in a flight suit and tennis shoes!

[Source: http://spaceflight.nasa.gov]

Quote

"The one thing [astronauts at NASA] have in common is the way that they got here—not by all taking the same path but by seeking out the things that they found interesting and doing them with great gusto—that's what works!"

— Kenneth S. Reightler, former astronaut
[Source: http://liftoff.msfc.nasa.gov]

Related Careers

Scientist, pilot, engineer

ATHLETE

The Basics

Athletes are the men and women of sports. They are the skiers, swimmers, and cyclists of the world. There are hundreds of sports, and in each one there is an athlete trying to make a buck playing it. Athletes must combine their physical abilities with their knowledge of the rules and strategies to excel at the game. In order to be paid for your athletic talent, there need to be people willing to spend money to watch the game. Without paying customers or a supporting sponsor, an athlete will need another job to support him- or herself. That's the difference between a *professional* athlete and a *recreational* athlete.

For most sports, it is nearly impossible to make a living playing the game (few dodgeball players earn money for throwing a dodge ball!). However, for the more popular sports in America, there is a very real possibility of fame and fortune. Top-level athletes are admired as heroes, live like celebrities, and *work* professionally at *playing*! It's the dream job for millions. But the road to sports stardom is more often filled with heartbreak than it is with glory. The degree of competition is fierce. Only a select few get to reach the upper levels of professional sports, and millions try. Age and injuries cause many athletes to fail. The job is physically and emotionally demanding.

Given the intense physical requirements for the job, athletes must train a lot. Athletes practice many hours every day, even during a season when they don't compete. For most sports, athletes also build their muscles with strength training. To stay in top shape, athletes maintain a proper diet as well. Motivated athletes may spend a great deal of time watching videos of themselves and their opponents. They do this to find the flaws in their own game and to possibly discover weaknesses of their opponents.

This is all well and good, but hard work and constant practice and training will only take you so far. You also need natural abilities and a bit of luck. If you play on a team sport, you may even need the help of your teammates to showcase your skills. For example, a football quarterback will have more chances to throw good passes if there is a good defensive line to protect him or her. (A talented wide receiver helps, too!) A good coach can also instruct athletes to make the most of their skills.

Here are just a few of the sports that professional athletes are actually paid to play:

- Archery
- Auto racing
- Baseball
- Basketball
- Boxing
- Cricket
- Cycling
- Figure Skating
- Football
- Golf
- Gymnastics
- Hockey
- Horse racing
- Jai alai
- Lacrosse
- Rugby
- Skiing
- Snowboarding
- Soccer
- Swimming
- Tennis
- Track and field
- Volleyball

Some people also consider games and other activities to be sports, such as billiards and bowling. You can get paid for playing these, too, if you win tournaments.

Preparation

High School

Practice, practice, practice. Practice in the morning, practice at night, and practice on the weekends. Join your high school team in whatever sport (or sports) you love. If that's not enough, sign up at a local league for more practice. A sports camp can teach you a lot about being an athlete. (You might spend all day enhancing your athletic talents.) Follow the stars, especially the young ones. If you go to high school and college games, you can get a sense of the talent level of your peers.

College

For many sports, college is the place to really fine-tune your abilities. Just be sure you attend a university with a good sports program. Almost all football and basketball players get drafted out of college. Some choose to leave college early to go pro and earn a big paycheck, but most attend even a year or two of higher education. (That doesn't include LeBron James, the basketball prodigy who went directly from high school to the NBA in 2003.)

Baseball players often go straight from high school to the minor leagues, but many teams draft college players as well. That's because college players are more mature, both physically and emotionally. College players are also more reliable because it's easier to gauge their competition. A handful of baseball players became good enough to go directly from college to the major leagues, such as John Olerud or Jim Abbott, the one-handed pitcher who threw a no-hitter in the 1990s.

Perhaps the most important reason to go to college is to provide a backup plan in case you don't make it in the big time. If you can get an athletic scholarship, take advantage of it! An injury can ruin your athletic career, and without a college degree it will be much harder to move on to another field. Even Mike Mussina, a star pitcher for the New York Yankees, earned an economics degree from Stanford. He did that while pitching for the school team, of course.

Possible Majors

Sport and leisure studies, athletic training, rehabilitation services, or virtually any major that interests you

Will I Be Rich?

You could be rich beyond your wildest dreams. Alex Rodriguez signed a ten-year contract with the Texas Rangers worth more than a *quarter of a billion dollars*. LeBron James signed a $90 million contract simply to endorse Nike. Sports is a huge moneymaking business, and the top athletes get their share. Even some of the less talented athletes at the top levels become incredibly rich. The *average* salary of a Major League Baseball player is roughly $2.3 million per year. The amazing Williams sisters have each made more than $10 million in prize money in their short tennis careers.

However, for each millionaire athlete, there are hundreds of athletes at the lower levels who are hoping to be able to pay for rent and food. For second- and third-tier athletes, playing at those levels is not glamorous, and it rarely pays much, if anything. For instance, top runners can earn enough in one big race, such as the New York Marathon or the Boston Marathon, to provide for a whole year. But finishing in sixteenth place won't earn you anything but blisters on your feet.

Fun Facts

Does Height Matter?

Height is an advantage in most sports, but you can still succeed if you're short. The average height in the NBA is about six feet six, but that didn't bother Tyrone "Muggsy" Bogues. Muggsy was only five feet three tall, about the average height of a professional jockey! He was quick and hard to defend. He scored more than 6,000 points and had more than 6,000 assists and more than 2,000 rebounds from 1987 to 2001. He even had thirty-nine blocked shots!

Unfortunately, you can be too short to be a Major League Baseball player. Eddie Gaedel was only three feet seven when he pinch-hit for the St. Louis Browns in 1951. (The number on his uniform was 1/8!) Because he was so small, it was difficult for the pitcher to throw him a strike. Gaedel walked on four pitches. Then he was replaced by a pinch runner. After that game, the league president made a rule that no similar stunt would ever be allowed again at a Major League Baseball game.

Related Careers

Coach, manager, umpire/referee, personal trainer, physical therapist, dancer, karate master

AUCTIONEER

The Basics

Auctioneers are the fast-talking sellers at public auctions. They try to get the highest bid from a buyer, selling anything from fine art and furniture to coins and other collectibles. To be successful, auctioneers have to have a good voice, charisma, quick wits, math skills, and solid ethics. They also need to be familiar with the property that they're selling. If an auctioneer misrepresents an item, for example, he or she may lose the buyers' trust.

Only a small fraction of an auctioneer's time is spent selling stuff. Auctioneers for big auction houses, such as Christie's or Sotheby's, have other specialty jobs. Some are art experts; others are businesspeople who work with numbers. An auctioneer often spends days at a time on the road, traveling to visit collections—and finding more business.

If you work for a large auction house, you may find yourself learning about many different fields. You might have to know about motorcycles for one auction and French impressionist paintings for another. Many auctioneers develop a specialty, but the learning process rarely stops. Even though an auctioneer has many roles, the actual auctioneering aspect of the job is usually the most fun part. You may be selling a famous piece of art for millions of dollars in front of thousands of people! That can be both thrilling and terrifying.

Preparation

High School

You'll need to be handy with basic math, so work hard in your math classes. You'll also need to be a confident public speaker, so it can help to participate in school debates or plays. Auctions are almost always free and open to the public, so visit them to see what they're like. If you can't get to an auction, many auction houses have traveling exhibitions of their property. Sales are sometimes broadcast on the Internet too!

College

You don't have to be an art history major, but it helps to specialize in something related to an item you might sell. Classes in finance, marketing, management, and even psychology can be a real bonus. An internship at a gallery or auction house is a great first step to establishing a career as an auctioneer. It's also a good idea to keep abreast of the art world by visiting museums or reading trade publications. Get to know your local museums.

Additional Training

Many states require that you obtain a special auctioneering license before becoming an auctioneer. You may also have to pass an auctioneering examination to get behind the podium. Many large auction houses also have an auctioneering school. These schools are basically training programs where you learn to be a top-notch auctioneer. You practice using your voice, physical mannerisms, and math skills with mock auctions—and even acting classes.

Will I Be Rich?

You can do very well as an auctioneer for expensive items. Auctioneers have been paid millions of dollars for holding a single sale. That's rare, however. Usually the money takes a backseat to the pleasure of selling the art or collectibles.

Fun Fact

In 1990, the auction house Christie's sold Vincent van Gogh's Portrait of Dr. Gachet—*within three minutes*—for $82.5 million. As of 2003, it is still the highest price ever paid for a work of art.

[Source: www.vangoghgallery.com]

Quote

"Auctioneers all have their own personalities, which come through with their voices. That's what auction houses are looking for. You're being rewarded for being who you are."

—Jamie Krass, auctioneer (Vice President,
Director of Bidding and Client Services), Christie's

Related Careers

Art dealer, salesperson, historian, art and antique restorer, museum curator, publicist

AUTO MECHANIC

The Basics

An auto mechanic maintains and repairs cars. He or she may specialize in repairing transmissions, doing tune-ups, fixing air conditioners, or be a one-stop shop for customers with car troubles. Although we generally think of auto mechanics as people who work in service stations, they also work in other environments—like on the sidelines of NASCAR races.

When a person with car problems goes to an auto mechanic, the mechanic asks the driver what's wrong with a car. The mechanic then tries to locate the problem by testing the car using equipment and reasoning skills. A mechanic may also choose to test-drive a car to understand the driver's complaint more clearly. Once a mechanic pinpoints the problem, he or she discusses options to fix the problem with the car's owner.

You'll need good diagnostic and problem-solving skills as an auto mechanic, as well as a love of cars and knowledge of how they work. Since most cars nowadays consist of advanced computers and electronic systems, you will need to be familiar with up-to-date advances in car technology. You'll also need to work well with hand tools and be comfortable taking things apart and putting them back together. Strong communication skills, sharp analytical skills, and a willingness to keep learning to meet the demands of the industry are the ingredients for a great auto mechanic.

Preparation

High School

Computer classes and math classes will be most important to your future career. If your high school has an automotive technology program, take it; if not, you may want to look into finding a high school that does offer that training. Ask a service station in your neighborhood if they need any after-school help. On-the-job training is invaluable!

Technical Training

After high school, you will need some additional training. Technical or vocational school programs can range from six months to a year, and most offer classroom training as well as hands-on experience fixing cars. Some community colleges offer automotive service technician training programs that are two years long. These programs include a range of classes, such as business and English classes, to help students gain a well-rounded education. After completing a program, students seeking certification will spend over 1,000 hours working on cars and must pass a written exam.

College

A college degree is not required in this field, but most colleges certainly offer classes that are relevant to this career.

Will I Be Rich?

You can earn a decent living as an auto mechanic, but be prepared to work long hours, including evenings and weekends. If you don't mind getting dirty and can handle the physically strenuous aspect of the job—you will be bending and lifting things all day—it's a very rewarding career. The daily problem-solving challenges of trying to diagnose what's wrong, along with the fast pace of changes in technology, keep it interesting. Plus, you get to meet and help a great deal of people!

Fun Facts

Think you know what a mechanic is talking about? Why not take this little quiz to find out.

1. A doughnut is

   a. a spare tire that is stored in a car's trunk.

   b. what you eat for breakfast with a milk chaser.

   c. a wrench you store in your glove compartment.

2. Why would you keep flares in your trunk?

   a. So you can flag down people who are driving the same car as you are driving and give them the thumbs-up.

   b. Flares keep your trunk warm in the winter.

   c. In the event that you have a flat tire, flares enable you to let drivers know you need help.

3. What does the acronym ABS stand for?

   a. Anything But Soda

   b. Antilock Brake System

   c. Air Bag System

Related Careers

Manufacturer, car salesperson, electrical engineer, mechanical engineer

Answer key: 1: a 2: c 3: b

BANKER

The Basics

Bankers make sure that banks run smoothly on a daily basis. Customer service, accounting procedures, and the technology systems that banks rely on are among a banker's priorities. Bankers are great with numbers, are superorganized, and have strong communication skills.

There are a number of different roles that you can fill as a banker. If you choose to be a *bank trust officer*, you will manage estates and trust funds. If you choose to be a *loan officer*, you will approve loans and make sure people receive them. As an *operations officer*, you will act as the link between banks and the computers that keep them up and running. If you are a *marketing officer*, you will make sure that the public knows about the bank's services and that customer needs are met. Regardless of which position you pursue, you will interact with bank officers in all of the other positions noted, as well as tellers and bank managers.

To be a banker, you must be trustworthy and have a strong moral nature. After all, you are dealing with other people's money. You will need to be a good decision maker as well. Since you will be discussing personal finance issues and interacting with the public a lot in this career, great interpersonal skills would be helpful. Your job will be intense, so the ability to stay calm and work well under pressure is important.

Preparation

High School

A part-time job in a local bank will provide you with great experience for this career path. Even a job as a cashier could be helpful because it will help you get comfortable dealing with numbers. Classes in math, computers, and English will help to develop the skills that bankers use on a daily basis.

College

If you want to be a teller or a bank manager, all you will need is a high school degree; to fill any other position, however, you will need to have a college degree. Take classes in accounting, business, calculus, finance, international business, investment management, economics, probability, and statistics.

Possible Majors

Business administration, business communications, actuarial science, finance, economics, accounting

Business School

Some bankers go to business school to get a master of business administration (MBA) after working for a few years or even straight out of college. In an MBA program, you'll gain a deeper understanding of business practices and principles, and you'll make a lot of connections. Plus, you may be able to earn more money in the job market once you earn the degree. Most MBA programs last for two years, but they can take longer if you attend part-time.

Will I Be Rich?

A banker's job is very challenging; it involves hard work and long hours. On a more positive note, you will get to help people make purchases and manage their money effectively. One banker said, "While the job is demanding, and the pace is often hectic, the satisfaction of making things happen and helping others is priceless." Most bankers make a pretty good salary after working a few years. For the really big bucks, try investment banking.

Fun Facts

Show Me the Money

Don Wetzel is the man we have to thank for inventing the modern ATM, or automated teller machine. The idea for the invention came to him while waiting in line at a bank one day, and in 1973, he got a patent for it. (Luther George Simian had taken the first stab at creating an ATM as early as 1939, but at the time, the idea just didn't catch on.)

Wetzel's first machine was not a full-service teller, but rather just a cash dispenser. The full-service teller machine, which enabled people to make deposits and transfer money, launched shortly after. Not everyone was permitted to use the first ATM machines, though. Only a few people with credit cards and great financial records received ATM cards.

[Source: http://inventors.about.com]

Related Careers

Accountant, investment banker, salesperson, financial analyst, stock broker

CAREER COUNSELOR

The Basics

Career counselors are personal advisors who help people look for jobs that will help build careers. They help people pinpoint their skills, values, and interests, and then present career options that suit their clients' goals and personalities.

As a career counselor, you'll counsel people of all ages. Sometimes you will work with college graduates; other times you will work with people who have worked in one career for over ten years and want to change fields. You use tests to learn more about your clients' goals and personalities, and from those results, you'll create career action plans for them to follow. You research careers to find out what qualifications are needed, what they are like on a daily basis, and details such as how much money your clients are likely to earn. You help your clients fix their resumes, set up interviews, and you give your clients interview tips.

You really have to be a people person to succeed as a career counselor. If you like to listen to people, analyze information they give you, and come up with solutions, this is the job for you. You need to remain objective and remember that you are helping people find jobs that are ideal for them, not you!

Preparation

High School

Start gathering information about different careers by asking your parents, aunts and uncles, and other adults what they do for a living. Read books like this one that explain different careers, and ask your guidance counselor about career possibilities. Classes in a wide variety of subjects will help, since you will probably counsel folks interested in all different types of careers.

College

College classes that help you to understand people will best prepare you for this career. They include communication, education, psychology, and sociology. You can also hang around the campus career center to find out about different jobs—and also to learn more about the career counselors who work there.

Possible Majors
Counseling, psychology, industrial psychology, clinical psychology, sociology

Will I Be Rich?

Your salary and workload as a career counselor may vary based on the type of clients you work with and whether you work at an agency or independently. One career counselor who loves her job said, "People have internal conflicts about what to do for a living—you are the one who helps them to work through those conflicts and move one step closer to finding their ideal job."

Fun Facts

Interview Tips

Not only will you use these tips when you go on your first interview, you'll also offer interview tips to your clients as a career counselor. Here are a few pointers:

Do's and Don'ts

Do:

- Have a positive tone
- Prepare for the tough questions
- Research companies before your interview
- Focus on what you have to offer a prospective employer, not what you want
- Learn about your rights as an interviewee
- Follow up with a note or a phone call

Don't:

- Attempt to use an informational interview to land a position
- Talk about money in the first interview
- Beg for a job
- Lie on your resume

Taboo Interview Subjects

- Citizenship and national origin
- Race, color, or sexual orientation
- Gender
- Love and marriage
- Age
- Disabilities
- Economic status
- Religious beliefs
- Criminal record

Quote

"A career is a terrible thing to waste. Be the terrific, alive, giving person that you were created to be. Everyone has a potential—have you discovered yours yet?"

—Gladys Kartin, career counselor

Related Careers

Guidance counselor, recruiter, psychologist, teacher, consultant, agent

CARPENTER

The Basics

A carpenter is a builder. He or she may build furniture, walls, boats, bridges, houses, or just about anything else. Carpenters use their hands—and some handy tools—to transform wood or other materials into useful products. The work that a carpenter does requires a lot of physical labor. Among their many duties, carpenters must chisel, drill, saw, and sand to create their products. They must lift, lay, measure, and use tools to double check their work.

Despite the hard physical labor, carpentry can be a very creative field. A client usually gives a carpenter blueprints for a design, but the carpenter may have to opportunity to choose the cut of wood and decide how to shape the parts. While drywall installation doesn't give carpenters a chance to be creative, furniture woodworking allows carpenters to focus more on artistic details. Whether their creations are artistic or straightforward, all carpenters get to enjoy the pride of creating a quality piece.

Some carpenters work in a studio; others work outdoors. Working outdoors may sound like fun, but it can be difficult if the conditions are rough. (Try hammering in the snow!) If you're a carpenter for a large construction business, you may work for a supervisor or a manager. If you build furniture, you may have many customers. In that case, if you sell your creations, you need people skills to communicate and negotiate. It all depends on what you want to make and for whom you end up working.

Preparation

High School

Start building! Build a birdhouse, a CD case holder, or anything you think you can use. You might be surprised how much fun it is—and how much money it can save your family! Take classes where you get to build with your hands, such as shop class. Work especially hard in your math classes because a lot of building requires you to work with numbers—particularly geometry.

College

Becoming a carpenter does not require a college degree, but many schools offer majors in related fields. In college, you can learn about carpentry from many different angles, including an artistic standpoint, a mathematical standpoint, and an industry standpoint.

Possible Majors

Math, carpentry, industrial arts, furniture design, sculpture, woodworking, interior design

Training Programs and Apprenticeships

Most carpenters learn to master their trade on the job, rather than in class. Watching experienced carpenters is one of the best ways to study carpentry. There are also special vocational training programs that teach the formal skills. If you don't attend a training program, make sure you participate in an apprenticeship. Being an apprentice gives you the chance to observe qualified carpenters under proper supervision. It can take a few years to learn the essential carpentry skills, but there's no other way around it.

Will I Be Rich?

Carpentry isn't a glamorous career. There aren't many famous carpenters in the world, and it can be hard at times to find steady work. Still, talented and hardworking carpenters can usually find work and are well compensated. And if you can climb your way up to a managerial position, you can earn a very good living.

Fun Fact

Harrison Ford the Handyman?

You probably own movies starring Harrison Ford, like Star Wars or the Indiana Jones series. But you might also own a piece of furniture that he built. That's right—Harrison Ford was a carpenter before he was a famous actor! He still builds furniture in his workshop—when he has time.

Related Careers

Electrician, engineer, plumber, furniture designer, interior designer, sculptor, construction worker, architect

CHEF

The Basics

Everyone knows that a chef cooks food, but most people don't realize how much work goes into being a professional chef. You have to deal with heat, fire, and sharp knives. You need to be able to stand for twelve hours straight and carry heavy objects. The work is hard, and the stress level can be through the roof. But passionate chefs will tell you that their job is artistic and entertaining, and it appeals to the five senses: sight, sound, touch, smell, and (of course) taste.

Most chefs work in restaurants, though others work on boats or in private homes. Some chefs even cook for celebrities as they travel, such as rock stars on tour. Chefs usually spend hours preparing the kitchen before they begin to cook. As a chef, you'll need to gather and arrange your ingredients each day; you need to set up the pots, pans, and other assorted cooking tools.

When the customers show up, the craziness begins. You may get hundreds of orders in only a few hours. To prepare meals properly and promptly, chefs often work with a team of people. Everyone has a job in the kitchen; perhaps three people work on a single plate. New workers are usually treated roughly, though; they need to prove they're reliable before they can be trusted as a chef. When the last meal is cooked, you need to rewrap all the useable food and figure out what you need for the next day. You'll have to clean the kitchen, and you may not get home until two in the morning.

Preparation

High School

Experience is the best form of education for a chef. If you can, work at the best restaurant that will take you, even if it means working for little or no pay and getting screamed at. If it's a good restaurant, your skills and techniques will improve and you will develop a good work ethic to carry throughout your career. When working for a chef, keep in mind that arrogance is the worst quality a young cook can have. You have to show a willingness to learn, and then more experienced chefs will teach you what they know.

College

Again, working in a restaurant is the best experience possible. Classes in accounting, business management, and psychology can improve your business and personal skills in the food industry. For the serious chef, chemistry, physics, and organic chemistry help you understand the scientific side of how cooking works.

Culinary School

Special cooking schools have their advantages and disadvantages. You learn various classic techniques, such as how to make a sauce or stock. But some take almost two years, and they can be very expensive. Even the most well-known cooking schools, such as the Culinary Institute of America, won't make you a chef; they'll just give you some useful skills and additional experience.

Will I Be Rich?

You can get stinking rich if you become famous. But it takes lots of hard work, years of sweating and learning, and luck. If you own your own restaurant, you can generate a lot of money—but of course you can lose money, too. A chef can become rich if he or she is famous and makes money from products, catering, banquets, and advertising. This happens a lot in Europe with the famous three-star (top-rated) chefs.

Fun Fact

More Famous Than Emeril!

George Auguste Escoffier may be the most famous chef of all time. He began his culinary career in France in the mid-1800s. He changed the professional cooking process by streamlining it with the "brigade" system. That's the line of different cooks working on different parts of a single plate.

Quote

"Being a chef is not a glamorous or fashionable job. You have to love what you are doing because success isn't a certainty, and a lot of sacrifice is required."

—Kenneth de Anda, apprentice chef at El Bulli

Related Careers

Critic, banker, artist, nutritionist, dietician

CHILD CARE WORKER

The Basics

A child care worker takes care of children while their parents or guardians are at work or away. It's the child care worker's job to feed and play with the child, and keep the child busy, safe, and entertained.

As a child care worker, you can work in a day care center, a community center, or an after-school program. Although your days will be devoted to the well-being and development of the children in your care, you will also interact with parents to update them on the progress of their children and discuss any concerns. If you work for an individual family, you may live with them or leave each night and return to your own home, depending on the arrangement you make. Child care workers who live with a family may also take on household responsibilities, such as cooking and cleaning.

Watching children learn and grow is highly rewarding, but it also requires a lot of work. You will need to be patient, creative, fair, firm, fun, energetic, and able to go with the flow—with children, you never know what is going to happen! That said, you'll need to know what to do in case of an emergency and remain calm under pressure. Great communication skills (including being a good storyteller) and super organizational skills are necessary, too. The more organized and levelheaded you are, the better for the safety and well-being of the child.

Preparation

High School

Take psychology if your school offers it. English classes will come in handy, too. Volunteer at an after-school program or a community center or babysit for family and friends of the family. Not only will these folks be grateful to you, but you will also get hands-on experience caring for children.

College

Although in some states a high school diploma will get you the job, a college degree will certainly not turn a potential employer away. Classes such as educational development, child growth and development, and psychology will be helpful. A job at a day care center or other type of child care setting will be extremely helpful in getting a job later on. Good references are important, too.

Possible Majors

Child care, child development, education, elementary education, psychology

Will I Be Rich?

How much you earn will depend on your working arrangement. Since child care workers are always needed, chances are that you will be able to work steadily and earn a decent living. Even though you may work long hours, you'll get to hang out with kids all day. You'll have the opportunity to play games and do all sorts of stuff that you can't do at most other jobs. Your days will be both physically and emotionally challenging, but if you've got the right personality type for the job, you'll love it more often than not. Helping children to learn and grow is not only fulfilling, but also just plain fun.

Fun Facts

Do You Have What It Takes?

If you're considering a career in child care, read through the statements listed below. Are any (or all) of these statements true for you? Are any false? If you come up with a lot more trues than falses, chances are that you could be a great child care worker.

I love young children.

I am very patient.

I can be flexible.

I am dependable.

I can think on my toes.

I am sensitive to the needs of children.

I have good communication skills.

I am sensitive to the needs and concerns of parents.

I am empathetic and responsive to children.

I am able to work with people from diverse backgrounds.

I am creative.

I am committed to the safety and welfare of children.

[Source: http://earlychildhood.miningco.com]

Related Careers

Teacher, guidance counselor, special education teacher

CHOREOGRAPHER

The Basics

Choreographers create new dances for dancers to bring to life. They are the behind-the-scenes artists who orchestrate the movements of a dance and then teach dancers to perform them. It isn't just the actual dance steps that choreographers take into account, either; they also consider the sequence of the steps, the transition between steps, the formations that dancers' bodies make onstage, the music, and the overall moods and themes of the dance.

If you become a choreographer, you will spend your days composing dances, auditioning dancers, and guiding and instructing performers at rehearsals. In some cases, you will work with a director to determine what type of dance to create. You will also coordinate with the musical director to find the right music for a particular piece.

Good choreographers are energetic, driven, and creative. They are patient teachers who can express ideas clearly and listen to the concerns of others. If you have a passion for dancing and excellent communication skills, you can go far—but you must also possess a great deal of knowledge about dancing.

Preparation

High School

Dancing is the best preparation for a career in choreography, so start dancing early on. Pay attention to the arrangement of dance steps in dance performances, and try to create your own combinations, either by yourself or with friends. If the drama club is putting on a musical, check to see if they need a choreographer for the dance scenes. And if you're taking dance classes, you may be able to act as a teaching assistant in a class for younger students. Just ask your dance teachers if they need any help.

College

Continue to take dance classes, and participate in college plays. Find out if any choreographers are needed for school productions. An internship with a dance company would be helpful; so would courses in dance history, drama, music, and visual arts. You'll need several years of experience as a dancer to become a choreographer, so keep on dancin'.

Possible Majors

Dance, dance therapy, dance education, theater, art, communications

Will I Be Rich?

Choreographers aren't loaded, but they do make more money than dancers. Expect to work long hours, including nights and weekends, and to travel with dance groups. It's a very social job, and you'll get the opportunity to work closely with many talented performers.

Fun Facts

Not Just for Tutu Wearers

Choreographers don't just create dances for ballet companies. They orchestrate the body movements of dancers in music videos, concerts, movies, musicals, festivals, and other performances. They work with many dance forms, too; African dance, Irish step dancing, bhangra (a type of Indian dance), break dancing, square dancing, ballroom dancing, and Japanese dance are just a few. Wherever there is an organized group of dancers, there is a choreographer.

These famous choreographers came from a variety of backgrounds and represent diverse dancing styles:

- Alvin Ailey
- Fred Astaire
- Cholly Atkins
- George Balanchine
- Mikhail Baryshnikov
- Trisha Brown
- Merce Cunningham
- Agnes de Mille
- Katharine Dunham
- Bob Fosse
- Martha Graham
- Judith Jamison
- Gene Kelly
- Tina Landon
- Mark Morris
- Rudolph Nureyev
- Jerome Robbins
- Ted Shawn
- Anna Sokolow
- Ruth St. Denis
- Paul Taylor
- Twyla Tharp

Quote

"If you love to dance, there is nothing like being a choreographer. Watching dancers onstage bring your ideas to life is like looking in a mirror and seeing a reflection of yourself that intrigues and amazes you."
—Nicole Brooke, a modern dance choreographer

Related Careers

Actor, dancer, producer, dance teacher, director, physical therapist, yoga teacher, personal trainer, athlete, music conductor

CITY PLANNER

The Basics

City planners develop the look, feel, and functionality of a city. They may create a new city from undeveloped land or redevelop an existing city. A city planner's goal is to make the best use of land and resources for people and businesses. City planners create maps of what a city will look like. They take into consideration details such as how tall buildings will be, where highways and airports belong, and where parks, schools, and libraries will be built. A city planner also considers the placement of roads, bridges, train tracks, and tunnels to best serve the community.

As a city planner, you will create solutions to answer many questions. How will the city adapt to change should its population increase? How can the city keep air pollution low? How can traffic jams be avoided? Aside from creating a city that is well organized and efficient, a city planner needs to create a city that is visually pleasing. An understanding of budgets and finance is essential, as you will need to estimate costs and then stick to your budget. You'll need to be familiar with different zoning and property laws, too. Expect to interact with the government, environmental groups, community groups, and architects to see your plans come to life.

What does it take to be a successful city planner? You'll certainly need to be creative, flexible, and detail-oriented, and you'll need superb management skills. In addition, you'll need excellent oral, written, and visual communication skills in order to write proposals and make presentations.

Preparation

High School

Geography, history, math, statistics, geology, and computer classes will come in handy in this field. Research the history of the town or city you live in and find out how it developed into what it is today. Try your hand at creating your own mock cities with games like *Sim City* by Maxis/EA Games.

College

A college degree is the minimum requirement to become a city planner. You will want to take classes in architecture, urban planning, computers, engineering, sociology, economics, English, finance, law, math, and statistics.

Possible Majors

Architecture, urban planning, civil engineering, public administration, urban studies, structural engineering

Graduate School and Licenses

If you go to graduate school for a degree in structural engineering, you'll be golden. It's not necessary, though. In addition, there are two different licensing tests city planners can take to earn extra credentials.

Will I Be Rich?

If you dream about seeing your visions become realities, being a city planner will leave you feeling rich. You can earn a pretty decent living, too, after ten to fifteen years of experience. Your working conditions will vary, and you will work for either the local government or a private company. The job does often require long hours and lots of time meeting with various people. Still, there's a great sense of accomplishment in creating something as incredible as a city.

Fun Facts

Street-Naming Fads

Up until about 1850, streets were named after landmarks, such as churches and monuments; features of the landscape, like hills and rivers; war heroes; or famous leaders. Two exceptions were New York, with its numbered streets, and Philadelphia, with streets named after different species of trees.

- After the 1850s, Philadelphia's tree species street names caught on and were a hit in many cities.

- After the Civil War, street names that included surnames (last names) were the rage. They were often named after private real estate developers.

- By the 1880s, "street" was old news. The word avenue became popular.

- From 1890 to 1910, the words boulevard, park, and court replaced street and avenue. Beauty and nostalgia for the past were motivating factors.

- After World War I, drive replaced avenue. The goal was to create pleasant street names that sounded light and airy. Streets were named after flowers and old English towns, and the suffixes wood and land were often added to names.

[Source: www.potifos.com/streetname.html]

Related Careers

Civil engineer, engineer, architect, inventor, train/subway engineer, real estate developer, construction worker, real estate agent

CLERGY MEMBER

The Basics

Most clergy members would agree that you don't *choose* a career in religion but are instead *chosen*. In fact, most will tell you that they are heeding a *calling* to devote their lives to teaching and practicing their religion. The role of these religious leaders—regardless of the religion they practice— is to provide educational, spiritual, and moral guidance to members of their congregation and to individuals who seek their help. A clergy member not only devotes his or her life to upholding the structure and scripture (sacred writings) of a religion but also to inspiring followers to do the same.

Since there are many different types of religion in this world, it's difficult to define religion; it has to do with a person's devotion to a faith or what a person believes in. Some world religions include Judaism, Christianity (which includes Catholicism and Protestantism), Hinduism, Confucism, Islam, Taoism, Buddhism, Mormonism, Jainism, and Sikhism. If you become a clergy member, expect a life of continuous challenges and hard work. Also expect a sense of intense fulfillment because you are helping others find their way in the world.

If a life devoted to religion is your calling, you will always be on call. People will expect you to be there for them when a loved one dies, when a baby is born, or when disaster strikes. You will need to be kind, compassionate, patient, supportive, dedicated, honest, and inspirational. Clergy members have the opportunity to show people other alternatives and to help people believe in what they thought was impossible.

Preparation

High School

Go to your local place of worship and speak with your clergy members about what a life in service is like. Study the religious texts and scriptures of your faith, and think about whether you could dedicate your life to upholding those virtues. Your class work in English, history, and psychology will allow you to better understand the scripture and to clearly communicate.

College

You don't need a college degree to become a clergy member, but additional education can only increase your understanding of the religion. In addition, you will have the opportunity to take classes that explore the meaning of religion.

Possible Majors

Religious studies, theology, theosophy, philosophy, Hebrew, Islamic studies

Vocational Preparation and Requirements

Depending on your faith, it may take years to complete the required training to become a clergy member. In addition, there are certain restrictions for some religious positions. For example, women cannot become Orthodox Jewish rabbis, Catholic priests, or ministers in certain Protestant denominations.

Will I Be Rich?

If you care about money, you are probably in the wrong field! While a career in religion will not bring you financial rewards, it will bring you priceless spiritual and emotional rewards. Some clergy members do receive a small salary, while most take a vow of poverty.

Fun Facts

Sneak Peek

If you want to experience life in a monastery, you can! Lots of monasteries have guest quarters in which they allow visitors to stay with them for anywhere from a night to a few weeks. Some monasteries that allow visitors include Mepkin Abbey in South Carolina and St. Joseph Abbey in Spencer, Massachusetts.

Myth v. Reality

Myth: Monks live in silence and do not engage in physical activities.
Reality: Some monks, called hermits, may take a vow of silence in which they live apart from other monks. Most monks, however, are not silent all the time and play sports just as we do! Jogging, basketball, and soccer are some sports that monks play. One Buddhist monk said, "I have some of my best meditations while I jog!"

Quote

"The one requirement to be a monk, aside from commitment to your teachers and a love for our planet, is the desire to help people heal."
—Brother Wayne, Plum Village Monk

Related Careers

Counselor, psychologist, social worker, professor, teacher

CLOWN

The Basics

Clowns make people laugh! They may perform skits, juggle, create balloon sculptures, do magic tricks, and mime. Clowns work at circuses, carnivals, amusement parks, parades, shopping malls, birthday parties, and children's hospitals. They can find work just about anywhere people want to laugh and have fun.

If you want to be a clown, you will first need to create your very own clown personality. That means that you need to choose a name for your clown self, make up a story about your history, and create a costume. You will also need to create your clown face or the makeup and expression that help define your personality. Are you smiling, frowning, or indifferent? Many clowns have big red noses, crazy hair, humongous shoes, and oversized pants, so you might want to consider some of those wild accessories. If you work in a circus, you'll rehearse your routines each day; you will probably have responsibilities, too, ranging from helping to set up for performances to cleaning up. If you work for yourself, performing at birthday parties and other events, you will need to schedule those events, promote yourself with advertisements, and manage the money you make.

A successful clown has a great sense of humor and loves interacting with people. Wearing lots of makeup and dressing up in your clown costume is part of the job, so you will need to feel comfortable in your clown getup. Above all else, you'll need to have a really positive attitude and tons of energy.

Preparation

High School

Now's your chance to be the class clown! But be sure not to be disruptive—even clowns need to do well in school. You need to start clowning around somewhere, so volunteer to be a clown for children's hospitals or for a birthday party. Art and drama classes will help with your act and costume, while math will help you manage your money. English and foreign languages will help you entertain kids from all different backgrounds. If you want to practice mime, try communicating with your friends and family without using any words.

College

Some people who become clowns start out attending college and pursue some sort of performance major. Others attend a clown training program. While the famous Ringling Bros. and Barnum & Bailey Clown College in Florida closed in 1999, aspiring clowns can still find related courses and conventions nationwide.

Will I Be Rich?

If making people smile is your main goal, you will love being a clown. You won't be the next millionaire, but you will have a lot of fun bringing happiness to others. Circus clowns are usually paid a yearly salary, while clowns who entertain at private events charge a certain rate per hour. Future clowns should expect to spend a lot of time in front of the mirror before each performance, perfecting both face and costume, in addition to long hours performing. And if you join a circus, you'll travel all the time, so try not to get attached to any one location.

Fun Facts

Would You Like Fries with That?

Willard Scott, a weatherman for NBC's *Today* show, was one of the most famous Bozos in the early 1960s. Then, when *Bozo the Clown* went off the air, Willard became the very first Ronald McDonald. He appeared in three commercials in 1963, but he looked very different from the Ronald we know today.

[Source: www.thejoyboys.com]

Clown Controversy: Who Created Bozo the Clown?

Alan W. Livingston claims that he is the true creator of Bozo the Clown, one of the world's most famous clowns. Livingston claims he created a Bozo at the Circus record in 1946 for Capital Records.

Larry Harmon, an entrepreneur and performer, is often considered the creator of Bozo. Livingston, however, claims that Harmon only played the part of Bozo and marketed the clown, while Livingston created Bozo's redhead look and helped come up with the famous clown's name.

[Source: http://abcnews.go.com]

Related Careers

Actor, magician, artist, comedian, dancer, talk show host, makeup artist

COACH

The Basics

Coaches teach athletes how to improve their abilities. They might help the athletes fine-tune their skills with drills, or they might help them understand the rules and the tools of the game they play. For team sports, coaches and managers also make the important decisions that affect the team. That includes deciding which players get to play, choosing the particular strategies, and encouraging a positive team spirit.

There are coaches at all levels of sports. Little League coaches usually volunteer for the job. Coaches for elementary and high schools usually teach classes and also coach for additional pay. College coaches and managers usually focus on their role full-time. For major teams, there may be many coaches: A head coach leads the team, and other coaches specialize in one area, such as hitting, defense, or strength training. There are coaches for just about every sport that is played professionally.

A coach can make all the difference for a talented athlete. A great coach has the ability to draw out an athlete's full potential. He or she can lead a team to greatness. A poor coach can impair an athlete's future. He or she can destroy a team's morale and chemistry. The power of a coach or manager is great and so are the responsibilities that go with the job.

Preparation

High School

It's never too early to be a coach. Volunteer at a local Little League or sports camp. Even if you can't be the head coach or manage the team, you should be able to help train others. Of course, that means you should know your game of choice—and be able to play it. Most coaches and managers get their start as an athlete because knowledge of the game and its finer points are so essential.

College

Continue to get real coaching experience, whether it's with your school team, a youth league, or a sports camp. That's the best preparation you can get, along with playing in a sport yourself. While you're in college, you can study psychology or communications because being a coach or manager requires you to build strong personal relationships. You can also take classes related to the physical training of sports. You should learn how to administer first aid, prevent injuries, and track the progress of the development of young athletes.

Athletic training, recreation management, sport and leisure studies, physical therapy, education

Will I Be Rich?

There are coaches who spend hundreds of hours a year coaching for nothing but the sheer enjoyment of helping others. Many coaches at the lower levels of professional sports still need other jobs to make ends meet. However, the further you can advance up the coaching ranks, the more money you can expect to make. The top-rated coaches and managers now make nearly as much as top athletes: millions and millions of dollars.

Fun Fact

Must You Go Pro?

You don't have to be an amazing athlete to be a marvelous manager. In fact, many of the greatest coaches and managers of all time never played professionally at the top level. More than one hundred managers of major league baseball teams became the leaders of their team without playing at that top level. That includes current manager Buck Showalter, who became manager of the New York Yankees at the age of thirty-five—which was younger than some of the athletes on the team!

Related Careers

Athlete, manager, referee/umpire, physical therapist, teacher, personal trainer

COLLEGE DEAN

The Basics

A dean oversees the daily life of students and faculty on a college campus. For students, a dean acts as an academic advisor, a source of information, and a counselor when it comes to resolving academic conflicts. A dean also is responsible for placing students with high grades on the *Dean's List*. When it comes to the faculty, a dean hires professors, prepares budgets, and creates and enforces academic policies and procedures.

Deans generally have an area of specialty. You may be the *Dean of Arts and Sciences, Dean of Business, Dean of Education, Dean of Math, Dean of Social Sciences,* or another type of dean. There's also a *Dean of Students* who coordinates admissions and strives to improve student life on campus. A dean's daily routine is pretty hectic. You will meet with students and faculty members throughout the day. You will be responsible for developing academic programs and helping students figure out what classes to take. In addition, you will set standards for your faculty and supervise them.

In order to become a dean, you will need prior experience as a professor or admissions counselor on a college campus. You'll also need to be confident, determined, and highly organized.

Preparation

High School

Run for class office to get some leadership experience. Try to get some office experience and teaching experience after school or during the summers. In school, make sure to show interest in your class work and study hard in all subject areas. You'll use what you learn in English, math, and computer courses the most in this job.

College

See if you can work part-time for a dean at your school. Seek out experience in teaching or admissions, even if that means becoming a peer tutor or helping administrators file applications. Classes in business will give you an edge on the technical and organizational aspects of leadership positions; English, computer classes, and communications will help you develop a plan of action and put it into effect.

Possible Majors

Education, education administration, business administration

Graduate School

A master's degree (and in some cases, a PhD) is a requirement for someone who wants to become a dean. Most deans have graduate degrees in their area of specialty. You will probably teach for a few years to immerse yourself in college life before working as a dean.

Will I Be Rich?

If you enjoy working with students and love being on a college campus, this job will offer you many rewards. College environments tend to be fun and full of energy; you will probably find that this setting motivates and inspires you. Expect to work long hours during the beginning and end of each semester—students and faculty will need your help during these busy times.

Fun Fact

The Dean of American College Deans

Herbert E. Hawkes was in a class by himself when it came to deans. Hired by Columbia University in 1910 as a math professor, he went on to become dean of the college in 1917 and held the position until his death in 1943. He was an advocate of core curriculum in college; this means that he believed in a complete education that included courses in many different subject areas before graduation. In addition, he supported new classes in the humanities, including contemporary civilization. He was inspirational to both students and his peers at Columbia.

[Source: www.college.columbia.edu]

Related Careers

College president, principal, college administrator, guidance counselor, professor, teacher, politician, consultant

COLLEGE PRESIDENT

The Basics

A college president is the head honcho on a college campus. He or she oversees all departments of the college, creates budgets, and plans and directs college events. The president also helps create college rules and policies and makes sure that everything runs smoothly.

As a college president, you will spend your days meeting with college faculty about everything from course curriculum to how to raise funds for the college. You will discuss future plans for the college with both college administrators and community leaders. You will figure out how to increase student enrollment, attract great faculty, and keep the college thriving. You will spend a lot of time at conferences and meetings with other college presidents, discussing budgetary issues and other topics that pertain to the world of higher education.

You should possess great organizational skills and a flair for public speaking if you want to run a college. You will need to be good with numbers, too. Dedication, hard work, and perseverance will come in handy for this career, as will the ability to motivate others. You will need to be a good decision maker, and you can't crumble under pressure.

Preparation

High School

You will want to get as much leadership experience as possible. Run for class office or aim for a leadership position in a job, club, or organization. Classes in communication, math, and English, as well as computers, will give you some of the skills you need to succeed in this job.

College

A college degree is necessary if you want to run a college. You can major in any field you'd like to teach; you'll probably have to teach before rising to the ranks of college president. In college, adding classes in business, education, and education administration will allow you to run a business in an educational environment.

Possible Majors

Education, education administration, business administration, communications

Graduate School

You will probably need to earn a master's degree and a PhD to run the show at a college or university. It's difficult to get a job as a college president; to raise your chances of success, do your best in school and get grades that make you stand out from the crowd. Continue to strive for leadership positions—the more experience you have, the more confident and efficient you will be as a leader.

Will I Be Rich?

You will work long hours, including evenings and weekends, if you are president of a college, not to mention the time you will spend traveling! You will attend many meetings, conferences, and community events, too. You will earn a good living in this career, but it takes time to work your way up to the top. Some college presidents compare the job to being the president of a small country!

Fun Facts

Notable College Presidents

Woodrow Wilson, the twenty-eighth president of the United States, was also the president of Princeton University from 1902 to 1910. He was extremely well respected; he made many contributions to Princeton's growth as a fine institution of higher learning.

[Source: http://etc.princeton.edu]

Charles Eliot was president of Harvard University from 1869 to 1909. He was the editor of The Harvard Classics, a series that includes notes and reading guides on major figures in literature and philosophy and other fields in the humanities.

Related Careers

Professor, principal, teacher, comedian, college administrator

COMEDIAN

The Basics

If you love making people laugh, you might be destined to be a comedian. Though all comedians earn a living making people laugh, success can come in many forms. You can be a stand-up comedian, an improvisational comedy wizard, or a comic actor, playing funny roles in movies or plays. Many smart comedians become comedy writers for such shows as *The Simpsons* or the *Late Show with David Letterman.*

A successful comedian needs to not only be funny but also distinctive. There are lots of people who can tell funny jokes; you have to find a way to do it so people will remember it was you who made them laugh. So you need to have a unique comic perspective on the world to go along with a strong sense of timing and rhythm.

To be a stand-up comic, you need to develop your art form at bars and small clubs. That's where you can build confidence and sharpen your delivery. To be a comic actor, you have to either audition for funny roles or make up your own comic characters. Comedy writers must submit their sketches and writings to sitcoms and other comic mediums. Steady work can be tough to find, however, so most aspiring comedians work second jobs to pay their bills. In the meantime, you have to pass your name out, spread the word of mouth, and hope for a big break. You have to be willing to stick it out.

Preparation

High School

While you're in high school, write a comedy column for your student newspaper. Create a spoof article, and come up with whatever funny ideas you can. Creative writing or playwriting classes can improve your writing, which will help make you a better comedy writer. Continue to try to make milk come out of your friends' noses.

College

If you study drama, you will learn how to show emotion. If you study journalism, you will learn to write and to get at the truth of a story. Comedy often mixes truth and emotion in ways that don't normally go together. While you don't need a college degree to be a comedian, you may need one to survive until you get there. In other words, you will probably need some college-related skills to pay the bills while you work the comedy circuit.

Workshops

There is no age limit—young or old—on going to an established improvisational theater and taking improv workshops. Almost every city has comedy clubs, and most will have classes that teach you how to be a comedian. Go sign up. If you love improv, study with the gurus in the improv mecca, Chicago. It helps to watch comedy films to learn what's funny—and what's funnier.

Will I Be Rich?

Just ask Jerry Seinfeld if you can get rich in comedy. *Forbes* magazine reported that Seinfeld made $267 million by 1998! But you can also try for years and years, never making more than a few dollars per gig. In fact, Jerry Seinfeld worked the stand-up circuit for eleven years before he got his big break with his sitcom.

Fun Fact

You probably know Conan O'Brien from his late-night talk show on NBC. But he wasn't always a star. He attended Harvard University, where he headed the Harvard Lampoon, *the world's oldest humor magazine. After he graduated, he wrote sketches for three years for* Saturday Night Live *and even won an Emmy award for it. He later wrote episodes for* The Simpsons *and produced the animated show, too.*

Quote

"Nothing is more fun than goofing off in front of a crowd and having them laugh and cheer and even pay you for it. But it's a battle to get there. The ones who make it are the ones who don't quit. You won't make it in a year or two."

—Orf, comic actor

Related Careers

Actor, clown, writer, screenwriter, producer, agent

COMPUTER PROGRAMMER

The Basics

Computer programmers are the men and women who create programs for computers. They write the programs in a special language called code, which tells a computer what to do. Programmers create computer software that performs a certain task. For example, that task may help people chat with each other on the Internet, or it may help businesspeople plug their sales numbers into a spreadsheet. There is an unlimited number of designs that a programmer can create. Most computer programmers work for large companies, and they are told what their program should accomplish by the program designer/analysts.

Some programs are simple and take less than a day to write. Other programs are complicated and may take more than a year. Complex programs may even require many programmers working on different parts of the program. Either way, you should expect to spend hours at a time working by yourself in front of a computer screen. You should be organized, because it can be a real challenge to keep track of a large program's structure.

Writing the program is only half the battle. You also have to test it to make sure it works properly and as perfectly as possible. So you'll need to exercise excellent problem-solving skills. You may also have to update or expand the program for future versions. Being a computer programmer can feel very much like getting paid to solve puzzles.

Preparation

High School

If you're serious about becoming a computer programmer, you can learn at least one computer language before you graduate high school. Even if you only learn the basics of a simple code (such as BASIC), it will help you know whether computer programming is for you. Take any programming classes if your school offers them, and practice. You can even write your own program. Maybe you can write software that tells you your grade point average—or even write your own video game!

College

A computer science degree will help prepare your programming career. But logic is important too because computers only understand logic (true or false). Learn as many computer languages as you can. Some of the common computer languages have names like C, C++, Java, and FORTRAN. Most programmers know more than one coding language; the more you know, the more jobs there will be available to you when you graduate. Depending on what kinds of programs you want to write, other classes can help. For example, if you want to write software for engineering applications, then an engineering degree can be useful. Just be sure to get real-life computer programming experience.

Will I Be Rich?

Most programmers spend their first few years on the job learning the trade. After a few years, you can earn more responsibility and begin to code more intricate systems. That's when the money becomes significant. To earn the really big money, you must move up from computer programmer to designer or analyst, which may not be as much fun because you usually spend less time on the computer. Starting your own business also gives the potential for more wealth.

Fun Fact

Debug This!

Computer programmers have to debug programs that they write. That means they get rid of the bugs—or the small problems—in their work. But did you know where the term bug comes from? Back in the 1960s, an insect caught in a computer caused it to malfunction, hence the term "debug."

Myth v. Reality

Myth: Computer programmers don't need to talk to people.
Reality: Many computer programmers work with executives, designers, and clients. They are the ones who tell you what the program should do, so you'll need to be able to talk to them.

Related Careers

Statistician, mathematician, computer scientist, physicist, engineer, video game developer, computer technician, web producer, web designer

COMPUTER TECHNICIAN

The Basics

A computer technician fixes computers. Computer technicians use their knowledge of computer hardware and operating systems to diagnose problems, maintain systems, and troubleshoot issues to prevent future problems. Many computer technicians work full-time for one company. It is possible, however, to work on a freelance basis and serve many companies and/or individuals.

As a computer technician, you will need to be prepared for anything and everything to go wrong. Computer problems come in as many varieties as people do, and you will respond to a lot of technological emergencies. In order to understand the problem, you'll need more than just technological skills—you'll need people skills, too, so you can interact easily with the users. In many cases you will interact with other information technology personnel to discuss solutions and get the job done. The type of work you do will depend on the company you work for, the size of the staff, and the type of computer equipment that's used in the company.

Calling all technology buffs: This may be the career for you. If you want a career as a higher-up in information technology, this job is a good place to start. In order to find logical, quick, and efficient solutions, you'll need strong problem-solving skills. And since technology is always advancing, you will need to keep learning by taking courses and attending training programs.

Preparation

High School

Start early. Learn how to build your own computer. Read up on the latest technological advances in computer magazines, and learn everything from office programs, to coding, to video games, to scanning and printing pictures. Math, science, computer science, and English classes will be most useful to you.

College

A degree in computer science or a related field is your best bet for grabbing a job after graduation. Experience is crucial in this industry, so a part-time job or an internship in computer technology will also be a big help for your future.

Possible Majors

Computer systems analysis, computer engineering, computer and information science, computer graphics, web design

Will I Be Rich?

The intellectual challenges you face as a computer technician will give you a good mental workout. And aside from helping you sharpen your problem-solving skills, this career will reward you with a pretty decent living. While the hours may be long, including some evenings and weekends, your days will not be dull. If you pay your dues, there is usually room for advancement.

Fun Facts

Did We Mention That You Should Start Early?

A high school junior, computer whiz kid Thomas J. Rothwell is no amateur when it comes to building websites and providing technical support. Thomas was the Webmaster for El Dorado High School's website when he was only 15. Now two years later, he manages the web pages, which include a school newspaper, and is the school's computer technician. He not only provides technical support but also restores and repairs computers for the school.

Quote

"People panic when their computers break down. They say that they will die if their computer doesn't work. When I tell them that it's all fixed, the smiles, the gratitude that people express always reminds me why I love this job!"

—Andrew Weiss, computer technician

Related Careers

Computer programmer, web producer, web designer, web editor, network engineer, systems analyst, professor, mathematician, webmaster

CONSTRUCTION WORKER

The Basics

Construction workers are responsible for building and maintaining the structures in our lives—from roads, highways, and bridges to schools, homes, and museums. A construction worker, also called a construction laborer, has many varied duties. He or she may prepare sites for construction, operate equipment such as drills and machines that mix concrete, load and unload trucks that carry heavy materials, or pour and smooth concrete. When construction workers aren't building brand-new structures, they also repair existing buildings and roads.

As a construction worker, you can specialize in building and repairing highways or tunnels, or you can serve as a general construction worker. If you choose the latter option, your roles will range from building homes and office buildings to removing hazardous waste materials from a site. At the beginning of each project, you'll receive instructions from the construction manager in the form of drawings or written plans. Then it'll be up to you to execute the job. You will usually work as part of a team, but you may also work alone on some jobs. Safety is always an issue, and it will be your job not only to stay safe yourself but also to make sure your site is safe for the public.

If you have a knack for building things (which many people don't!), you might enjoy being a construction worker. You'll need to be hardworking and reliable and to have great problem-solving abilities. A lot of what you do will rely on physical strength and an ability to follow directions.

Preparation

High School

Take classes in technology education, industrial arts, and drawing and sculpture. Any class where you can use your hands—whether to draw or drill—will be helpful. Find a building or repair project to tackle at home. Your parents will be grateful, and you'll gain some great hands-on experience while building muscles. Classes in math, computers, physics, and chemistry will be helpful, too.

College

You won't need a college degree to work construction, but it won't hurt. Besides, you can learn a great deal about the structures you'll be working on in the future.

Possible Majors

Structural engineering, architecture, mathematics, sculpture

Formal Apprentice Programs

Formal apprentice programs are not required, but they save time by combining classroom lessons and on-the-job training. It may take you from two to four years to complete the program, but you'll learn everything you need to know about reading blueprints for projects, using tools, and following safety procedures. You will need a high school degree to enter a formal apprentice program, and you must be physically strong. You can choose to concentrate on building construction, highway construction, or environmental cleanup.

Will I Be Rich?

As a construction worker, you can expect to hear loud drills, smell fumes, and operate dangerous machinery. You will work long hours, get dirty, and shed a lot of sweat. Since the work often depends on projects and the weather, there may be times when you are out of work. But if you like to build things and work outdoors, this job may suit you. "There's something really fulfilling about working hard each day and knowing you are creating something," said one Brooklyn construction worker. As a construction worker, you can make enough money to get by; become a construction *manager*, and you'll start seeing larger paychecks.

Fun Facts

Reality TV?

Joe Millionaire *star* Evan Marriott *pretended to be a superwealthy bachelor to win a wife on television, while in real life he was a construction worker!*

Ancient Construction Sites

Stonehenge, in Wiltshire, England, is one of the greatest construction mysteries of all time. No one knows for sure who constructed the massive stone arrangement, but we do know that the construction began over 4,000 years ago and that Stonehenge took approximately 2,000 years to build!

[Source: http://exn.ca]

Myth v. Reality

Myth: Construction workers are always goofing off on the job.
Reality: Construction workers work hard for their money! Their jobs are incredibly demanding, and they're also dangerous.

Related Careers

Plumber, electrician, architect, city planner, carpenter, interior designer, engineer

CORRECTIONS OFFICER

The Basics

Corrections officers, also called detention officers, watch over criminals in jails and prisons to make sure that they follow the rules. They oversee inmates' activities, including their meals and their work assignments, and they help transfer inmates from one location to another. Corrections officers also search criminals' cells for weapons and drugs and for fire hazards that may make the cell unsafe for the prisoner. They also try to stop prisoners from trying to escape. If a fight breaks out between inmates, it's a corrections officer's job to break it up and maintain order.

As a corrections officer, you'll spend a lot of time around prisoners. Aside from making routine checks to verify that cell doors and exits are secure, you'll have to search packages from visitors to make sure they don't contain weapons. You will write up daily and weekly reports on inmates, noting their behavior, and provide oral reports to your supervisors, too. In case of a prisoner acting up or an uprising, you'll have to call for help immediately! That's because you won't be carrying a weapon; the objective is to keep weapons as far away from inmates as possible. A corrections officer's law enforcement powers only exist when he or she is at work in a jail; he or she does not patrol the streets like a police officer.

Physical strength, good health, and a strong moral and ethical nature are necessary to be a corrections officer. You will need to remain calm under pressure and have good logic and reasoning skills to work with criminals on a daily basis.

Preparation

High School

In order to be physically suited for this job, you'll have to develop strength—gym class is a start, but you can also get involved with sports and take some self-defense courses. You should also work on building up your communication skills early on. You'll learn the basics in English. Beyond that, you can learn a lot about people through psychology, sociology, social work, and conflict resolution.

College

While not a requirement, a college degree can give you some bonus skills on the job. For example, you can learn more about criminals in psychology and criminology.

Possible Majors

Criminology, psychology, sociology, forensic science

Additional Requirements

In order to be a corrections officer, you must be at least eighteen to twenty-one years old and have a high school degree and a clean police record. There are training programs that teach the law, self-defense, and interpersonal communication skills. Programs vary from state to state and may have additional requirements. For example, some require that applicants pass eyesight and hearing tests, while others may require that you know how to use a weapon safely and effectively.

Will I Be Rich?

The job of a corrections officer is incredibly important. If you understand this and are willing to work in a dangerous environment in order to protect others, this may be the job for you. As a corrections officer, your working conditions will vary. While some jails are clean and well-lit, with good ventilation, some are old, dirty, noisy, and overcrowded. In any case, you won't become rich in this field. Since inmates need to be supervised twenty-four hours a day, seven days a week, you'll work different shifts, during the day and at night. Over time you may advance to corrections sergeant, supervisor, or warden.

Fun Facts

Prison or Jail?

The difference between a jail and a prison is that a jail is a temporary holding place, whereas a prison is a long-term holding place. If a suspect is found guilty of a crime, he or she is moved from a jail to a prison.

Island Prisons

Located in New York City, Riker's Island is home to more than 15,000 jailbirds! It may sound bizarre, but the concept of using islands to contain prisoners is nothing new. Alcatraz Federal Prison, on an island off the coast of San Francisco, was home to notorious criminals like Al Capone and George "Machine Gun" Kelly from 1934 to 1963. Robben Island, off the coast of Cape Town, South Africa, became internationally known because it was used to imprison those who were opposed to apartheid.

Related Careers

Police officer, detective, security guard, probation officer, criminologist, special agent

COSTUME DESIGNER

The Basics

Costume designers create new costumes or alter existing costumes for television, movies, and plays. If you don't think it's an important job, think again: The clothing worn by an actor truly affects how you perceive his or her character. One of the most important factors that costume designers must take into account is a story's setting; the time period, location, and environment in which a story is set largely determine clothing styles. Each character's personality and economic status, as well as the overall tone of the movie or play, helps to determine his or her wardrobe.

As a costume designer, you will sketch ideas for costumes and discuss the sketches with a director, designer, and stage manager. Once all of you agree on the look and feel of the costumes, you will create a budget and a production schedule. You will then shop for the right fabrics and accents for your designs, create patterns, and sew the costumes. If you're aiming for a strange effect, you may have to dye, paint, or dirty the fabric to make it look just right. Finally, you will tailor the costumes to fit the actors. You may also create hats, shoes, and other accessories such as handbags. In some cases, you will simply alter existing costumes so they can be reused in different productions.

To be a great costume designer, you must have a vivid imagination and know how to sew and sketch well. You must also have great multitasking skills and a keen attention to detail. It's not easy to make it big as a costume designer, so you'll have to be strong willed and determined.

Preparation

High School

Watching a variety of plays and movies is a great way to become familiar with the work of costume designers. Ask yourself: What, if anything, would I have done differently if I created that character's costume? Try out some of your own sketches for characters in books you have read. Then, to get some hands-on experience, help to create costumes for school plays. Art history and other history classes will teach you the styles associated with different periods of time. Art, drawing, sewing, and computer graphics classes will help prepare you to turn your costume ideas into outfits.

College

If you study costume design in college, you'll get to work on the costumes for campus theater productions. You will probably assist the main costume designer and create some of your own designs. Take a figure drawing class—it'll enable you to sketch realistic bodies for your designs. Any kind of history, but especially costume, art, and theater, will be important resources.

Costume design, fashion design, fashion merchandising, art, illustration, painting, theater

Graduate School

If you want to go on to work as a costume designer for a university and teach there as well, a master of fine arts or a PhD in theater design is necessary.

Will I Be Rich?

You may be rich if you work on a major film, but most costume designers are richer in passion for their career than in dollars. You will need to stick around to fix costumes at all stages of a performance or film shoot until the actors hang up your costumes for good; in other words, depending on the project, your schedule may be hectic and include some very long days. Some highlights of the job are that you get to work with interesting and creative folks and see your designs onstage or on the tube.

Fun Facts

All Dolled Up

Costume designers helped bring to life the characters in the following films (and their sequels):

- Dracula (1931)
- Gone with the Wind (1939)
- The Wizard of Oz (1939)
- Willy Wonka and the Chocolate Factory (1971)
- Star Wars (1977)
- Superman (1978)
- Star Trek (1979)
- Excalibur (1981)
- Edward Scissorhands (1990)
- The Last of the Mohicans (1992)
- The Age of Innocence (1993)
- Don Juan de Marco (1995)
- Emma (1996)
- Gulliver's Travels (1996)
- Mulholland Falls (1996)
- Austin Powers (1997)
- Dr. Seuss' How the Grinch Stole Christmas (2000)
- X-Men (2000)
- Crouching Tiger, Hidden Dragon (2001)
- Moulin Rouge (2001)
- Spider-Man (2002)

Related Careers

Fashion designer, makeup artist, seamstress, artist, director, producer, set designer, hairdresser

COWBOY/COWGIRL

The Basics

When you think of the words cowboy or cowgirl, do you picture someone who tends land and raises cattle? Or does the image of an amazing athlete riding a bull in the rodeo come to mind? You may even imagine a sharpshooter of the Old West, with a ten-gallon hat, chaps, and boots with spurs, or a chart-topping country singer, decked out in country-style clothing. As far as careers are concerned, there are two different types of cowboys and cowgirls: those who tend cattle and other livestock, and those who compete in rodeos for money.

A cowboy or cowgirl who works on a ranch is also called a *cowhand*. He or she works the land and tends cattle year-round. In addition to his or her outdoor duties, a cowhand may also work in an office and handle paperwork for the ranch. The most important trait for a cowhand is the ability to work well with animals. Most cowhands spend a lot of time on horseback while working, gathering cattle and moving them to new pastures. Some cowhands love riding so much that they take a stab at riding for money.

If you seek a life of adventure, a career in rodeo competitions might interest you. There are many different rodeo events for cowboys and cowgirls, including bull riding, bareback riding, calf roping, team roping, breakaway roping, goat tying, steer wrestling, and barrel racing. Although these competitions sound super fun, beware: Rough falls, broken bones, and even concussions are not uncommon in bull riding and other dangerous events. You'll need to be in excellent physical shape to compete in rodeo events. And if and when you fall, you'll need to have the determination to get back up and try again.

Preparation

High School

No matter which type of cowboy or cowgirl you'd like to be, you'd better learn to ride horses and rope calves. Try to find some work on a farm, and take some riding lessons (many cowboys and cowgirls have been riding practically since they could walk, so try to catch up!). Check to see if there are any horse riding camps or classes in your area for a more intense learning environment. Stay in great shape, so you can make the most of your training.

College

You don't need a college degree to tend cattle or ride in the rodeo. But if an injury puts you out of the loop, it's good to have a degree to fall back on.

Will I Be Rich?

Ranch cowboys and cowgirls—cowhands—usually earn a modest living. But if you own your own ranch or farm, the stakes are higher. As for professional rodeo cowboys and cowgirls, it can go either way. The very top professional riders can earn over $100,000 a year. On the other hand, those who fall walk away with nothing but a bruised-up body. The perks of this lifestyle, like the excitement and travel, are countered by the risk and danger involved.

Fun Facts

No Boys Allowed

Bull riding is generally considered a male sport, as it's extremely dangerous, but a number of brave cowgirls do compete. Women have to ride the bull for six seconds; whereas men ride for eight seconds. In the early 1900s, women were featured in some Wild West shows, including Buffalo Bill Cody's. These days, the Professional Women's Rodeo Association has over 120 members. Each year, it oversees or approves more than twenty female-only rodeos and seventy events. The finals competition hosted by the PWRA each year offers leading ladies over $50,000.

[Source: www.wpra.com]

Clowning Around with Cowboys

Ever hear of rodeo clowns? They do much more than entertain! When a cowboy takes a fall, the rodeo clown distracts the crazed bull or bronco long enough so that the cowboy can run for cover. Underneath the clown suit is not only a brave soul, but protective clothing to keep the rodeo clown safe!

[Source: www.texasstampede.org]

Related Careers

Athlete, jockey, race car driver, farmer, veterinarian, zoologist, park ranger

CREATIVE DIRECTOR

The Basics

A creative director basically directs a whole crew of people to create a product. The creative team may consist of artists, writers, marketing people, and production assistants. The creative director will outline what a client wants and then parse out responsibilities to different members of the team.

As a creative director, you may work for a publishing company, an advertising firm, or a design firm. You may be involved in creating designs and copy (written material) for book projects, magazines, newspapers, television, posters, or packaging for products. Regardless of what you are working on, you will oversee your creative team. You will give the team feedback on their work; brainstorm with them to develop concepts or designs that fit the client's needs; and create a schedule so the project will be completed by the deadline. You will review the final product and approve (or disapprove) what the creative team has put together. Finally, you will present the final product to the client.

You will need to be creative, flexible, and decisive to succeed as a creative director. Great communication skills are required to understand exactly what your client wants and to explain it to your team. You'll also need to have good management and organizational skills to be able to coordinate all of the details of multiple projects.

Preparation

High School

You will want to take lots of graphic design, art, and English classes to prepare for a career as a creative director. Join the staff of your school newspaper and/or yearbook. It'll give you some experience laying out pages, creating ads, and working with a creative team of people. If you have the opportunity to lead the production of either the paper or the yearbook, that's even better!

College

A college degree is highly recommended for this career. Sign up for courses in advertising, art, graphic design, business, computers, photography, English, and marketing. Continue to pursue opportunities at the school newspaper, yearbook, or other productions. Assisting with set or costume design in school productions can even provide some creative teamwork experience. An internship at a magazine, publishing company, or advertising agency will be a great way to break into this field.

Will I Be Rich?

Creatively, you will be very rich. You will work alongside talented, innovative people. Your creative visions will help shape some fantastic products. The hours may be long, and pressure to meet deadlines is sometimes intense, but if your client loves the product, you'll have a great sense of accomplishment. On top of all that, you can earn a pretty good living as a creative director. You'll have to work your way up, though; you'll probably start your career as a member of the creative team.

Fun Fact

MTV's Creative Director

If you love MTV programs such as Beavis and Butt-Head, Liquid Television, Cartoon Sushi, *or* Daria, *you have Abby Terkuhle, president of MTV Animation and creative director of MTV to thank. Terkuhle is the creative force behind MTV's funky animation for movies and television. Before working for MTV, Mr. Terkuhle was a producer for* Saturday Night Live *and* Showtime/The Movie Channel.

[Source: www.cencom.org]

Related Careers

Advertising executive, artist, graphic designer, writer, publisher, printer, publicist, filmmaker, illustrator, animator

CRIMINOLOGIST

The Basics

Criminologists study the behavior of criminals and the crimes they commit to understand what makes them tick. They search for patterns among criminals. By finding patterns, criminologists are able to figure out what type of criminal—what age group or gender, for example—is most likely to commit certain crimes, like robbery or assault. This information is very helpful to the police, as it can often enable them to solve crimes. Criminologists also evaluate how criminals respond to their punishments.

Your life as a criminologist will never be boring! You will spend your days questioning suspects to see if they fit the crime under investigation; attending autopsies (that's when they examine a body to figure out the cause of death); and performing research. One New York criminologist said of his job: "It's not easy trying to make sense of senseless crimes, but it is certainly intriguing work!" If gory details horrify you, however, beware: This job is not for the faint of heart.

You will need to be analytical, creative, detail-oriented, insightful, and logical to do well in this field. You'll also have to be a great problem solver who steps back to see the whole picture when you're investigating a case. Patience and commitment are necessary for this job, as is a sense of determination.

Preparation

High School

You'll need to develop your logical thinking skills early. Pay attention in your general math and science courses, and try logic or statistics, too. Try taking psychology and sociology courses if they're offered at your high school—you'll want to get a head start at getting inside people's minds. In addition, some schools have crime-solving programs that seek to get to the bottom of school and community crimes.

College

You will need to earn a college degree in order to become a criminologist. Classes in computer science, criminology, English, law, logic, research methods, sociology, and writing will come in handy.

Will I Be Rich?

The cogs in your mind will always be in motion if you're a criminologist. If you love a challenge and enjoy solving problems, you will be very happy in this career. Expect to work long hours and to travel to interview or interrogate suspects. Your initial paycheck won't break the bank, but the level of excitement should help make up for it. Plus, if you stick with it, there's room for advancement.

Fun Facts

Comparing Crime Rates

Criminologists in different parts of the country will have to consider the unique population and culture of the community they work in because crime rates vary from city to city. For example, in 2002, there were 508 robberies for every 100,000 people living in New York, New York; there were 465 robberies for every 100,000 in San Francisco, California; and there were 830 robberies per 100,000 people in Miami, Florida. (Okay, so it's not exactly a fun fact, but let's face it: The job of a criminologist is pretty serious.)

[Source: www.realestatejournal.com]

Related Careers

FBI agent, detective, police officer, corrections officer, lawyer, scientist, special agent

CRITIC

The Basics

A critic shares his or her experiences and opinions with the public. He or she publishes reviews in newspapers, magazines, or on the Internet. Then people use this information to help them decide whether they might enjoy the same experience, whether it's a musical or a five-course meal.

Here's how it works: Critics must first perform research. They may watch movies, plays, concerts, or dance performances; they may read books; they may attend art shows; or they may dine at various restaurants. Then, no matter what the subject matter, the critic writes a review summarizing his or her experience and offers an opinion about its quality. They also provide an overview—this can be a heads up on the plot, subject matter, or style of work, or a description of a particular dish.

If you want to be a critic, you'll have to become somewhat of an expert in the field in which you write reviews. After all, you can't very well review a ballet if you don't know the first thing about dance. For example, if you are an *art critic*, a background in art history or firsthand experience as an artist will give you the authority to comment intelligently on another artist's work. If you are a *literary critic*, you should know about other books by the author you are reviewing, as well as authors writing in the same style or genre. As a *food critic*, your most valuable feature will be a big appetite; you'll also need a good working vocabulary of culinary terms. Strong writing skills and a passion about your area of specialty are crucial for success as a critic.

Preparation

High School

In your free time, write reviews of movies, video games, art, music, or whatever else you enjoy. Then try publishing some of your reviews in the school newspaper—it's a great place to make your debut. Take classes to develop knowledge in your area of interest. Writing skills are essential for any kind of critic, so make sure you do well in English and creative writing.

College

Check out movies, performances, art exhibits, and other events on campus. Submit reviews to your college newspaper, as well as magazines and local papers. (Inquire about submission guidelines if you're not sure whether they'll print your reviews.) Keep track of your published reviews so you can start to build a portfolio. Keep taking English and writing courses. Continue your specialized studies so you can become an expert critic.

Possible Majors

English, English composition, English literature, journalism, creative writing, art history, art, film, theater

Will I Be Rich?

You'll be happy as a critic if you're critiquing what you really enjoy, but you probably won't strike it rich. You will be working with a lot of deadlines—sometimes for multiple publications—and you may have to review an event that you don't even want to go to. You will need to be flexible to attend a lot of after-hour events, but there are plenty of perks. You'll see some great shows or consume some amazing meals while on the job!

Fun Fact

Thumbs-up, Thumbs-down

Roger Ebert is an incredibly famous movie critic. He cohosted the television show Siskel & Ebert *with Gene Siskel for twenty-three years and now cohosts* Ebert & Roeper *with Richard Roeper. Wondering how he got started? Ebert became a sportswriter for a newspaper when he was only fifteen years old!*

[Source: http://tvplex.go.com]

Quote

"As a food critic I get to eat at the hottest new restaurants, order whatever I want, and then get to tell people about my meal. It's the greatest job in the world aside from being a chef!"

— *Christiane Bennett, food critic and chef*

Related Careers

Journalist, writer, artist, editor, chef, taste tester, actor, dancer, musician

CROCODILE HUNTER

The Basics

It may sound cruel to hunt a crocodile for its skin, but back in the day, that's exactly what crocodile hunters did. For many years, shoes, handbags, and other crocodile-covered accessories were in demand. It wasn't until the number of crocodiles declined that some crocodile hunters became concerned. If they wanted the species to survive, they would have to stop hunting crocodiles. Thus, a new wave of crocodile hunters was born with the chief goal of protecting the animals. Now crocodile hunters find crocodiles in danger and move them to areas where they can breed and stay safe.

If you choose to become a modern-day crocodile hunter, you will need to be incredibly brave and adventurous. Crocodiles are powerful creatures, so there are physical requirements for this job. You'll have to be strong and able to move quickly and quietly to avoid bodily harm. Good hearing will keep you on your toes, and keen eyesight will help you pick camouflaged crocodiles out of the surrounding terrain. You'll also have to handle the crocodile with care so you don't hurt it during relocation. To do this properly, you'll need to know about the crocodile's anatomy and physiology. In fact, there are a lot of little details that go into the successful capture and relocation of crocodiles.

Crocodile hunters work for wildlife parks, crocodile farms, and zoos. Some are wildlife biologists who do research for various wildlife organizations. Many also lecture and teach at colleges and universities. In order to be a great crocodile hunter, you will have to love crocodiles and animals in general. You must be patient, persistent, careful, and calm to get the job done right.

Preparation

High School

Volunteer at a local animal hospital. Classes in biology, anatomy, chemistry, English, and physics will get you started in the right direction. In your free time, read up on crocodiles; learn about their diet, natural habitat, and behavior early on. Take trips to the zoo to see some crocs in person.

College

If you really want to be a crocodile hunter, you'll have to work hard. Biology, animal physiology, anatomy, and principles of wildlife management will be the most useful subject areas. If at all possible, try to get some hands-on experience working with a crocodile hunter.

Possible Majors

Biology, animal physiology, zoology, ecology, environmental science, wildlife management

Will I Be Rich?

While you may work in dangerous situations, if you love crocodiles and aren't afraid of their snapping jaws, this is the career for you. You may work long hours into the night—crocodiles are nighttime creatures—and you may have to travel a lot, depending on whether or not you live near crocodile territory. Chances are that you will work with a team of people to capture and transport the crocodiles. Most crocodile hunters don't make a ton of money; instead, their good deeds provide a different type of fulfillment.

Fun Facts

Did You Know?

- There is just one species of crocodile in America, called Crocodylus acutus. It's also known as the American crocodile.

- The order Crocodilia includes crocodiles, alligators, caimans, and gharials. Caimans are small crocodilians that live in Central and South America; gharials have long thin snouts, and they live in India, Burma, and Pakistan.

- Crocodiles are an endangered species—there are fewer than 500 in the wild in North America. Alligators, on the other hand, are not so much at risk. In North America, there are 1,000 alligators for every 1 crocodile in the wild.

[Source: www.gatorland.com, the website of Gatorland in South Orlando, Florida]

A Must-See

For more info about the life of a real live crocodile hunter, watch The Crocodile Hunter Diaries on Animal Planet. You'll see Steve and Terri Irwin and the zoo team at the Australia Zoo in action as they tend to some of the zoo's most dangerous animals.

Related Careers

Veterinarian, researcher, environmentalist, environmental scientist, ecologist, zoologist, park ranger, farmer, fisherman

DANCER

The Basics

Dancers use their bodies to communicate with an audience, expressing ideas, rhythms, and stories. Dancers may specialize in classical ballet, modern dance, jazz, tap, or a variety of cultural dances. They can work in groups, with a partner, or as soloists.

As a dancer, your days will consist of auditions and rehearsals. If you're a quick learner, you'll have an advantage; you will have to learn the timing and sequence of many different dance steps at auditions and rehearsals. You may perform in ballets, operas, movies, musical theater, music videos, or television shows. You won't be perfect for every role, though, so you'll have to be tough. The sooner you recover from rejection, the sooner you can go on your next audition!

Talent, dedication, energy, patience, endurance, and a love of dancing make for a great dancer. You'll need to be in peak shape to make it through long, physically demanding rehearsals. Good listening skills and an ability to work well with others and be open to feedback are necessary for dancers, too.

Preparation

High School

Get involved early! Sign up for dance classes to gain some formal training and join drama or dance clubs at school and in the community. Check out some local dance performances. Learn more about the performing arts by taking courses in music, drama, art, and art history. To find colleges with dance programs, you may wish to consult *Dance* magazine's *College Guide,* available at www.dancemagazine.com.

College

College isn't a requirement for professional dancers. But if you want to teach dance later on down the road, you can complete your degree now rather than later. Classes to take include choreography, communication, dance history, drama, kinesiology, musical theater dance, and movement analysis.

Some dancers attend professional dance schools instead of or in addition to college. These schools often have their own dancing troupes that dancers may perform with while attending school.

Possible Majors

Dance, dance therapy, dance education, communications

Will I Be Rich?

Most dancers will tell you that they're doing what they've always wanted to do. That's why the job brings satisfaction to many dancers, even though it doesn't pay tons of cash. The life of a dancer can be stressful and exhausting, but also exciting and invigorating. If you're in a troupe that tours, you'll have the added perk of traveling often. Sometimes, between jobs, dancers will have to find other work to supplement their income.

Fun Facts

This is Crazy

Ever heard of Dance Dance Revolution? It's a video game by Konami for Sony PlayStation in which players must follow programmed dance moves, competing either with the computer or with another player. In the arcade version, players dance on a platform, while the shy beginner can play on a mat at home. In July 2002, Damian Sarcuni was declared world champion of DDR Max 2, a recent version of the game. Damian's total score was a whopping 315,802,020 points! If you've ever played it, you know how impressive that is!

[Source: www.twingalaxies.com]

Dance-athon!

If you need to learn some moves to fuel an upcoming dance contest, check out any of the flicks listed here:

- Saturday Night Fever (1977)
- The Turning Point (1977)
- Fame (1980)
- Flashdance (1983)
- Staying Alive (1983)
- Beat Street (1984)
- Breakin' (1984)
- Breakin' 2: Electric Boogaloo (1984)
- Footloose (1984)
- A Chorus Line (1985)
- Fast Forward (1985)
- Girls Just Want to Have Fun (1985)
- White Nights (1985)
- Dirty Dancing (1987)
- Tap (1989)
- Lambada (1990)
- Strictly Ballroom (1992)
- Shall We Dance? (1997)
- Dance With Me (1998)
- Mad About Mambo (1998)
- Center Stage (2000)
- Save the Last Dance (2001)

Related Careers

Actor, choreographer, artist, dance teacher, physical therapist, yoga teacher, personal trainer

DETECTIVE

The Basics

Detectives investigate people, places, and events in order to solve crimes or mysteries. How do they gather information? Well, they try to track down clues through interviews, research, and evidence from crime scenes. Detectives may work for a local, state, or federal police force, or they may be private detectives, hired by an individual or organization to perform an investigation.

The activities that fill your days as a private investigator will vary, depending upon what type of case you're working on. You could be doing anything from performing a background check to carrying around a photograph of a missing person. If you work for a law enforcement agency, you will dress in plain clothes, unlike a police officer. You will conduct interviews, review records, track suspects, and take part in arrests and raids. You may specialize in a particular area, like fraud or narcotics. If you are a private investigator, you'll fulfill your duties to your client and report the results. Sometimes you will have to give your client bad news; at other times, your findings will relieve your client of his or her fears.

You will want to keep a low profile as a detective so you can get your job done without arousing suspicion. Therefore, you'll need to be calm and careful. Having some decent acting skills wouldn't hurt, either! You will also need excellent communication skills, dedication, and a willingness to take risks to succeed in this field. Good vision, hearing, and physical strength are important, too, as you must be prepared to defend yourself.

Preparation

High School

Reading up on mystery novels is a pretty good start to becoming a detective. Of course, you'll also have to study the law to learn what constitutes a crime; sociology and psychology to learn about human behavior; and writing and speaking in public to be able to communicate your findings. You can also solve mini mysteries in your own daily life, but beware—you need to have a warrant to search through someone's stuff for evidence.

College

While a college degree isn't necessary, it's always a safe bet. A two-year associate's or four-year bachelor's program in criminology or criminal justice is recommended for aspiring detectives. Your classes may include sociology of law, statistical analysis, and theories of crime.

Possible Majors

Criminology, criminal justice, sociology, psychology

Police Training

If you choose to work for a law enforcement agency, you will need to go through police training. You'll spend from six to nine months training full-time at a police academy, and you'll learn a range of skills required to protect people and defend yourself. You will need to work as a police officer for a few years before being promoted to detective. Most private detectives also gain experience in law enforcement before starting their private practice.

Will I Be Rich?

Detectives often work long or irregular hours, including evenings, weekends, and early mornings. Most detectives are constantly on the go, trying to obtain information for their case in any way possible. Depending on the case you are working on, your job may be stressful and dangerous. You won't earn a ton of money as a detective on a police force, but you will do a great service to your community; private investigators may earn more. If you crave excitement, are great at solving problems, and love to help people (and spy and pry!), this may be the career for you.

Fun Facts

Everybody's Favorite Crime Solvers

Tune in or pick up a book to check out some of TV and literature's most famous sleuths and mystery shows:

- *Sherlock Holmes (1883)*
- *The Hardy Boys (1927)*
- *Nancy Drew (1930)*
- *Dragnet (1951)*
- *Hawaii Five-0 (1968)*
- *Columbo (1970)*
- *Charlie's Angels (1976)*
- *Magnum, PI (1980)*
- *Scooby-Doo and the Mystery, Inc. Gang (1980)*
- *Inspector Gadget (1983)*
- *Miami Vice (1984)*

- *Murder, She Wrote (1984)*
- *Law & Order (1990)*
- *NYPD Blue (1993)*
- *The X-Files (1993)*
- *Ace Ventura: Pet Detective (1994)*
- *The Mystery Files of Shelby Woo (1996)*
- *Nash Bridges (1996)*
- *The Profiler (1996)*
- *CSI: Crime Scene Investigation (2000)*
- *Monk (2002)*

Related Careers

Criminologist, corrections officer, police officer, security guard, FBI agent, lawyer, secret agent

DISC JOCKEY

The Basics

Disc jockeys play music on the radio or in clubs. Your main goal as a DJ is to attract followers and keep them tuning in or dancing the night away. To do this, you'll have to know what people like and form a relationship with your audience. You'll have to love music and know a lot about it, too. You could be playing Top 40 hits, classic rock, reggae, or any other kind of music, depending on what type of station (i.e. college radio) or club you work for.

Your responsibilities as a disc jockey will vary depending on whether you work in a station or a club. If you work at a radio station, you'll need to know how to use technical equipment in the DJ booth. You'll also do quite a bit of talking—you may report on the news, traffic, weather, sports, or conduct interviews in addition to playing music. If you work at a club, you'll mix songs, using high-tech turntables and other sound equipment. Since you'll be performing in front of a live audience, you can watch the crowd to gauge whether they like the songs you're playing; if people are leaving the dance floor, you can try to round them back up with a classic!

Disc jockeys are creative, spontaneous music lovers with charismatic personalities and voices. They have the ability to make people happy with the music they play and popularize a band by playing their music! The radio station or club you work for will usually dictate the type of music played; however, you'll still likely have a lot of freedom to choose which songs will be in your set.

Preparation

High School

Intern for your local radio station or throw parties and be the DJ. Of course, you'll need to have a decent music collection and a place for friends to dance. Start making demo tapes of your DJ sets early on. You can learn about your presentation by listening to your demos. Classes in music, voice, computers, theater, and psychology will be helpful.

College

A college degree isn't necessary for an aspiring DJ. Still, experience working for a college radio station can be extremely beneficial to your future plans. Classes such as audience research, broadcasting, broadcast management, communication, ethics of mass media, and media criticism will provide a solid base for your career. Keep making demo tapes, and send them to local radio stations.

Will I Be Rich?

Unless you become a star radio personality or a well-known DJ, chances are that you will not make millions at this job. You will, however, get to be creative and have a lot of fun. Plus, working at the radio station, you may get to meet artists and see concerts for free! Music lovers: As long as you can go with the flow and be spontaneous, and you are open to having an odd work schedule, you have the potential to excel in this job.

Fun Facts

A Star Is Born

DJ John "Jellybean" Benitez produced and remixed over thirty top hits and more than ninety top-ten singles. He introduced Madonna's music to the club scene, creating remixes of her early songs. He also founded the record label H.O.L.A. Recordings in 1995.

How did he get started? He began by mixing music as a kid. Soon enough, he became a famous DJ in the Manhattan club scene, performing at clubs such as Studio 54, Funhouse, and Xenon.

[Source: www.discostepbystep.com]

Quote

"I see being a DJ as an art form, a way of building a musical bridge to connect people to something that is greater and beyond themselves."
–Michele Arcand, DJ, Portland, Oregon

Related Careers

Journalist, musician, music executive, rock star, promoter, music conductor, VJ, recording technician

DOCTOR

General practitioner • dentist • optometrist • opthalmologist
pediatrician • podiatrist • cardiologist • surgeon

The Basics

Doctors safeguard our health. They examine patients, diagnose problems, prescribe treatments, and treat injuries and diseases. They also help prevent future illnesses by teaching their patients how to stay healthy. We trust our doctors to prescribe only the best treatment for our medical problems; basically, we trust them with our lives. That's not a responsibility that doctors take lightly! Many medical students swear by the Hippocratic oath—promising to work honorably for their patients' health and well-being and exercise sound judgment—before becoming doctors.

It takes a great deal of knowledge, confidence, hard work, and courage to become a successful doctor. Devotion to your patients and a strong desire to help others will keep you going, challenge after challenge. There are a lot of interpersonal skills you'll need, too, as clear communication with your patients is crucial. Whether you're explaining the steps a patient should take to get better or speaking with a patient's family member about a serious illness, you must remain clear, tactful, professional, and compassionate.

There are many different types of doctors out there. Which do you wish to become? Here are a few of your options:

A *general practitioner* is usually the first doctor that a patient consults if he or she would like an overall checkup or if something doesn't feel right. General practitioners can also send patients to different types of *specialists* for additional testing and more specialized treatment.

A *dentist* treats teeth and gums. Dentists give checkups, diagnose cavities and gum problems, discuss treatment options with patients, and treat their patients. They also provide helpful tips about tooth and gum care to avoid developing problems in the future.

If you are interested in helping people improve their vision, you may want to be an *optometrist* or an *ophthalmologist*. Optometrists check a patient's focus and depth perception and test to see if a patient is nearsighted, farsighted, or has a stigmatism or another eye problem. They then prescribe glasses or contact lenses and eye medications if necessary. Ophthalmologists specialize in the treatment of eye diseases and perform eye surgery. They may also prescribe contact lenses and glasses.

If you love kids and want to keep them healthy, you may consider becoming a *pediatrician*. A pediatrician focuses on children's health issues. He or she provides routine checkups and immunizations for kids. Pediatricians also diagnose and treat diseases, injuries, and infections in children. A pediatrician's job requires a lot of patience and skill, since many children are less than thrilled to visit the doctor's office.

A *podiatrist* diagnoses and treats foot problems, such as circulation problems, diabetes-related foot problems, and ingrown toenails. The goal of a podiatrist, aside from treating foot problems, is to educate their patients about how to care for their feet (thus preventing more foot problems!).

A *cardiologist* diagnoses and treats heart disorders. Cardiologists use electrocardiograms (electrical recordings of the heart), echocardiograms (images of the heart created by ultrasound waves), and X-rays to learn more about a patient's heart condition. Based on the results of these tests, a cardiologist prescribes a treatment for the patient. Medication, a healthier diet, and exercise are some of the treatments a cardiologist may prescribe. In cases that are more serious, a cardiologist may have to operate.

A *surgeon* performs operations to correct or repair bones, tissues, or organs. There are many different types of surgery. Preventive surgery stops diseases from spreading. A surgical procedure can remove an infected organ or implant a new organ in a patient's body. Surgeons can treat patients by scheduled appointments or work in emergency rooms and operate on critical patients who are rushed into the hospital. Surgeons may specialize in a number of different areas, such as plastic surgery, reconstructive surgery, heart surgery, brain surgery, and preventive surgery.

The above is just a sample of a few different types of doctors. Here's a list of a few more:

- Allergist
- Anesthesiologist
- Chiropractor
- Dermatologist
- Endocrinologist
- Gynecologist
- Neurologist
- Oncologist
- Psychiatrist
- Radiologist
- Urologist

Preparation

High School

Volunteer or work part-time job at a hospital or a health care facility; you'll gain some experience in a health care environment, and you'll observe doctors and other medical staff at work on a daily basis. Courses in science, especially biology and anatomy, will be most helpful in your pursuit of medical knowledge. But psychology, English, and communications classes will help you develop an indispensable sensitivity toward people and an ability to communicate with them. Your grades will have to be excellent in order to qualify for medical school admission, so make sure to study!

College

You will need to earn a college degree in order to apply for medical school. You don't have to pursue a pre-med major, but you'll do best to take your share of science courses—otherwise, you may have to take additional classes in order to qualify for medical school. These may include organic chemistry, biology, physiology, or a number of other medical or scientific courses. A diverse background in science will serve as a useful reference in your daily life as a doctor.

Possible Majors

Biology, chemistry, genetics, pre-medicine, pre-optometry, pre-dentistry

The MCAT

You will need to take the Medical College Admission Test (MCAT) to apply for medical school. Start preparing early. Admissions are competitive, and you will need to earn a high score to get into the best medical schools. Some fields have additional testing requirements. For example, if you choose to go to school for optometry, you will need to take the Optometry College Aptitude Test (OCAT).

Medical School

If you get into medical school, celebrate, and then get ready to study like crazy! For the next four years your time will be split between working in a hospital or medical practice and taking classes. After four years, you will take the United States Medical Licensing Examination (USMLE). If you pass the USMLE, you will receive a medical degree. After that, you must complete an internship and residency, which can take from three to eight years, depending on your specialty. Once you have completed these requirements, you will need to continually keep up to date on advances and changes in medical procedures.

Additional requirements may apply for certain specialties. For example, if you are pursuing the path of an optometrist, after four years of optometry school, you will receive a doctor of optometry (OD). Then you must pass the state board exam to receive a license to practice optometry in your state. If you wish to become a dentist, after four years of dental school, you must pass state exams to receive a license to practice dentistry in your state.

Will I Be Rich?

You can earn a great deal of money as a doctor, but expect to contribute much of your time and energy to your work. Being a doctor is physically, mentally, and emotionally exhausting. You will have to work incredibly long hours (especially when you are a resident!) and remain kind, compassionate, and caring. The life of a doctor is one in which you are always learning and growing, and always trying to help people. If you love working with and helping people, the satisfaction you gain from this profession will far outweigh its drawbacks.

Fun Facts

America's television-viewing audience just can't get enough of the drama that surrounds the daily lives of courageous doctors. Check out the list below to find out what hit TV shows provide a behind-the-scenes look at the lives of doctors and their patients:

- General Hospital (1963)
- St. Elsewhere (1982)
- Doogie Howser MD (1989)
- Chicago Hope (1994)
- ER (1994)
- Hilltop Hospital (1999)

Doctor Tips

Here are some of the ways doctors try to better communicate with their patients:

- Show your patients your pearly whites—a smile can ease their tension. Be sure to shake hands with your patients, and when you speak to them, look them in the eye.

- Remember that your patients are people, not body parts or diseases!

- Don't use doctor lingo when you talk to your patients—keep it simple so that they understand what you're talking about.

- Show your patients what you are talking about by using pictures and diagrams to help them understand what you're explaining.

[Source: www.piscesonline.ca]

Quote

"You have to love humanity to be a doctor. If you do, your job will always be your greatest reward."

—Paul Friedman, dentist

Related Careers

Veterinarian, scientist, physical therapist, nurse, holistic doctor, massage therapist

EDITOR

The Basics

An editor is a wordsmith; much like a carpenter works with hammers and nails or an auto mechanic works with car parts, an editor works with words. Editors take an author's written words and improve them, shaping the text so that it reads properly. An editor takes into account much more than grammatical accuracy—he or she must also consider the style, tone, audience, and organization of any written piece.

You can be a newspaper editor, working on a daily publication and sharpening the stories on each day. You can be a magazine editor, working on a weekly, monthly, or bimonthly publication that usually has a focus (sports, fashion, weddings, anything). Or you can be a book editor, which means you might be editing anything from science fiction novels to a book like this one.

Depending on your specific role, your work may vary significantly. Newspaper editors, for example, often work late at night under tight deadlines, helping to craft the stories of the day. Book editors may have more time, but their projects are much bigger. Chances are you will also have to work with writers on a regular basis.

To be an editor, you have to have a passion for the English language. You should love to read, and you should love to write, too. Because while authors aren't perfect, an editor's job is to make their writing appear that way.

Preparation

High School

Read as much as you possibly can. Read books, magazines, even the backs of cereal boxes. Read critically, too; look for ways to improve upon existing writing with a reworded sentence, a different adjective, or even an extra comma. Most high schools have a school newspaper. Get involved, and help improve other writers' stories. Help your friends with their papers and reports, and you'll learn to edit.

College

Most companies require their editors to have a college degree. Editors don't need to specialize in any one field of study—they just need to make sure they have a strong English background. (A journalism degree would be more useful than a math degree, for example.) Don't be afraid to study something you love, such as history or archaeology, as long as you get the chance to write and edit.

Be active in campus newspapers or magazines, and donate your time to a local media organization if they're willing to have you around. If you can get some practice editing on a professional publication while you're in college, you'll be in great shape by the time you graduate.

English, English composition, English literature, creative writing, history, journalism, technical writing

Will I Be Rich?

Editing isn't the most glamorous career. Authors are the ones who get their names on the covers of the books, and if their name even appears at all, editors' names appear a few pages later in the book. Good editors are well compensated, but few really strike it rich. To be a very successful editor, you have to manage a team of writers and other editors. This position—often called managing editor or editor in chief—earns the big bucks.

Fun Fact

Every writer needs an editor. That's true for even the best writers. Ernest Hemingway had a favorite editor, Maxwell Perkins, who was devoted to helping turn Hemingway's writings into works of art. The professional relationship between Hemingway and his editor blossomed, and Hemingway even called Perkins his "most trusted friend."

Quote

"The hours may be long and the deadlines can be a little stressful, but an editor is paid to solve puzzles and use their brain. Plus, you get to work around some very smart people. When your work is done, it's a very satisfying feeling to hold the finished product in your hands."

—Michael Bagnulo, editor

Related Careers

Writer, publisher, printer, translator, literary agent, journalist/reporter

ENGINEER

*Aerospace engineer • chemical engineer • civil engineer
electrical engineer • mechanical engineer • robotics engineer*

The Basics

There are many different types of engineers, and each one does a very different job. But whether you're an *environmental engineer* or a *nuclear engineer,* the basic principles are the same. Engineers use math and science to improve the design of a product or to create new products. The product can be a telephone or a bridge; it can be anything!

An engineer might design a robot that helps with farming or help improve the space shuttle for NASA. There are millions of possible jobs, and they all require problem-solving skills. Engineers have to not only find the solution to a problem, but also they need to know how to make that solution happen. In addition, they have to be sure that the project doesn't take too much time or cost too much money.

Engineers aren't done after they've built or improved their products, either. Engineers have to test the product to make sure it works properly. They also have to maintain their products, making sure that they know why something might go wrong. Some engineers work as supervisors in factories or out in the field. Other engineers even work in sales because engineering know-how can be important in business. There are so many jobs an engineer can have, it's no wonder they're always in demand!

Check out some of the different types of engineers:

Aerospace engineers—otherwise known as rocket scientists—create, develop, and test aircraft, spacecraft, and missiles. In addition, they oversee the manufacture of products they create and develop new ways to improve space exploration and aviation.

Chemical engineers figure out how to develop the products that chemists invent in labs. They come up with safe, efficient, and practical methods to manufacture chemicals, fuel, food, or environmental products and take part in all the stages of manufacturing.

Civil engineers design and create everything from bridges to sewer systems for a city. Before a civil engineer gets to build anything, he or she checks out the land, reviews the plans, and decides how much money and resources will be needed for a job. A civil engineer also sets schedules, hires staff, and orders building materials. Once all the pre-building responsibilities are met, it's time to build. When a project is complete, a civil engineer makes sure that everything works properly and makes necessary adjustments.

Electrical engineers create, develop, test, and improve electronics. They are the brains behind the electronic devices you use every day, such as televisions and stereos. Electrical engineers work in teams to design and implement new electrical products used in homes, hospitals, and other areas.

Mechanical engineers design and develop machines, tools, and other mechanical devices, from engines to elevators. Apart from machines that we rely on in our daily lives, mechanical engineers also design machinery that is used in manufacturing and agriculture.

Robotics engineers develop and create robots that are used for everything from operating machinery to flying to other planets. A robotic engineer's focus is to create technology that helps robots think for themselves.

Preparation

High School

Engineering is based on math and science. Make sure that you're really, really comfortable working with numbers. More importantly, explore how things work around you. For example, take apart an old phone and put it together again. (Please ask your parents first or we'll get in trouble!) Build your own home computer. Use your curiosity to discover how technology works.

College

An engineering degree alone could take you pretty far. But you could use a science degree in physics or geology, too. It depends on exactly what you want to do as an engineer. Use your time in college to discover your specific passion. See which classes you like best and focus on them. For example, if you like building robots and motorized cars, take more mechanical and robotic engineering classes. An internship at an engineering firm will give you insight into the real world of engineering.

Possible majors

Aerospace engineering, applied physics, architectural engineering, bioengineering, civil engineering, chemical engineering, computer engineering, electrical engineering, engineering design, industrial engineering, nuclear engineering, petroleum engineering, mechanical engineering, physics

Graduate School

Go-getting engineers use their time in graduate school to hone in on their skills or to learn a broad skill-set (such as management). Some of the most specialized engineering fields, such as nuclear engineering, may even require a graduate degree. Many times, however, engineers earn graduate degrees because they want to teach. It's not uncommon for a company to pay for an employee's master's degree.

Additional Preparation

Many mid- and large-sized engineering companies will train you. The knowledge you can gain from these work classes may be priceless. Take advantage of whatever comes your way, especially if it's free.

Will I Be Rich?

Most engineers work for a company that pays pretty well. To really strike it rich, however, you have to use your engineering skills to become an inventor. You can get rich with one useful invention that lots of people use.

Fun Fact

Did You Know?

Engineers are responsible for some of the most fun things in the world. They design roller coasters to be safe and exciting. They create special effects to make movies seem realistic (and sometimes scary). An engineer even invented the snowboard!

[Source: www.americanengineeringcampaign.org]

Quote

"The best part of the engineer's job is being able to come to solutions, either by yourself or in a team. There is a real feeling of gratification to making something work that either didn't exist, or making it work like it never did before."

—Max Cascone, senior software engineer, Motorola

Related Careers

Scientist, mathematician, statistician, designer, entrepreneur, computer programmer, computer technician

ENTREPRENEUR

The Basics

An entrepreneur uses his or her own resources to start a business. Entrepreneurs work for themselves and get to be their own bosses. Of course, owning your own company is hard work. It requires that you have a keen business sense, as well as the money to open your own business. To keep your business afloat, you must also be hardworking and responsible.

What kind of business can you start as an entrepreneur? The possibilities are endless. You can start your own commercial photography business, for example, or a company that provides a groundbreaking technological service. In any case, you'll start by developing a business plan and rounding up enough money to get the ball rolling. You will research your competition to figure out how to make your company and products unique. You'll manage your money and oversee every single detail of company production, from stocking office supplies to marketing. Your company can be tiny—with you as the only employee—or you can manage a team of employees. On the one hand, if your company is profitable, you may be able to expand your business. On the other hand, you are taking a risk, and your business may fail.

Motivated, dedicated, passionate, and creative are some of the adjectives that describe the type of people who own their own businesses. Entrepreneurs are talented leaders with a strong knowledge of business and finance.

Preparation

High School

Start your own business from your home. You can take photographs, build websites, make jewelry, or even walk dogs—and you can sell all of these products and services. Find out where your passions lie, and then think of what type of business you could run that relates to those passions. If you love acting but don't want to be a professional actor, you could eventually open your own playhouse.

College

Now it's time to round out your expertise in a certain area—be it technology, advertising, or basically anything—with business courses. Classes in accounting, finance, marketing, management, probability, and statistics will help you figure out how to plan your business. Find out what other similar companies are out there. Seek out others who have started their own companies for advice and inspiration.

Possible Majors

Business administration, business communications, accounting, finance, marketing, or whatever field you plan to start your business in

Will I Be Rich?

Expect to spend most of your time working if you are an entrepreneur—at least for the first few years. There's a lot of hard work involved in opening up your own business. But if your business succeeds, you will reap great rewards. Though there are ups and downs to owning your own business, most entrepreneurs love not having a boss to report to. If your business never takes off, don't despair. Each project is a learning experience, and you can make your next endeavor more successful.

Fun Facts

Young Entrepreneurs

Juan Riera Pol was born in Manacor, Spain and started working with computers when he was seven. In 1995, he became the youngest Microsoft Solutions Provider in Spain, at only ten years old. In 1997, at age twelve, he formed his company, Babysoft S.L., working with his sister and father.

[Source: www.islaweb.com]

Adam Stites was only fifteen in 1995 when he first started his business selling paintball products online. The website, xtremex.com, offers paintball products and other "extreme" stuff, like skateboards and snowboards, to countries all over the world. Adam won wide recognition in the Northwest for being the youngest entrepreneur in the region and was voted "Most Likely to Succeed" by his high school class.

[Source: www.xtremex.com]

GlobalTek Solutions Inc. is run by Shazad Mohamed, a fifteen-year old who lives in Lewisville, Texas. Mohamed started building websites for his friends around age nine and made his Web development company official at age twelve.

[Source: www.globaltechsolutions.com]

Quote

"To start something from the ground up and watch it soar is amazing."
—Rosemary Vargas, founder and owner of Yoga Bums, NJ

Related Careers

Accountant, lawyer, banker, financial analyst, consultant, programmer, Web designer, store owner

ENVIRONMENTALIST

The Basics

A person who works to preserve the environment can have many different jobs, although almost nobody has the actual job title "environmentalist." Environmentalists can be lawyers, planners, scientists, activists—even accountants. As long as someone works with the goal to conserve and preserve our planet (the air, land, water, animals, etc.), he or she is an environmentalist. An environmental lawyer, for example, can protect lands by arguing to change or enforce laws. A scientist can study the effects of human development on the environment; scientific research helps change laws, too.

Many people who are passionate about environmentalism become advocates. That means they work for groups like the Sierra Club or the Defenders of Wildlife. These organizations try to protect nature in many ways. They may get signatures on petitions, push for stricter pollution laws, or teach people how to recycle. Anybody who works for these groups can call his- or herself an environmentalist.

You don't have to work for an advocacy group to help the environment, though. A photographer can take beautiful pictures of nature. A writer or a poet can write about animals. These people tell stories about the environment and help raise awareness. There are so many ways to help and influence new laws! In any case, you'll need to communicate your ideas and opinions effectively. You will try to persuade both the public and the decision makers to see things your way.

Preparation

High School

Most high schools have environmental clubs. Join yours, and you can be an environmentalist. Take field trips to nature preserves and start a recycling program. On weekends or in the summer, you can volunteer at a local nonprofit environmental group. You might end up stuffing envelopes, but you'll be helping—and getting experience. In order to communicate your ideas about nature, focus on your science and English classes.

College

If you want to be an effective environmentalist, you need a college degree. Environmental degrees are nice, but you don't need one. Remember that even accountants can work to protect nature. A background in the natural sciences will give you a better understanding of natural processes, which can help a lot. Try to get experience as a volunteer, intern, or assistant, and go out there and lend a hand!

Possible Majors

Environmental science, agronomy and crop science, agriculture, biology, ecology, forestry

Graduate School

If you want to be a lawyer or a scientist to help the environment, you'll need a graduate degree. Figure out what it is about the environment that interests you—air, water, traffic, endangered species—and move in that direction. If you can specialize in something that you believe in strongly, you'll be better off.

Will I Be Rich?

Environmentalists choose to pursue a noble cause rather than wealth. You won't get rich working for a nonprofit agency or for the government, where most environmental jobs are. You might do well as a manager or an attorney, but even environmental lawyers make less money than lawyers in other fields.

Fun Fact

Presidents for Planet Earth

Theodore Roosevelt may have been the first true environmental president. While in office, he established five national parks, 51 wildlife refuges, and 150 national forests. In fact, he set up the U.S. Forest Service. Roosevelt once said, "The nation behaves well if it treats the natural resources as assets which it must turn over to the next generation increased, and not impaired, in value."

Myth v. Reality

Myth: If you want to do something for the environment, it's bad for the economy.

Reality: What's good for the environment is often good for the economy. Property values go up because of environmental measures.

Quote

"Environmentalism requires a passion. If you don't have the passion, you're not going to last long. It is inherently difficult. You lose a lot more battles than you win, so you need to stick with it and be committed to what you're doing."

—Jon-Paul Harries, program director, League to Save Lake Tahoe

Related Careers

Lawyer, volunteer, scientist, zookeeper, park ranger, veterinarian, writer, researcher, crocodile hunter, farmer, fisherman

FARMER

The Basics

A farmer, by definition, is someone who works on a farm. And a farm can be either a tract of land or water used to cultivate crops, raise animals, or both. Farmers either own their own farmland (or water) or rent it from a landowner. A farmer's responsibilities will vary, depending on the size of the farm, the number of people who work on the farm, and the number of crops or animals being tended to.

There are many different types of farmers. If you are a *crop farmer*, you will grow cotton, grain, fruit, or vegetables. If tending to plants and flowers and getting them ready to sell is your passion, then a career as a *horticultural farmer* may be your calling. If you like working with animals—feeding them and making sure that their living conditions are safe and clean—the life of a *livestock, dairy,* or *poultry farmer* will appeal to you. If you choose to be an *aquaculture farmer*, you will raise fish or other aquatic animals.

Regardless of the area you specialize in as a farmer, you will need to be physically healthy and strong to handle the strenuous work. You will need to be familiar with a wide variety of tools and machinery and keep up with new trends and technology in the farming industry. You'll also have to keep track of your finances and be aware of the changing market price for goods; these prices will affect the money that you can charge for your products and in turn affect the money you earn each year. You will spend a lot of time alone with the earth and your crops or animals, so a love for nature and its creatures is important.

Preparation

High School

Try growing crops in your own backyard or create a garden at your school. You can grow different foods, vegetables, or flowers depending on the seasons; the tomato plant is a fine experiment for beginners. Spend some time on a farm if possible—you can observe the methods used to raise crops and tend to farm animals. Classes in biology, agriculture, and math will be helpful. Better yet, find out if your school or one nearby has a special agricultural program.

College

Attend a school that's near a lot of farmland so you can get some major hands-on experience outside of the classroom. No matter which area of farming you choose to specialize in, you'll want to take classes like farm management, agricultural mathematics, and agricultural mechanics. Classes like these will give you the background information and confidence to run a farm.

Possible Majors

Agriculture, agronomy, feed science, grain science, soil science, horticulture, animal science, agricultural business and management, agricultural economics, agricultural education, agricultural engineering, agricultural journalism, agricultural mechanization

Will I Be Rich?

As a farmer, you will spend your days performing strenuous physical labor that often involves using dangerous farm machinery. You'll probably start working at the crack of dawn, too. You may not have to bust your hump *every* day; crop farmers, for example, work their hardest during certain seasons. Farmers don't pull in a ton of money, but if you crave a quiet lifestyle that includes spending a lot of time outdoors, this may be the career for you!

Fun Facts

Pig Tales

Check out these three stories in which pigs rule!

In George Orwell's novel Animal Farm, farm animals revolt against the farmer and farmhands who are less than kind to them. Old Major, a prize pig who is about to die, encourages the animals to fight for their freedom.

In the movie Babe, a pig that didn't quite fit in dares to be different. Raised by Fly, the sheepdog, Babe goes on to win the world sheepdog championship!

In the novel Charlotte's Web, by E. B. White, Charlotte, a wise spider, rescues Wilbur, a bashful pig, from his fate. In this story of courage and friendship, the pig survives!

Related Careers

Environmentalist, ecologist, park ranger, veterinarian, agricultural engineer, cowboy/cowgirl, crocodile hunter, fisherman, florist

FASHION DESIGNER

The Basics

A fashion designer turns ideas into clothing and accessories. Some designers create a full range of clothing, from winter jackets to bathing suits. Others may focus on jeans or evening gowns. What all fashion designers have in common is creativity, fashion know-how, and the perseverance to see ideas through to fruition.

As a fashion designer, you will need to have a good eye for color, style, fabrics, fashion trends, and a sixth sense about what people want to wear. You will need to be able to draw your clothing designs by hand or on the computer. Then, in order to see your creations come to life, you will need to find the right fabrics for your designs, create patterns, and sew the material. Since fashion changes from season to season, you will need to keep up to date on trends and continue to be innovative and creative in your designs.

Although working as a fashion designer is demanding and competitive, it's also very exciting. In addition to designing and creating new clothes, you will shop, travel, and research trends and fashions. If you're successful, you may even open your own boutique to sell your designs. Attention to detail, a creative mind, and an artistic sensibility are necessary for fashion designers. Since you need to be good at promoting yourself and your work, excellent communication skills are key.

Preparation

High School

Art, art history, home economics, and computer graphics will give you a head start on your career as a fashion designer. Sketch out some of your design ideas and keep an eye on fashion magazines—if your designs seem cutting edge, you're probably on the right track. Learn how to sew, using existing patterns to start, and then create your own designs and patterns.

College/Art School

Most fashion designers earn a degree from art, design, or fashion schools. It is possible, though, to earn a degree at a regular four-year college and then enroll in a fashion program afterward. At a fashion institute, you'll gain a lot of useful specialized skills. Classes that will help you get started in your career include the business of fashion, fashion illustration, history of costume, fashion art and history, textiles, merchandising, and manufacturing. Internships are crucial for getting your foot in the door in the fashion industry.

Possible Majors

Fashion design, art history, art, advertising, interior design, fashion merchandising, costume design

Will I Be Rich?

If the public loves your designs, you can hit the jackpot. If your designs *don't* make you rich, well, don't give up. You never know when one of your designs may catch on and make you famous. As a designer, you'll get to exercise your creativity on a daily basis and meet many talented and interesting people. As an added bonus, you'll always know what to wear!

Fun Facts

International Fashion Proverbs

"Borrowed garments never fit well."—English proverb

"The style is the man himself."—Greek proverb

"Every fashion goes out of style."—Japanese proverb

"Fashion is more powerful than any tyrant."—Latin proverb

[Source: www.infomat.com]

Fashion Quotes

"Fashion is a form of ugliness so intolerable that we have to alter it every six months."—Oscar Wilde

"I base my fashion taste on what doesn't itch."—Gilda Radner

"Every generation laughs at the old fashions but religiously follows the new."—Henry David Thoreau

"Fashions fade, style is eternal."—Yves Saint Laurent

[Source: www.quotationspage.com]

Myth v. Reality

Myth: You have to spend a fortune on clothes to look good.

Reality: Not true! If you wear clothes that make you feel good, you will look good, regardless of the price tag. A piece of clothing isn't cool just because it costs an arm and a leg.

Quote

"I'm a fashion slave and I love it!"

—Denise Smilowitz, executive designer, vice president of Jonden Clothing, New York, New York

Related Careers

Costume designer, seamstress, artist, illustrator, graphic designer, photographer, interior designer, product designer, retail salesperson, textile manufacturer, fashion merchandiser

FBI AGENT

The Basics

FBI agents work for the Federal Bureau of Investigation and investigate people who are suspects in federal or national law cases. That means that they are interested in people who commit crimes that span across state borders. Serial killers, bombers, bank robbers, kidnappers, organized crime leaders, hijackers, and drug traffickers are just some of the criminals that FBI agents pursue. FBI agents track stolen property across states, set up surveillance cameras to keep a lookout for criminals, and wiretap phones to listen in on suspects' phone calls.

As an FBI agent, you will research and gather information on suspects. You'll analyze evidence and do lots of behind-the-scenes investigation. While you will need to be secretive and quiet as you do your research, it's your job to share the information you uncover with government agencies. While a criminal is being apprehended, you may already be deep into your next case.

Your work as an FBI agent will often involve top secret information; that means you will need to refrain from telling friends and family about what happens every day on the job. An ability to work alone and handle a lot of tasks at once is crucial in this job. While the work of an FBI agent can be dangerous and stressful at times, it is also adventurous and intellectually stimulating. Stealthy, trustworthy, analytical people are best suited for this career.

Preparation

High School

Just as we prescribed for detectives in training, future FBI agents should start by building up their problem-solving skills, especially in solving crimes and mysteries. Where to get some practice in this field at such a young age? Mystery books and movies are good places to start. You can also study real-life mysteries and criminals and learn about criminal law to get a head start. Classes in English, math, psychology, and science will help prepare you for this career.

College

In college, you should study criminology, psychology, sociology, and theories of crime. You'll need a college degree to serve as an FBI agent. Any experience that involves heavy research and investigation will help to develop your skills in this difficult field.

Possible Majors
Criminology, pre-law, political science, psychology, sociology

Additional Requirements

If you want to become an FBI agent, you must be a U.S. citizen who is between twenty-three and thirty-seven years old and is physically strong. The application process to become an FBI agent includes written tests, interviews, and background checks. If you make it through the intense screening process, you will choose from the five programs of study that the FBI offers: law, accounting, science, language, and diversified (where candidates focus on a little of each topic). In addition, you will learn self-defense, investigation strategies, and how to use a gun.

Will I Be Rich?

You will live dangerously as an FBI agent, and you'll help put criminals behind bars. While you may earn a pretty good living, money is usually not the motivating factor for choosing this career. Your job may involve a lot of travel and long, stressful hours, but the amount of adventure and the extreme importance of this job can make it well worthwhile.

Fun Facts

Directors, Then and Now

Robert S. Mueller, III, is currently the sixth director of the Federal Bureau of Investigation. J. Edgar Hoover, the most famous FBI director, served from 1924 to 1972.

FBI's Ten Most Wanted Fugitives (as of July 2003):

- Michael Alfonso
- Osama Bin Laden
- Hopeton Eric Brown
- James J. Bulger
- Robert William Fisher

- Victor Manuel Gerena
- Glen Stewart Godwin
- Richard Steve Goldberg
- Eric Robert Rudolph—CAPTURED!
- Donald Eugene Webb

[Source: www.fbi.gov]

Quote:

"There's nothing like the thrill of narrowing in on a criminal that belongs behind bars. The long hours and the stress of the job are worth it when you realize that you are helping to make the world a safer place."

—Anonymous FBI agent

Related Careers

Criminologist, police officer, detective, corrections officer, politician, special agent

FILMMAKER

The Basics

Filmmakers tell a story using moving images and sound. The purpose of their story can be to entertain or educate an audience. Many people may work on a film, from the actor and the costume designer to the best boy and the key grip. However, directors and producers are the people who have the greatest influence on the production of a movie.

The director is the one who runs the show from a creative point of view. A director is responsible for translating a script into a film; in other words, he or she interprets and adjusts the script as necessary to bring it to life. The director also chooses camera angles and hires the actors and the rest of the staff. In fact, the director is responsible for just about every facet of a movie, from the music to the makeup. The producer is the one who oversees the whole production of the film. A producer finds a movie script, locates sources of funding, takes care of finances, and works with the director on hiring a cast and on other major aspects of making the film.

Most major movies are currently made by one of the large Hollywood studios. There is, however, a growing number of independent filmmaking companies that make smaller budget movies. You can even make movies for yourself—and you won't have executives over your shoulder—but the risk is great because many movies lose a lot of money. Raising money is a big part of the business, and it requires you to sell yourself, your ideas, and your movie to the folks with the loot.

Preparation

High School

Get a video camera and make your own movies! Your films don't have to be masterpieces, but the experience of making even a crummy short film will help you develop your craft. Study the great directors; rent every Hitchcock movie. Also go to your high school plays; if you watch the performers, you can learn to recognize good acting talent.

College

If you want to be a filmmaker, you'll have to earn a film degree in college or film school. That's where you can learn the technical and artistic aspects of filmmaking that you will use later in your career. Film classes can open your eyes to the visual world of composition and frames. You'll also have your first opportunity to meet people and network, which is a giant part of the filmmaking business. Take drama classes or study drama earnestly. You don't have to actually get onstage, but get as much experience working with actors as you can. Interning for a movie studio is an awesome way to see how the filmmaking world works, but competition is fierce.

Film, theater, art, photography, playwriting, screenwriting

Will I Be Rich?

It's certainly possible to make a ton of money as a filmmaker. It's a big-bucks business, and the directors and producers of popular films get compensated very well. Only a few make it to the top level, but if you get there, you'll have a unique opportunity to be highly creative and extremely well paid.

Fun Fact

It takes a great deal of determination to make it as a filmmaker. Even Steven Spielberg, one of the greatest directors and producers of all time, had to start somewhere. Before a studio ever hired him, Spielberg used to pretend that he worked at Universal Studios. He would wear a suit and tie and sneak into an old janitor's office. That helped him learn all about the film industry that made him a multimillionaire!

[Source: www.filmmakers.com]

Quote

"More than anything, you need to have a conviction for your own way of doing things. Realize that you have a unique point of view, and stick with it. If you have perseverance and confidence, eventually you'll hook up with someone."

—Andy Sidaris, filmmaker/director for Andy Sidaris Films

Related Careers

Screenwriter, actor, film editor, camera operator, photographer, artist, creative director, writer, editor, costume designer, stage technician

FINANCIAL ANALYST

The Basics

Financial analysts help businesses make decisions about where to invest their money. They research companies, analyze their financial pros and cons, and recommend whether or not a company is worth investing money in. Their goal is to direct companies to make solid investments so they can make more money over time.

As a financial analyst, you may study an entire industry in addition to specific companies to determine if the industry is profiting or losing money. You will meet with company bigwigs to learn more about a corporation, and then share your information with your clients. You may work for a bank, an insurance company, or a securities firm. If you are a personal financial analyst, you will do a lot of the same stuff, only you will work for individuals who want to invest their money, rather than companies. In either case, keeping up with industry trends will be your daily responsibility, so you'll do a lot of reading and researching.

You will need to have a deep understanding of finance to succeed in this field; if you're good with numbers and are interested in the stock market, you're off to a great start. Other than outstanding math, business, and computer skills, you'll have to be extremely organized and adept at communicating with people. You'll also have to be honest and persuasive to earn the trust of your clients. After all, their money is in your hands!

Preparation

High School

Strive to get good grades in your math classes and make sure your computer skills are up to speed. In order to practice using the stock market, you can make some mock investments. Pretend that you've been given $100,000 to invest. Perform some research to find out what companies have been making more money lately. Set aside some of your investment money to buy stocks. Keep a record of your mock investments. Have you lost money? Gained money?

College

You do need a college degree to become a financial analyst, but you don't have to major in business. Almost any undergraduate degree will be suitable, as each company trains its financial analysts when they are first hired. Still, a background in business, math, or science may put you at an advantage over liberal arts majors.

Possible Majors

Business administration, accounting, finance, economics, applied mathematics, computer and information science

Will I Be Rich?

You will work hard for your money, but you'll most likely earn a lot of it. Expect to work long hours, including evenings and weekends, with co-workers to meet deadlines and to have tons of responsibility. Depending on the location of your clients, you may travel a lot. Don't count on having too much time for leisure travel, though; financial analysts do not have a lot of free time outside of the office. The yearly bonuses are great—they can make all the hard work worthwhile. Over time, you can become a senior financial analyst or open your own firm.

Fun Facts

Need Some Guidance on Your Mock Investment Strategies?

Investment Challenge is the self-proclaimed "#1 real-time stock market simulation program for students." High school or college students in the United States or Canada can learn all about trading and investing here.

[Source: www.ichallenge.net]

YoungInvestor.com, run by Liberty Funds, features a library of information about money and investments, tools like the Allowance Calculator, and a whole batch of money-themed games.

[Source: www.younginvestor.com]

Myth v. Reality

Myth: If you listen to your financial analyst's advice you will get rich fast.
Reality: Maybe, maybe not. While your financial analyst will try to steer you in the right direction, sometimes things happen overnight that he or she could not have predicted. While your investment might be safe, sound, and profitable, it may also flop.

Related Careers

Accountant, stockbroker, banker, actuary, lawyer, agent

FIREFIGHTER

The Basics

The wail of a fire engine's siren might startle those nearby. But for the firefighters on deck, it's a sound that moves them to action. Firefighters put themselves in harm's way to protect people and property against fires. They respond to accidents and emergencies that often involve fire or explosions. They work as a team to put out the fire, rescue people from unsafe buildings, and treat anyone who has been hurt at the scene. They also work to preserve the wilderness, as is the case with a blazing forest fire.

Today's firefighters do a lot more than fight fires. As a firefighter, you might handle floods, icy roads, a dangerous bridge, or lightning damage. In an urban setting, you may help with an elevator rescue, a gas leak, a car fire, or a medical emergency where there aren't enough paramedics. Your days will be a mixture of downtime (waiting for calls) and fast, hard work. On a fire call, you will connect hoses to hydrants, position ladders, and rescue victims. You will ventilate areas that are full of smoke and do your best to save lives and property. Between calls, expect to clean and maintain equipment, run practice drills, and inspect buildings for fire exits, fire alarms, and an escape plan. Educating both adults and children about fire safety will also be part of the job.

Firefighting calls for courage, strength, and the ability to make tough decisions under pressure. You will need to be alert and ready for action at all times. Dedication and a commitment to others are necessary for this rewarding career.

Preparation

High School

If your local fire department offers it, join their Fire Explorer program, for potential firefighters ages fourteen to eighteen. Take classes in English, science, and math. Many fire departments rely on computers, so brush up on your skills. Participate in gym classes and sports; firefighters need to be in excellent shape! Take a class from the Red Cross in first aid or CPR—many departments require their firefighters to be certified EMTs (emergency medical technicians).

College

A college degree is not a requirement for becoming a firefighter. Because of the obvious risks firefighters face in their careers, it doesn't hurt to have something to fall back on.

Possible Majors

Forestry, wildlife management, environmental science, architecture, natural reserve conservation, physics

Special Requirements and Training Program

Firefighters need to be eighteen to thirty-one years old and have a high school degree or equivalent. If you qualify, you will need to take a series of written exams and physical tests that show strength, stamina, and coordination. Once you pass, you will have several weeks of training. You'll learn firefighting techniques, fire prevention, local building codes, emergency medical procedures, first aid, and hazardous materials control. You will learn to use fire extinguishers, ladders, and rescue equipment. Then you will join a fire company and go through a probation period.

Will I Be Rich?

Basically, no. But many firefighters wouldn't trade their job for any other—they love what they do. Expect to work long, hard hours—some shifts run for twenty-four hours, followed by forty-eight hours off. The job is physically, emotionally, and mentally tiring, not to mention dangerous. But you will work alongside other dedicated people who share your bravery and love of humanity. Promotions to a position like fire chief require more exams, a great job performance, and a certain number of years on the job. A college degree in fire science or a related field may be necessary as well.

Fun Facts

In the Beginning. . .

The first volunteer fire company in America started in 1736 in Philadelphia, Pennsylvania. The Union Fire Company's first volunteer fire chief was none other than American printer, author, diplomat, philosopher, and scientist, Ben Franklin!

[Source: www.kirksvillecity.com]

Related Careers

Police officer, paramedic, nurse, detective, FBI agent, park ranger

FISHERMAN

The Basics

Fishermen, also known as fishers, are men and women who catch and trap fish. They are generally self-employed and physically strong. They work long hours and are often at the mercy of weather conditions.

As a fisherman, you can expect to spend a majority of your time in or near the water. If you work on a fishing boat or vessel, you may live on the sea and away from your family for long stretches of time. In addition to using a fishing rod, you will use a variety of tools to fish, including nets, rakes, hoes, hooks, and shovels, as well as dangerous fishing machinery. You may use pots and traps to catch shellfish such as lobsters or crabs. Expect to handle your catches and prepare them for sale by cleaning and icing them. You will need to make arrangements to sell your catches, too.

You will need to be good at fixing things and have great coordination skills to be a fisherman. Physical strength and a love for life at sea are necessary, too. You never know what Mother Nature will serve up while you're out at sea, so a sense of adventure and fierce determination to survive are crucial.

Preparation

High School

Go fishing with friends and family, and read up on a wide variety of fish and other marine life. If you can spend some time on a real professional fishing boat, you'll be able to witness fishermen at work—and you'll be able to get accustomed to using your sea legs. In fact, spending time on any kind of boat will help in that respect. Of course, visiting aquariums is also a great way to buff up your aquatic intelligence. You'll need to be a good swimmer, too, in case of emergencies, so make sure your skills are up to par.

College and Training Programs

No formal education is necessary to be a fisherman. Still, the more you know, the better your chances of surviving and making a living out on the seas. Some secondary schools—often those that are in coastal towns—offer two-year vocational-technical programs for fishermen. In addition, some community colleges and universities offer fishery technology and related programs that may include the following courses: seamanship, vessel operations, marine safety, navigation, vessel repair and maintenance, health emergencies, and fishing gear technology. Most courses include hands-on experience.

Possible Majors

Fishery technology, oceanography, marine biology, ecology

Will I Be Rich?

If you enjoy peace and quiet and have a lot of patience, the life of a fisherman may appeal to you. When fog, storms, or heavy winds set in, however, your life will be far from peaceful! The close friendships that develop on board fishing vessels usually make the hours away from the comfort of home bearable. The best seasons for fishermen are summer and fall when the weather is good and the demand for seafood is high. During the off-seasons, many fishermen work alternate careers—some in fishing-related industries, such as selling fishing gear, to supplement their income. While you won't make millions as a fisherman, if you love the sea, are hardworking, and have a sense of adventure, it's a career worth pursuing.

Fun Facts

Famous Literary Fishermen

- The Old Man and the Sea *by Ernest Hemingway*

  In this sea adventure, an old Cuban fisherman named Santiago battles with a huge marlin.

- Calm at Sunset, Calm at Dawn *by Paul Watkins*

  In this novel, twenty-year-old James Pfeiffer takes to the waters off the Rhode Island coast to become a fisherman against his family's wishes. The novel follows his adventures on a dilapidated scallop trawler.

- Moby-Dick *by Herman Melville*

  In this classic novel, Captain Ahab pursues the great white whale Moby-Dick.

Related Careers

Sailor, marine biologist, chef, farmer, military personnel

FLIGHT ATTENDANT

The Basics

A flight attendant has two main jobs: to make sure that a flight is safe and to help passengers have a comfortable and enjoyable trip. A flight attendant's job begins before an airplane leaves the ground. He or she checks that first-aid kits and emergency equipment is working and greets passengers and helps them to settle in. Once the passengers are seated, a flight attendant reviews safety procedures, ranging from how to fasten a seat belt to what to do in the event of an emergency. During the flight, a flight attendant distributes food and drinks, brings passengers blankets and pillows, and assists passengers if the plane runs into any turbulence.

Your additional job responsibilities will vary, depending upon the needs of the passengers you serve. A young passenger flying alone may require your help to reach his or her destination safely. A passenger with a headache may request an aspirin. A nervous flyer may even need a pep talk to get rid of the jitters. If there are any major problems with passengers, you will communicate this to the pilot.

As a flight attendant, you will need to be attentive, patient, and even-tempered—in other words, you need great service and communication skills. You'll also need to have a strong stomach; the airsick traveler need not apply. Since you will travel often and spend the night at hotels at various destinations, you'll need a passion for travel and a willingness to be away from home often.

Preparation

High School

Foreign language classes will come in handy when talking to passengers on international flights. Geography classes are useful, too, as you'll be flying all over the map. Try to work part-time in a customer service position so you can gain some experience and develop your communication skills. Even a job as a waitress would be suitable early training for this position.

College

Although a college degree isn't required, it's recommended, as is experience working with the public. Classes that will be useful include communication, education, foreign languages, and psychology.

Possible Majors

Communications, hospitality, tourism

Additional Training

A one-to-two-month training course is required before you can become a flight attendant. As a trainee, you will learn emergency procedures, first aid, CPR, water survival techniques, and how to handle disruptive passengers. You'll need to pass a security exam as well as a physical exam to graduate. At the end of the training program, you will be assigned to a practice flight.

Will I Be Rich?

You won't earn a ton financially, but you'll be rich in experience. You'll meet new people each day, travel often, and accumulate a long list of great stories to tell. Since you'll be able to get airline tickets at reduced rates for yourself and your family, you can travel in your free time. Job advancement is also possible; many flight attendants study to become pilots or take tests to work in the business departments of an airline, such as marketing or food service.

Fun Fact

The chief flight attendant on each flight is the person who determines when drinks and food are served. Here are some of the choices you'll find on a major airline:

- Bland/Soft Meal
- Diabetic
- Gluten Free
- Lactose Free
- Low Calorie
- Low Fat/Cholesterol
- Low Sodium
- Vegetarian (non-dairy)
- Vegetarian (lacto-ovo)
- Hindu
- Kosher
- Moslem

[Source: www.aa.com]

Myth v. Reality

Myth: After flight attendants serve meals and clean up, they just hang out.
Reality: The job doesn't end until all the passengers are safely off the plane; flight attendants are always busy working.

Quote

"If you enjoy meeting people from all over the world, love to travel, and don't mind being away from home a few times a week, a flight attendant is the perfect career choice!"

—*A chief flight attendant from Air France*

Related Careers

Pilot, travel agent, hotel manager, tour guide, salesperson

FLORIST

The Basics

A florist cuts and arranges flowers according to a customer's order. Florists create arrangements for an assortment of events, including weddings, proms, award ceremonies, and even funerals. They may also create floral arrangements to add a decorative touch to restaurants, businesses, and homes. In addition to bouquets, florists also put together corsages and boutonnieres, wreaths, arches, hair pieces, and centerpieces. They may work with live, dried, or artificial flowers, depending on the customer's request.

As a florist, you will probably work in a retail flower shop or in the floral department of a larger store. Your responsibilities will include growing, buying, trimming, and arranging flowers, but you may do much more than that if you run your own shop. You will have to coordinate the details of a customer's order to make sure you get it right. These details may include the type of occasion, the color and type of flowers to be used, the total amount they would like to spend, and when they'd like to pick up the order or have it delivered.

A love of and knowledge about the wide variety of flowers is essential for florists. The creation of decorative floral arrangements is an art form. To be a successful florist, you'll need to have an eye for color coordination, beauty, and design. Creativity, imagination, and an ability to work independently are important traits for a florist, too. Since you will work with the public on a daily basis, patience and good communication skills are a must.

Preparation

High School

Art classes, including sculpture, ceramics, painting, and photography, will train you to see form, color, and composition. Science courses like biology will add another dimension to your studies, as will courses in botany, horticulture, or agriculture. Try growing some flowers at home or at school, if possible. And if you can score an after-school job in a florist shop or greenhouse, you will get some great on-the-job experience.

College

While a college degree isn't necessary, a two- or four-year degree in a related major will come in handy should you decide to run your own floral business. Continue to develop your floral knowledge in both the scientific and artistic sense, and add some communication courses into the mix.

Possible Majors

Floriculture, horticulture, botany, floral design, art, biology, business administration, sculpture

Vocational Programs

Some technical schools offer training programs in floral design that can be completed within a year. Although these courses are not required, they might help you develop a wider range of skills—especially business skills, which you will use in the shop. If you want to pursue a career as a florist, but don't want to spend four years in college, this may be a practical choice for you.

Will I Be Rich?

If you love flowers, there's nothing like spending your days surrounded by them! You probably won't make tons of dough, though. You may have to work on holidays and weekends, but the job enables you to interact with people and also spend time alone, creating. The joy you bring to others through your designs makes it all worthwhile.

Fun Facts

This Gift Says "I Love Ya"

Mother's Day is the most profitable day of the year for florists, followed by Valentine's Day in a close second.

[Source: http://abcnews.go.com]

A Rose Is a Rose. . .Or Is It?

There are seven types of roses that florists choose from when making floral arrangements. Check out the basic categories:

- Fancy Roses
- Extra-Fancy Roses
- Spray Roses
- Sweetheart Roses
- Medium-Stem Roses
- Long-Stem Roses
- Import Roses

Roses also come in what seems like a zillion different bizarrely named colors, including osiana (pink peach), fire 'n' ice (white on the outside, red on the inside), and ravel (hot pink).

Related Careers

Botanist, landscape artist, artist, horticulturist, farmer, wedding planner, sculptor, interior decorator

FURNITURE DESIGNER

The Basics

Furniture designers create, develop, and manufacture furniture that is comfortable, long lasting, and looks good. Furniture designers use wood and other materials, such as metal and fabrics, to create everything from bedroom sets to couches to kitchen tables. Some furniture designers work for themselves and sell their creations to stores and to individual clients, while others work for companies, designing furniture for specific stores.

As a furniture designer, you will usually meet with clients or people within your company before starting a project. You will learn more about the type of furniture they'd like you to create, and then you'll sketch some ideas by hand or using a computer. Once all of you agree upon a design, you will make a large-scale drawing of your idea to show how the furniture will be put together. In addition, you'll either build the furniture or help solve any problems that arise during the production process.

Creative people who like not only to come up with big ideas but also turn them into realities will enjoy this career. You will need to have a working knowledge of the history of furniture and remain up to date on new trends in furniture styles. You'll also need to be strong, innovative, and determined to formulate your own designs and create furniture that is appealing, comfortable, and practical.

Preparation

High School

Look around your home—what piece of furniture would you make for your living room or bedroom? Don't just think about it—make sketches! Take some woodshop classes at school to become familiar with a wide range of tools and techniques. The elements of form and shape will come into play in your designs; art and art history courses will provide a good foundation in this respect. Study hard in your math courses, too—measurements of the length of different pieces and angles in your design must be precise.

College

Many art and design schools offer furniture design as a major, but you may also be able to take furniture design courses at other colleges and universities. You'll probably start with the basics—sculpture, art history, drawing, and art theory—and turn to specialized classes that will teach you how to make furniture out of wood, metal, and other materials. If you plan to sell your own designs, you may want to grab a few business classes, too. You'll maintain a portfolio throughout your college career, which you can use to secure jobs later on down the road.

Furniture design, art, interior design, industrial design, sculpture

Will I Be Rich?

If you have a knack for putting things together and love to work with your hands, you'll love this job. It may sometimes be strenuous to rework and compromise your plans to please clients. Still, any job where you can see your artistic designs come to life is incredible. You will use your imagination all the time and get to work with other creative folks. Your salary will vary depending on whether you work freelance or for a company; the price range of furniture that you create will obviously also make a difference.

Fun Facts

Form and Function

To find out more about different furniture styles (and for a little inspiration), check out the following famous architects and furniture designers:

> Salvador Dali
>
> Charles Eames
>
> Alexander Girard
>
> Eileen Gray
>
> Josef Hoffmann
>
> Le Corbusier
>
> Frank Lloyd Wright
>
> Charles Rennie Mackintosh
>
> Ludwig Mies van der Rohe
>
> Jacques-Emile Ruhlman
>
> Eero Saarinen

Related Careers

Architect, interior designer, artist, carpenter, sculptor, fashion designer, shoe designer

GRAPHIC DESIGNER

The Basics

Graphic designers are the people who are responsible for how a product looks. They design everything from candy wrappers to business brochures. They also design company logos and the layout of publications, such as a newspaper or a magazine. They might even work with film, designing the credits to a movie or TV show.

Being a graphic designer takes a lot of creativity. It's your job to take raw materials—shapes, colors, patterns, text, images, logos, etc.—and turn them into a layout for your client. You can work on a really small scale, designing business cards, or create layouts for massive billboards. Your jobs can range from designing posters for a rock concert to creating promotional materials for a political candidate. At any rate, it's your job to make the product, service, or company look as attractive as possible. Customers often buy a product depending on how its packaging looks, so your designs may play a big role in the sale of a product. As a graphic designer, you can work full-time for a large company or work several smaller part-time jobs for different companies. About a third of all designers are self-employed.

Although many graphic designers use pencils and paper to create a design, computers are very important in this profession. There are several programs that are essential tools for graphic design. Apart from knowing these programs like the back of your hand, you'll also need a strong artistic sense to become a successful graphic designer.

Preparation

High School

It takes a special eye to know what looks good and what doesn't. Whenever you buy a product, study its design. There is a reason for every color, every font. While you're in school, take as many art classes as you can. You'll need experience to learn proper aesthetics. And it's never too early to learn some important designing software, such as Adobe Photoshop™, Illustrator™, or PageMaker™.

College

A bachelor degree is a requirement for most graphic design jobs. It is especially important to get your start. Some colleges have great graphic design or product design programs and many offer art or art history majors. Although these are great ways to gain an eye for art aesthetics, you may want to consider attending art school and earning your bachelor of fine arts in graphic design. Since much of your paid work will be in advertising, business and finance classes can help you gain a competitive edge. While in college, offer to design layouts for school publications and posters for promotional events.

Will I Be Rich?

It's not likely that you'll get extremely rich working as a graphic designer, but you can live comfortably. If you work on a freelance basis, it may be difficult to find work regularly to pay the bills. If you can find some high-paying clients, though, you're all set. The best part is that you get to be creative, and you can be your own boss if you are self-employed.

Fun Fact

Swoosh

The Nike logo, the "swoosh," is one of the most famous logos in the world. Tiger Woods wears it on his hat, and you can see it on sneakers across the country. A graphic designer created the "swoosh" in 1971. The designer was a college student named Carolyn Davidson, and she was paid only $35 for the logo. (She later received company stock for her valuable contribution.)

Related Careers

Architect, artist, computer scientist, engineer, photographer, webmaster, Web designer, illustrator, creative director, art director

GUIDANCE COUNSELOR

The Basics

A guidance counselor helps students plan for the future. Over the next few years, a guidance counselor will help you sign up for classes and possibly apply to college or technical school. Looking further ahead, he or she will also provide information about careers based on your interests and talents. If it's nonacademic guidance you crave, fear not; a guidance counselor can also help you deal with social issues, relationships, and mental health. Basically, if you're upset or confused about anything at school, the best place to go is your guidance counselor's office.

As a guidance counselor, you will spend a lot of time listening to the dreams and fears of students. For example, one of the biggest decisions that high school students face is whether they'll apply to a four-year college, a two-year college, a technical school, or pursue another career path. You'll provide a lot of information to help students make this decision. For students who do apply to schools, you'll have to help them with their applications, financial aid, and scholarships. You may also administer tests to help determine a student's strengths and weaknesses.

Are you a mentally and emotionally strong person with great communication skills? You'll need to be to survive in this job. Above all, you will need to be comfortable with teenagers and have an ability to connect with them. The best guidance counselors are caring, trustworthy, open-minded individuals who have a strong desire to help others.

Preparation

High School

In high school, you can get a head start on understanding others through sociology and psychology. Be sure to meet with your school guidance counselors and ask if you can assist them in any way. They know a lot about careers; they'd probably be happy to talk about theirs. Also, volunteer at a community center to get experience interacting with a wide range of people.

College

You'll have to earn at least a bachelor degree to become a guidance counselor. Your undergrad schedule will probably include behavior modification, counseling, education, psychology, public speaking, school counseling, and statistics.

Possible Majors

Counseling, communications, education, social work, sociology, psychology

Graduate School or Certification?

Some states require school counselors to have school counseling certification and/or teaching certificates. A master's degree in counseling and teaching experience may also be required for a school counseling certificate. Check with your state Board of Education Department to find out your state's specific requirements.

Will I Be Rich?

You will earn a decent living in this challenging career. Although you may work the same hours as teachers, be warned; the emotional and mental commitment to this job is intense. If you like working with teenagers, though, the job is very rewarding, as you will help students uncover their potential.

Fun Facts

Analyze This

As a guidance counselor, you may help students figure out what career path is right for them. Below are some of the questions you may ask students to consider:

- If you had to describe yourself in three words, what would they be? What are your personal strengths and weaknesses?

- What are your academic strengths and weaknesses? Are your grades a good indication of your abilities? Why or why not?

- What's your favorite class? Why?

- What is your least favorite class? Why?

- What are you most interested in learning about?

- If you could be anything in the world, what would you be?

Related Careers

Career counselor, recruiter, teacher, professor, social worker, sociologist, psychologist, principal

HAIRDRESSER

The Basics

Hairdressers shampoo, cut, style, and color hair to make people look and feel good. They customize each hair appointment to the customer's needs and may perform a wide variety of duties. A customer looking for a haircut, for example, will get more than just that—his or her hair will be shampooed, rinsed, cut, dried, and styled. Some customers want their hair dyed, bleached, highlighted, frosted, or streaked with color. Others want their hair permanently waved (permed) or straightened. Some are looking for hair or scalp treatments. Still others simply want their hair styled for a special event like a wedding or prom.

As a hairdresser, you will listen to your customer's requests and provide suitable haircut or style options. You'll have to keep up to date with new products and techniques to best meet your customers' needs. You'll use a ton of different tools in this line of work, including scissors, clips, and razors to trim locks and facial hair, and combs, hairbrushes, hair dryers, curlers, curling irons, and straightening irons to style. You may advise your clients on hair care and recommend hair products. If you work at a smaller salon, you may also record appointments in a schedule book, take payment from customers, and assist with cleanup each day.

A great hairdresser is a good listener who is attentive, caring, and creative. If you listen closely and give your clients what they want, they'll keep coming back; plus, your client base will expand to include their friends and their friends' friends. If you are a people person and love to chat while you work, you might feel at home at a hairdressing salon.

Preparation

High School

Try cutting a friend's hair. You could always practice on a cheap wig if you're afraid you'll mess up. Pay attention to the techniques hairdressers use at salons, and ask them to explain what they are doing. Art classes like sculpture will be most relevant to your future career, but observing the haircuts of your fellow classmates is a good idea, too.

Possible Majors

Art, graphic design, sculpture, communications

College or Vocational School

Although college is not a requirement, you can pick up on some crucial design elements in an art program. Vocational schools offer training programs for aspiring hairdressers. Through training, you will learn how to cut hair and administer hair treatments such as chemical styling and hair dyeing. The best part is that you'll have the opportunity to work on clients' hair while an instructor watches—that way, you can't mess up! Most hairdressing programs are between nine months and two years long.

Will I Be Rich?

If you work in a salon, you will receive a salary or commission plus tips and possible bonuses. You probably won't become wealthy working at a salon unless you have a tremendous following and some movie star clients. If you work for yourself, however, your chances of doing well are a bit higher. Expect to work irregular hours, including evenings, weekends, and lunch hours—whenever your clients can squeeze in an appointment.

Fun Facts

Celebrity Cuts

Jose Eber, a hairdresser in Hollywood, California, has a star-studded list of clients. Among them are Cher, Elizabeth Taylor, Barbra Streisand, Meg Ryan, and Farrah Fawcett.

Christophe, a hairdresser with a salon in Beverly Hills, California, once gave former President Bill Clinton a $200 haircut. Some of his other clients include Nicole Kidman, Sally Field, Goldie Hawn, Ted Danson, and Kate Capshaw.

[Source: www.seeing-stars.com]

Hair IQ

Think you know one hairstyle from the next? Test your knowledge of hairstyles through the ages by matching the name with the number.

1.   2.   3.   4.   5.

- Afro
- Bald
- Beehive
- Bob
- Bouffant
- Bowl cut

- Braids
- Bun
- Comb-over
- Cornrows
- Crew cut
- Dreadlocks

- Duck butt
- Feathered
- Flat top
- Flip
- Marcel wave

- Mohawk
- Mop top
- Mullet
- Page boy
- Pigtails

- Pixie
- Pompadour
- Ponytail
- Rat tail
- Spikes

Related Careers

Makeup artist, cosmetologist, massage therapist, artist, sculptor, florist

Answer key: 1. Pixie 2. Bowl cut 3. Beehive 4. Dreadlocks 5. Mullet

HISTORIAN

The Basics

A historian works to discover, explore, and investigate events in history. He or she researches stories with historical importance and writes articles or books about them. Most historians also work for a university, teaching their knowledge of history to students of any age.

Successful historians need to be patient. They must be willing to dig into public archives, looking for documents that may contain important facts in order to complete a story. They may spend days looking for a letter that describes what happened on a single day in history. And they may never find it. It takes a certain person to be willing to sort through boxes and folders, taking careful footnotes and notations. Still, the true historian will relish the quest, cherishing the challenge of the hunt for historical facts.

Historians not only get their information from public archives but also from interviews. Depending on the event in history, historians can interview people who witnessed or participated in an event. If the event took place in ancient history, they can interview other historians who have done similar research. In all, the role of a historian is to gather historical information and explain it to an audience. That audience can be a nation of bookworms, readers of historical magazines, or a classroom full of college kids.

Preparation

High School

You can't be too young to do your own original research. Go to the archives and follow your passion. You can perform research with oral history. Talk to your mayor, councilpeople, and even your history teachers to learn about your town's history. This will teach you to interview and to realize that there are many untold stories waiting to be written. Once you start interviewing people, you never know in what direction your research will take you.

College

You should study history in college, but a journalism or English degree will also teach you how to find and report information. Read history books, and prepare to write one, too. Pick a subject and dive into the research. Write an article that you can submit to a history journal. You can also serve as a research assistant or an intern for a historian at a university. You might have to do busy work such as retrieving clippings or transcribing interviews. But you may also get to help with the interviews and actively take part in the historical learning process.

Graduate School

It is necessary to get a graduate degree in order to teach in college, which most historians do. You can be an independent historian, writing books and articles while teaching yourself what you need to know. You don't need to go to grad school for that. Still, if you really have a passion for learning history and want to be a historian, graduate school is the logical next step.

Will I Be Rich?

The only way to get *rich* as a historian is to become a best-selling author of a popular history book. But that's incredibly uncommon. More likely, you will earn a good living as an educator and have the freedom to learn history on your own time.

Fun Fact

History ReenACTed

David McCullough is one of the most famous historians in America. He wrote three books about United States presidents: John Adams, Truman, *and* Mornings on Horseback (*Theodore Roosevelt*). The book about John Adams won him a Pulitzer Prize, and his book on Harry S. Truman was adapted into a movie.

Quote

"To be a historian, you have to care about the stories. You have to be obsessed and be curious and wonder why the world is the way it is. You have to want to figure out what happened ten, twenty, fifty, one hundred years ago, or further back in time."

— Kai Bird, journalist, author, historian

Related Careers

Professor, teacher, journalist, writer, anthropologist, paleontologist, art and antique restorer

HOLISTIC PRACTITIONER

Acupuncturist • ayurvedic practitioner • herbalist • reflexologist

The Basics

Holistic medicine is a type of medicine that treats the whole patient rather than treating a specific body part or illness. For example, if a person has a cold, a holistic practitioner (someone who practices holistic medicine) may ask the person about his or her sleeping patterns, eating habits, and whether any other body parts hurt before treating the cold. Holistic practitioners, like doctors, are concerned with helping people get better and preventing them from getting sick in the future.

Holistic medicine may seem strange and unusual to new patients because of its alternative approach to health. Therefore, great communication skills and the ability to answer patients' questions clearly are necessary. New research is constantly being performed in the field of holistic medicine, so it's your job to learn about new findings and techniques. Most holistic practitioners study many different types of holistic medicine; you may start out as a reflexologist and then take courses to become an acupuncturist.

Some of the different types of holistic practitioners include the following:

Acupuncturists insert fine needles into the body at specific points to relieve a person of pain or a disorder and to balance energy. Acupuncture is a practice that's based on the ancient Chinese theory that people are healthy when their energy is balanced. Acupuncturists can treat a variety of disorders having to do with the ear, eye, nose, throat, stomach, breathing, or muscles. If a patient has chronic knee pain, back pain, or migraines, acupuncture can help those ailments, too.

Ayurvedic practitioners try to balance a person's energy through attention to diet, breathing, and herbs. Like acupuncturists, they try to get rid of sickness and make people feel focused and full of life by balancing their energy. Among other things, ayurvedic medicine has been successful at treating digestive problems, arthritis, asthma, skin conditions, anxiety, insomnia, and viral infections.

As an *herbalist*, you will prescribe herbs to your patients in order to treat or prevent pain and sickness. Herbs serve a number of functions: They can cleanse and purify the body; regulate glands that may not be functioning normally; provide vitamins, nutrients, and extra energy to the body; and wake up the immune system.

Reflexology relieves tension, improves circulation, and creates a sense of balance by restoring the body's natural energy flow. *Reflexologists* believe that certain pressure points on the hands and feet are linked to internal organs. As a reflexologist you will apply gentle massages to the hands, feet, and ears of your clients to stimulate the body's natural healing energy. Soothing, healing hands are a must for this career.

Preparation

High School

Volunteer in nursing homes, hospitals, shelters, or other places where you can gain experience working directly with people in a health care situation. Part-time work in a gym or spa also provides exposure to basic therapy techniques. If there's a holistic practitioner in your area, try to set up an informational interview to learn more about their specialty. English, health, math, and science classes will be helpful.

College

Many people who become ayurvedic practitioners are already nurses, medical doctors, or physical therapists. They use ayurvedic medicine to help when treating patients. If you'd like to enter one of these careers before learning holistic medicine, you'll have to take many science classes and get proper medical training. See the career profiles for nurse, doctor, and physical therapist for more information.

Possible Majors
Pre-medicine, rehabilitation services, nursing, physical therapy

Training Programs

There are a lot of different training programs available for holistic practitioners. Many of them require you to take courses in biology, chemistry, herbs, human anatomy, nutrition, physiology, and psychology. If you wish to study herbs, expect to take a wide range of courses that include plant identification and herbal gardening. Future reflexologists need to complete up to 200 hours of training for certification. If acupuncture appeals to you, check out your state's requirements. You can expect to commit to two to four years of training in order to become a licensed acupuncturist.

Will I Be Rich?

You will be rich in knowledge if you are a holistic practitioner; you just have to be willing to work long hours and remain on call for your patients. You never know when one of them will have an emergency and call on you to help relieve pain or suggest a remedy. If you are detail-oriented, love working with people, and are analytical and compassionate, this may be the career for you. And if you're good at what you do, you can develop a large group of patients (translation = more money).

Fun Fact

Ayurvedic medicine suggests that there are three different energies that may rule individual people. These energies, called Doshas, are Vata, Pitta, and Kapha. Each of the Doshas describes different personality types and different physical characteristics. For example, Vatas are generally thin people with small eyes who are not able to sit still. Pittas have medium builds, reddish or yellowish complexions with freckles, and are good decision makers. Kaphas are strong and well-proportioned, have large eyes, and are calm. An ayurvedic doctor diagnoses your Dosha based on your physical appearance and information gathered about your personality, and by listening to your pulse points. A Vata's pulse is rapid and thin; a Pitta's is quick and full; and a Kapha's is steady and regular.

Related Careers

Doctor, nurse, physical therapist, massage therapist, yoga teacher

HOMEMAKER

The Basics

A homemaker is someone who works at home and manages household affairs. But a homemaker is more than just that—he or she is a coordinator, educator, facilitator, manager, motivator, negotiator, nutritionist, and peacemaker who takes care of a family and a home. If reading that list made you feel weary, you can imagine how a homemaker feels!

As a homemaker, your days will vary; you may clean up, do laundry, prepare meals, and run errands one day, while the next day you help your children with a school project and pay the bills. The ability to multitask and a go-with-the-flow attitude are a homemaker's secret weapons to getting through each day. If you work as a homemaker, your family may rely on you for everything from waking them up in the morning to buying them their favorite cereal. You will need to settle disputes when they come up (and they will!) and remain calm and cool. Patience is a virtue that homemakers cannot do without.

Since you will be managing a whole range of responsibilities and tending to a variety of personalities, a flexible attitude will make your life as a homemaker much easier. You will need to be able to prioritize the needs of others, solve problems, make decisions, and motivate other people. On top of all that, you'll have to reserve enough energy to move on to the next task. There is one drawback to being a homemaker: Since you work *and* live at home, your work technically never ends!

Preparation

High School

You're probably doing things in your daily life right now that will help prepare you to be a homemaker. The most difficult part of the job is probably figuring out how to run a home efficiently, so take note of how different people do it. If your room is a total pigsty, and you can never remember what homework is due tomorrow, you've got a long way to go in terms of your organizational skills.

College

A college degree isn't necessary to be a homemaker, but the more you know, the better! It's often difficult to work as a homemaker due to the lack of pay; unless you know that you will be able to afford to stay at home, it's probably best to have a backup plan. You can always get a college degree and decide to be a homemaker later on in life.

Possible Majors

Child care, home economics, education, sociology, psychology, art, accounting

Will I Be Rich?

You won't receive a paycheck as a homemaker; your fortune will depend on the salary of your spouse or any inheritance you may have. You certainly won't waste any money on your commute! The rewards of this job are endless—you will get to see your family grow day by day because you'll spend tons of time with your kids. It's hard work taking care of a family and a home, but in the end, most homemakers agree that it's worth it.

Fun Facts

Famous Sitcom Homemakers

- I Love Lucy's *Lucy Ricardo* (1951)
- The Brady Bunch's *Carol Brady* (1969)
- All in the Family's *Edith Bunker* (1971)
- Happy Days' *Marian Cunningham* (1974)
- The Jeffersons' *Louise Jefferson* (1975)
- The Cosby Show's *Claire Huxtable* (1984)
- Family Matters' *Harriet Winslow* (1989)
- The Nanny's *Fran Fine* (1993)
- Everybody Loves Raymond's *Debra Barone* (1996)

Myth v. Reality

Myth: Stay-at-home moms have it easy!

Reality: So not true! There is always business to take care of at home, especially when you have young children. A homemaker doesn't even get to leave work behind at the end of the day like many people who work nine-to-five jobs.

Quote

"Being a homemaker is the hardest job in the world, but a worthwhile one. Each day you learn something new about life and love, and look out at the world with different eyes. It reminds you that there are so many things that you have yet to learn!"

—*Karen Weiss, homemaker*

Related Careers

Child care worker, teacher, guidance counselor, wedding planner, chef, nurse, volunteer, manager

HOTEL MANAGER

The Basics

Hotel managers monitor the daily operations of a hotel. They take care of hotel staff and guests and make sure the hotel is clean and comfortable. In addition, they hire new staff members, order hotel supplies ranging from toilet paper to couches, and oversee improvements to the inside and outside of their hotel.

If you are a hotel manager, expect to juggle a lot of different things at once. You will have to answer phone calls about the hotel, serve guests, and manage a staff of employees. Financial decisions regarding the hotel and maintaining an operating budget are your responsibility, too. Since you will interact with all types of customers on a daily basis, you need to be friendly and accommodating. In emergency situations, you'll have to take charge and restore order; an ability to remain calm under pressure and solve problems is crucial. You never know what issue a guest or employee may bring to your attention or when you'll have to settle a dispute between your own employees.

If you are detail-oriented, have good organizational skills, and love to work with the public, this may be the career for you. Expect to spend a lot of time listening to people and making them feel comfortable and cared for.

Preparation

High School

Apply for a job at a local hotel or another customer service job to gain some experience working with the public. This job requires you to be a jack-of-all-trades, so make sure you get a well-rounded education and do well in each of your classes. Math, English, and sociology will be the most important subjects in your schedule.

College

Many schools offer a major in hotel management or hotel administration—these programs would be your best bet. Other classes that will be help prepare you to run a hotel are communication, finance, accounting, foreign languages, and business management.

Possible Majors

Hotel management, hotel administration, hospitality, business administration, finance, management

Will I Be Rich?

You could make a lot of great friends and have fun as a hotel manager, but you will work long hours, sometimes on holidays, and be on call at all times. Plus, you won't likely take home large paychecks. Since a hotel serves customers all night long, an emergency can happen at any hour of the day. Despite any problems that might crop up, you will need to wear a smile on your face and be friendly to customers. Lots of energy and enthusiasm are necessary for this job, as guests can be very demanding.

Fun Facts

Chelsea Girls

New York City's famous Chelsea Hotel, a favorite spot for artist Andy Warhol, has been home to many artists and writers, including the following:

- Leonard Cohen
- Jane Fonda
- Milos Forman
- Jimi Hendrix
- Dennis Hopper
- Janis Joplin
- Jack Kerouac

- Arthur Miller
- Vladimir Nabokov
- Edith Piaf
- Sam Shepard
- Patti Smith
- Tennessee Williams

Posh Places

Check out the following luxury hotels in four fine cities:

- New York, New York: Hudson Hotel, The Pierre, The Peninsula
- Chicago, Illinois: Hotel Burham, Palmer House Hilton, Ritz-Carlton Chicago
- Los Angeles, California: Beverly Hills Hotel, Hotel Bel-Air, Beverly Wilshire
- Boston, Massachussetts: Four Seasons, Le Meridien Hotel, Fifteen Beacon

Quote:

"I always feel as if I am on a vacation!"

—Mr. Lloyd, hotel manager

Related Careers

Restaurateur, store owner, flight attendant, travel agent, wedding planner,
landlord, caterer, chef, human resources director

INTERIOR DESIGNER

The Basics

Interior designers plan the interiors of homes, hotels, offices, stores, restaurants, hospitals, theaters, and other buildings. They create a certain look and feel for each room by using a combination of furniture, light fixtures, wall coverings, colors, and patterns. The designer always takes his or her customer's needs and preferences into consideration when creating layout plans.

As an interior designer, you will probably specialize in a particular type of building, such as office buildings or homes, or a specific type of room, such as kitchens or bedrooms. You may design rooms for brand-new structures or for existing buildings that are being renovated. You may also work with architects, electricians, and carpenters to safely and effectively plan your designs. The supervision of the whole design project, from ordering all necessary supplies to making sure that final coat of paint goes on perfectly, will be your responsibility.

Flexibility, creativity, organization, and the ability to listen are crucial for this career. Some knowledge of finance will also help you on a day-to-day basis, as you will have to stick to your client's budget for each project. You will also need to know federal, state, and local interior design codes and keep them in mind as you work.

Preparation

High School

Draw, paint, take pictures—be creative! Go to furniture stores and check out furniture styles, patterns, and colors. If you could redo your home, how would you design it? Why not sketch a plan and share it with your family? Since you will draw your layout plans by hand or on a computer, classes in art, art history, and computer graphics will get you started in the right direction.

College

Classes in art, art history, furniture styles, color and theory, and computer graphics will give you the skills you need to be an interior designer. You will start to develop a portfolio of your ideas and designs, which you will show potential clients or employers. An internship with an interior designer is a great way to get hands-on experience.

Possible Majors

Interior design, art, art history, architecture, engineering

Will I Be Rich?

Although clients can be frustrating, the fact that you will get to be creative and innovative makes it all worthwhile. You always need to be prepared for the unexpected as an interior designer—at the last minute, you may fall behind schedule or a piece of furniture may arrive late; as long as you keep telling yourself it will be fine, then you will keep your sanity. You won't start off seeing a high salary, but you can learn more as you gain experience. Expect to work longer hours when a project is in full swing. As one interior designer told us, "Nothing is as exciting as seeing your plans come to life!"

Fun Facts

What Is Feng Shui?

In Chinese, feng shui means "wind and water." If your living or work space leaves you feeling overwhelmed and crowded, feng shui may just be for you! The goal of feng shui is to make you feel balanced, calm, and comfortable. When it comes to feng shui, less clutter and more living space is important. Designers apply feng shui principles to create serene kitchens, bedrooms, and offices.

Interior Design Styles Include:

- Bauhaus: stresses the beauty of basic, unadorned materials, functional furniture
- Minimalism: plain, furniture with no details, light colors such as beige and white
- Country: calm, peaceful, comfortable, rustic furniture
- Mediterranean: simple, lots of stone and wood, functional and light-colored furniture
- Feng shui: calm, peaceful, open spaces, simple furniture

[Source: www.home-improvement-decorating.com]

Quote

"Being an interior designer satisfies the artist part of my mind."
—Pauline Raiff, interior designer, New York City

Related Careers

Interior decorator, furniture designer, architect, artist, art dealer, graphic designer, costume designer

INVENTOR

The Basics

Inventors make brand-new things. Every item we use was invented by a person or team of people, from CDs to computers to dishwashers to cars. The best thing about being an inventor is that the sky's the limit—you can create absolutely anything, as long as you have (or can develop) the technology to make it happen.

The road to completing an invention can be a long one. Inventors must perform experiments, conduct research, make samples of their inventions, and test them to make sure that they work. They also have to make sure that their invention is unique—that someone else hasn't already invented it. Once the invention works, they need to find a company or person to manufacture it as a product. It's important for an inventor to get a patent for his or her invention at this stage to ensure that other people can't copy the idea. You will also need some marketing, or advertising, for your product, so people will know that it exists.

As an inventor, you may work in a lab or a research and development department, or you may work out of your home. Regardless of where you work, it's not easy to turn an idea into a reality. Expect to fail and to keep trying over and over again until you get it right. You'll need to be really persistent to complete your inventions, as well as creative, motivated, and dedicated. You'll also need a good business sense to figure out whether people will buy your invention.

Preparation

High School

If you've been busy trying to make a robot out of old clock and vacuum cleaner parts, you're already on the right track to becoming an inventor. To further develop your skills and satisfy your curiosity, read up on robotics, electronics, engineering, science, and math. Art courses, including sculpture, will help you develop aesthetically pleasing inventions; woodshop and other hands-on courses will teach you about construction and manufacturing; and English classes will help you articulate your ideas to others.

College

In college, you can get down into the nitty-gritty of developing ideas and constructing prototypes. You'll probably want to major in engineering design or a related field to make sure you get all the required skills to get your projects off the ground. Courses in finance, business, and marketing will also come in handy when it comes time to sell your inventions. If you can find a part-time job or an internship in a lab or research and development department, that will be your best bet.

Possible Majors

Engineering design, mechanical engineering

Will I Be Rich?

Expect to work long hours and be persistent if you wish to invent things for a living. You can make a lot of money as an inventor, but only if your invention appeals to a lot of people. You will need to be patient, too, since it takes a long time to see your project through to completion. You may work alone or with a team of people, depending on the scope of your project.

Fun Facts

Inventors' Hall of Fame

Can you match up each of these inventors with the inventions they helped develop?

1. Alexander Graham Bell
2. Thomas Alva Edison
3. George Washington Carver
4. Henry Ford
5. Orville and Wilbur Wright
6. Philo Taylor Farnsworth
7. Roy J. Plunkett
8. Percy L. Spencer
9. George de Mestral
   a. Peanut butter (1890s)
   b. Teflon (1938)
   c. Electric lamp (1879)
   d. Television (1927)
   e. Airplane (1903)
   f. Velcro (1955)
   g. Telephone (1876)
   h. Automobile (1896)
   i. Microwave oven (1945)

[Source: www.invent.org]

Related Careers

Engineer, artist, entrepreneur, researcher, scientist

Answer key: 1. g 2. c 3. a 4. h 5. e 6. d 7. b 8. i 9. f

JOURNALIST

The Basics

Journalists (also called reporters) collect news and information and explain it to people. A journalist might write about sports for a small community newspaper. He or she might discuss what's going on in other countries around the globe or provide coverage of an ongoing investigation. A journalist's work can appear in newspapers, magazines, books, television, radio, or the Internet.

A journalist usually interviews other people to gain information and learn about something. Then the journalist has to write and report the story. Unfortunately, tight deadlines mean that many journalists usually have less time to write than they would like. That's simply part of the job. Another aspect of being a journalist is keeping long and sometimes strange work hours. You may have to work through the night to cover an important event that happened during the day. Of course, that's also a plus for those who dislike predictable nine-to-five routines. Journalism can be very exciting if you're in the right spot.

The role of a journalist in society is a significant one. You'll impart important information to your readers, viewers, or listeners. You also have to report an article or story accurately and without bias. That means you should be fair and objective. It takes hard work, but the public is counting on you.

Preparation

High School

If your high school has a student-run newspaper, get involved. Student newspapers are great introductions to the world of journalism. Submit any cool stories to a magazine that you think might like it. Or start your own magazine; you can write articles and collect writing and visual art from friends and classmates and turn them into your very own Xeroxed zine. Work hard in your English classes. You'll need to be an exceptional writer to be a journalist.

College

A journalism degree is an obvious way to start your journalistic career. You can focus your skills on the medium you like most—print, television, or online, for example. But there are other paths to a journalism career. An English or communications degree teaches you to write well. A political science degree will help you learn about politics and government in the world you'll write about. Experience is essential, so work at your local school newspaper or magazine. Even if you spend your weekends working for free, you can learn the trade and add necessary lines to your resume.

Possible Majors

Journalism, English, English composition, English literature, radio and television, political science, communications, sociology, psychology

Will I Be Rich?

Journalism isn't a very high-paying field. Considering the long hours and high pressure, that may come as a surprise. But many journalists enjoy the experience. And they get some perks, too. For example, a music journalist earns free concert tickets, and many journalists often travel to cover news stories. If you get to be a famous television reporter or work for a premiere newspaper like *The New York Times*, you can do pretty well. But you'll need experience first—and lots of it.

Fun Fact

Woodward and Bernstein

Have you ever heard of Robert Woodward and Carl Bernstein? They may be the most famous journalists of all time! Woodward and Bernstein were reporters for the Washington Post in the 1970s. They investigated—and wrote about—the link between a burglary at the Watergate Hotel and President Richard Nixon's administration. About two years after they published their first article about Nixon's wrongdoings, the president resigned from office!

[Source: www.heroism.org]

You Run the Show

Looking for a place to get started? There are plenty of websites, newspapers, and even TV stations where students can write and report news stories. Nickelodeon has a cable news show called Nick News (see www.nick.com), while Time magazine also prints Time for Kids (www.timeforkids.com) magazine. Check out these additional sites, featuring material written by teens, for teens:

- News by Teens International
www.newsbyteens.com
- Teen World News
www.teenworldnews.com
- Teen Ink
www.teenink.com

Related Careers

Critic, news anchor, writer, editor, publisher

JUDGE

The Basics

A judge regulates court proceedings to make sure local, state, and federal laws are applied to court cases. Presiding over cases in a courtroom is a huge responsibility; the importance of this job makes it an incredibly well-respected profession. After all, a judge is responsible for protecting the legal rights of the plaintiff and the defendant in every court procedure by ensuring a fair trial.

As a judge, you will spend most of your day sitting in either a courtroom in your formal black robe or in your chamber. Before a case even makes it to a courtroom, you will meet with lawyers to decide whether there is enough evidence to hold a trial. You will also decide whether suspects should remain in jail while waiting for their trail or if they should be set free on bail. In the courtroom, you will listen to attorneys as they present their claims and settle any disputes. In cases where a jury decides the guilt or innocence of the person on trial, you will assist the jury in interpreting the law. When a jury is not present, you will decide whether the accused is guilty or innocent based on the lawyers' statements and your knowledge of the law.

As a judge, you will need to be honest, trustworthy, and fair. You'll also have to pay close attention to detail and think analytically to process legal evidence and draw conclusions.

Preparation

High School

Join your high school's debate team and serve as the mediator. It will be your job to make sure the speakers stick to the topics and present fair, clear comments. English and psychology classes will help you understand and communicate with people. American history and government courses will provide you with a strong foundation for your law studies.

College

Although majoring in pre-law can get you started in the right direction, it's not necessary. You'll use what you learned in English, history, logic, philosophy, political science, psychology, public speaking, and writing in your career as a judge. Summer internships at a law firm or local court will provide indispensable experience.

Possible Majors

Pre-law, criminology, political science, psychology, public administration, American history

The LSAT

Before you can attend law school, you need to take the Law School Admissions Test (LSAT). A high score will help you get into more competitive law schools, so study and prepare accordingly.

The Bar Exam

Even if you've aced law school, you're not out of the woods yet. To practice law legally, you'll need to pass the bar exam, a two- or three-day test that proves you know your state's laws. Most states have their own bar exam.

Law School

Your law school curriculum will cover a wide range of topics, including contracts, constitutional law, property, trusts, and estates. A majority of students intern at law firms or in the court system during the summer. Once you finish law school, you will need to pass a two-day written examination called the state bar exam, which tests your knowledge of the laws in your state.

Will I Be Rich?

Expect to work long hours en route to becoming a judge and to be emotionally and mentally exhausted more often than not. Your work as a judge will be deeply satisfying because you play a role in releasing innocent people and placing guilty people behind bars. If you have a deep-rooted dedication to truth and justice, the long road to becoming a judge will be worth it.

Fun Facts

Famous Judges

Benjamin N. Cardozo (1870–1938) was a lawyer in New York City who later went on to serve as Chief Judge of the Court of Appeals of New York and then Associate Justice of the Supreme Court of the United States. Yeshiva University's Benjamin N. Cardozo School of Law in New York City bears his name.

Oliver Wendell Holmes (1841–1935) was famous for his lecture series, The Common Law (1881). He served on the Supreme Judicial Court of Massachusetts before he was appointed to the United States Supreme Court, where he was an Associate Justice.

Related Careers

Lawyer, professor, detective, police officer, counselor, corrections officer

KARATE MASTER

The Basics

You mean people actually practice karate for a living? Some karate masters do. They've spent years studying this martial art that is used in combat or self-defense. If you've seen a movie starring Bruce Lee, Jackie Chan, Jet Li, Michelle Yeoh, or Chow Yun-Fat, you've seen some great martial artists in action.

People practice karate to learn self-defense, to stay in shape, and because it's fun. Some love to compete; others find that the confidence they build in practice helps them in other areas of their lives. One karate student said, "It not only makes you physically strong, it makes you mentally strong, too. After practice, I feel as if I can take on the world!"

While people of all ages and backgrounds practice karate, only those who have a deep commitment and devotion to the art form become masters, or black belts. (And only a fraction of those people actually practice karate as a job.) It takes many years and lots of hard work to progress from a white belt up through the ranks to a black belt.

As a karate master, you may compete in national and world competitions, teach at a karate school, or—watch out, world—star in karate movies! No matter how you earn money doing karate, you will practice your moves every day with basic drills, work on your form, or *kata*, sparring, and doing exercises such as sit-ups and push-ups to keep strong. The best karate masters have discipline, dedication, and focus.

Preparation

High School

It can take many years to become a first-degree black belt, so the sooner you get started, the better! Lots of gym classes and physical activities will keep you strong and develop endurance. Keep up with your studies, too—strong mind, strong body.

College

While a college degree isn't necessary to become a karate master, college is a great place to learn about Asian languages and cultures. If you have plans to teach karate, consider taking education classes and getting certified in CPR and first aid.

Possible Majors

Japanese, Chinese, Korean, East Asian studies, physical education, sport and leisure studies

Promotion and Certification

You enter karate as a white belt. When your teacher feels you are ready, you take a test to move to the next level, often a yellow belt. Different karate schools use different color belts to show progress, but generally, the darker the color of the belt, the higher the rank. It takes about three to five years of steady practice and commitment to pass the many tests and become a black belt of the first, second, or third degree. Many never make it. To teach at a karate school, you may need certification by an organization such as the National Korean Martial Arts Association.

Will I Be Rich?

You will be strong physically and mentally—and bonus: Your job title has the word *master* in it. Who can argue with that? If you star in movies or win lots of championships, you'll be all set. More realistically, if you teach at a karate school, you are likely to make a decent living. You may teach a few classes of different skill levels each day, and you may train serious students one-on-one. If you love karate, you can't beat the life of a karate master!

Fun Facts

The Legend of Superfoot

Due to a chronic injury, karate master Bill Wallace was only able to kick with one foot. But he wasn't deterred in the practice of karate—Bill "Superfoot" Wallace still won plenty of championship karate titles using only his powerful left leg.

[Source: www.superfoot.com]

Translation: Japanese to English

- Karate: *empty hand*
- Gi or Dogi: *traditional karate uniform*
- Dojo: *martial arts training hall*
- Kata: *form (how you move your body when you practice karate)*
- Sensei: *karate teacher*
- Obi: *karate belt*

Quote

"Karate is not what you do, it's who you are."

—Rocco Seccafico, black belt

Related Careers

Personal trainer, teacher, athlete

LANDLORD

The Basics

A landlord owns property and rents it out to tenants. Whether a landlord owns a small apartment building, several floors of office space, or a whole bunch of fancy historic homes, screening the tenants before they move in is an important part of the job. Those properties are an investment! A landlord can't afford to have someone using the space who will mess it up or not pay the rent on time. A landlord looks for people he or she can trust and should check the references of every applicant. Once the tenants are in, a landlord handles the repairs and maintenance of the building, including plumbing, electricity, and overall upkeep.

As a landlord, you may live far away from the space you rent or right there in one of the apartments. Landlords who own more than one building often hire a superintendent, or "super," to manage them. Superintendents take care of a building's daily chores—like mowing the lawn or painting the hallways. Landlords and/or superintendents are on call at all times. If a tenant has a complaint or emergency—let's say the heat stops working on a cold January night—the tenant will contact you and expect immediate results. Landlords and supers also deal with a building's security, such as fire alarms, door locks, and, in some cases, keeping a doorman on duty.

Communication skills, a sharp business sense, and attention to detail are vital for a landlord. Good managerial skills, problem solving, and the ability to juggle many things at once are important qualities as well.

Preparation

High School

Each landlord will have different tales of the experience, so talk to as many as you can. Classes in English and math will help build up your business skills. Shop class would be handy as well. As a landlord, you may find yourself fixing things!

College

A college degree isn't crucial, but classes in accounting, business, communications, engineering, finance, and management will build the right skills. If you can find a job working for a landlord, go for it. You will need to start somewhere, and anything you learn—whether in a landlord-owned building or a real estate office—will put you on track to get properties of your own.

Possible Majors

Management, business administration, business communications, finance, real estate

Will I Be Rich?

Expect to work long hours and to be on call all the time. Unhappy tenants will track you down! Strong communication skills are important, as is a commitment to your tenants. You will need to keep your buildings up to date on safety and maintenance codes. Insurance and liability prices can be steep. If you want to earn more money, buy more property, and buy it wisely. Look for up-and-coming areas of town where property values will surely increase over time.

Fun Facts

Landlord University

Think it's easy to sit back and be a landlord? Not a chance. Landlords need to keep up to date on their rights—and those of their tenants—to prevent legal issues or other problems. One way they do that is by joining local landlord associations to meet with other landlords and swap ideas. Some landlords even have local education opportunities:

- The Department of Neighborhood Services in Milwaukee, Wisconsin, offers a free Landlord Training Program for those interested in managing property.

- The police department of Hollywood, Florida, offers a Landlord Workshop to educate property owners.

- The Neighborhood Stabilization Team of St. Louis, Missouri, holds an annual Landlord's Conference with workshops and resources from experts in the field.

Quote

"Knowledge is great, but experience is the best teacher. As a superintendent, you learn from experience each day. No two tenants are the same, and no two complaints are, either. You need to pay attention to what people say—listen to them. That's how you learn and help people to live more comfortably."

—Luis Berrios, resident superintendent, New York, New York

Related Careers

Real estate agent, real estate developer, banker, carpenter, plumber

LAWYER

The Basics

A lawyer is one of the most respected professions in the world. As the name suggests, lawyers deal with all matters concerning the law. Lawyers have the ability to send crooks to jail or protect innocent people from being falsely convicted. They also have the ability to protect land or get money to help people who were injured. In fact, there are literally thousands of possible jobs that a lawyer can have.

You can be a *prosecuting* or *plaintiff's attorney,* which means your role is to convince a judge or jury that a person or company has done something wrong (is *guilty*). Or you can be on the other side—a *defense attorney.* Defense attorneys try to convince judge and juries that a person or company is *not guilty* of the charges.

Whatever your specific role as a lawyer may be, expect to do a lot of reading, writing, and speaking in public. You can also expect to spend a lot of time doing research, reading up on prior similar cases and just about any other information relating to a case.

Preparation

High School

If you want to become a lawyer, aim for good grades in high school. Join your school's debate team to prepare for public speaking and learn how to take sides and argue. Follow the legal news and take as many civic and government classes as you can. Take a trip to your local courthouse to see how the law process works firsthand.

College

Good grades in college will help you get into a top law school. While you're in college, you can study just about anything that interests you, but it helps to learn about political science, English, or legal studies. A specialization can help your specific law career; for example, an environmental studies degree can help you become a great environmental lawyer. Keep debating, and be prepared for the law school entrance exam, the LSAT.

Possible Majors

Pre-law, English literature, history, legal studies, philosophy, political science

The LSAT

Before you can attend law school, you need to take the Law School Admissions Test (LSAT). A high score will help you get into more competitive law schools, so study and prepare accordingly.

Law School

You simply must go to law school if you want to practice law. It involves three years of intense studying, critical thinking, writing papers, and preparing for difficult, high-pressure exams. It's not easy, but many lawyers agree that it gets easier after the first year.

The Bar Exam

Even if you've aced law school, you're not out of the woods yet. To practice law legally, you'll need to pass the bar exam, a two- or three-day test that proves you know your state's laws. Most states have their own bar exam.

Will I Be Rich?

If you can last long enough in the profession, you can earn a lot of money. Young lawyers have to tough it out—they often work six days a week, twelve to fourteen hours a day. The long hours and hard work cause some lawyers to change professions, but successful lawyers will usually tell you the pain was worth the gain.

Fun Fact

More than half of all United States presidents were lawyers. The last president to be a lawyer was William Jefferson Clinton, who was the Arkansas attorney general from 1976 to 1978. He then became the governor of Arkansas from 1978 to 1980 and 1982 to 1992, then the forty-second United States president from 1993 to 2001.

Myth v. Reality

Myth: You can tell a lawyer is lying because his or her lips are moving.
Reality: In reality, lawyers are ethically obligated to tell the truth and must keep secret private information from a client.
Myth: Lawyers are only in it for the money.
Reality: Lawyers are responsible for some of the most significant social changes, such as civil rights.

Quote

"Although becoming a lawyer is a difficult and lengthy process, you can accomplish wonderful things. I get to use laws to protect our environment and punish those who pollute."

—*Jordan Kahn, environmental lawyer*

Related Careers

Judge, politician, criminologist, detective, police officer

LIBRARIAN

The Basics

The basic role of a librarian is to help people access information. The immense amount of resources—from books to microfiche to the Internet—can be overwhelming for some. That's why the librarian is there to help you find exactly what you are looking for. Librarians also order new books and resources that will best serve the patrons in their community. They may also organize outreach programs in the community; these programs bring books and other learning materials to people who don't have access to libraries.

You can work in a variety of departments in a library. Fiction and nonfiction books are separated by age—adult, young adult, and children's books. Then there are periodicals, reference materials, and media resources (including music and art books, CDs, books on tape, VHS, and DVDs). Regardless of which department you work in, you'll work with the Dewey decimal system. Each library material is assigned a Dewey decimal number by the Library of Congress in Washington, D.C. It's your job to use this national system to locate materials and keep track of what is checked out.

If you work in a small library, you will probably have additional duties; you may check out books, sort and file materials, and enter new materials into the system. At a large library, you'll probably focus on a more specific task. At some types of research libraries, you may also gather and prepare materials for patrons. Organization should be a strong point for future librarians; the desire to continuously learn and teach is important, too.

Preparation

High School

Explore your local library to get familiar with all that a library has to offer, including fiction, nonfiction, and mystery books, as well as magazines, newspapers, films, art slides, CDs, and DVDs, too. Also, check out your local library's newspaper to find out about cool events at your library, such as book clubs, movie nights, and more. English classes, as well as computer classes, will be a big help.

College

A college degree is necessary to be a librarian, and in many cases, so is a graduate degree in library science. Sign up for classes in computer science, English, and education. A library internship or part-time job will provide you with great hands-on experience.

Possible Majors

Library science, American studies, classics, education, English literature, history, great books

Graduate School

Although you can get some jobs in libraries without a master of library science, you can move up in the ranks if you earn one.

Will I Be Rich?

You'll certainly be rich in knowledge as a librarian! You will work closely with people and also spend some time alone doing research and organizing library events. The library environment is generally calm, quiet, and soothing; that helps make a librarian's job less stressful. Most folks who work in libraries love learning and sharing information each day.

Fun Facts

Can I Help You?

Although we know J. Edgar Hoover as the former director of the FBI, he first worked in the Library of Congress for five years as a cataloguer. Mao Tse-dung, former chairman of the Chinese Communist Party, worked in the journals section of the Beijing University library before he came to power.

[Sources: www.fbi.gov and www.wikipedia.org]

Myth v. Reality

Myth: Librarians are nerds who wear glasses and hide behind books.
Reality: Librarians are people who love books. They can come in any shape, size, or style, and some even have 20/20 vision.

Quote

"If you love to teach, enjoy working with people of all ages, like to do research, and are an information junkie, this is a great field to pursue."
–Tony Traguado, librarian, Port Washington public library

Related Careers

Researcher, teacher, professor, art dealer, museum curator, consultant, guidance counselor

LOBBYIST

The Basics

You've probably lobbied on an amateur level many times: for a higher allowance, a later curfew, or your own big-screen TV and cell phone. Professional lobbyists work for organizations, specific people, or the general public. They try to bring about change by persuading politicians or organizations to agree with their point of view. Lobbyists are well-informed and self-confident individuals who arm themselves with facts, figures, and research that they use to "lobby"—or promote what they believe in.

As a lobbyist, your goal will be to sway politicians to vote on laws that you (or the group you represent) support. You'll want to get to know as many politicians as possible. While you may be the voice behind the change, politicians are the people who officially put a plan for change in motion.

There are two types of lobbying that you may take part in. As a *direct lobbyist,* you will meet with congresspeople in person, phone them up, and write letters to specific people to express your point of view, either for or against a proposed law or bill. As an *indirect lobbyist,* you will be in the public eye less often. You will spend a lot of time talking on the phone, writing letters and articles, creating petitions, and organizing rallies.

Patience, persistence, and a deep-rooted dedication to what you believe in are necessary to be a lobbyist. Outspoken, influential people will do well in this career. Sharpen your communication and leadership skills if you are interested in becoming a lobbyist.

Preparation

High School

Get as much practice as possible in public speaking. Run for a position in student government or join the debate team. Even giving reports in front of your class or emceeing a school talent show will give you a chance to develop your confidence in front of an audience. What you learn in history and government classes and the newspaper (keep up with current events!) will help prepare you for a life in politics.

College

Get involved in your student government. Try to get an internship with a politician. The more politically active you are and the more contacts you make early on, the better it will be for your lobbyist career. Your studies will probably include classes in economics, history, political science, political philosophy, politics, religion, sociology, and statistics.

Possible Majors

Public policy analysis, international studies, sociology, American studies,
journalism, economics, political science, pre-law, history

Will I Be Rich?

You may not be rolling in dough, but if you put in your time, you may see meaningful changes happen because of your hard work. While the job can be demanding and stressful, knowing that you are fighting for a cause you believe in tends to make it worthwhile. You will do a lot of behind-the-scenes research, but you will also meet a lot of people and sometimes find yourself in the media spotlight. Working with people who are fighting for the same things you are is a plus. Remember, though, you will also be working alongside folks whose views clash with yours; this means that on-the-job frustration levels can run high if you can't keep your cool.

Fun Facts

Anyone Can Speak Up!

In June 2003, 200 children with diabetes and their families voiced their opinions in Washington, D.C. The bottom line is that they want American lawmakers to help them find a cure for diabetes. These lobbyists came from all fifty states and were from two to seventeen years old.

[Source: www.jdf.org]

Also during the summer of 2003, high school students protested beer manufacturers, claiming that their beer advertisements targeted children. The students chanted and carried signs that showed the advertisements while marching in front of the Beer Institute's offices in Washington, D.C.

[Source: www.whatkidscando.org]

Related Careers

Politician, journalist, news anchor, reporter, professor, advertising executive

MAGICIAN

The Basics

Magicians provide audiences with a sense of awe and wonder by reminding people that anything is possible. They may perform in a variety of settings, including magic shows, birthday parties, carnivals, or circuses.

There are a few different types of magic you can choose to perform. First, there's *closeup magic,* where you perform right in front of your audiences' faces. Close-up magic often includes coin tricks or card tricks. You can perform *stand-up magic,* where you do your act on a stage before an audience. Stand-up magicians sometimes perform illusion tricks, such as sawing a person in half, or quick escapes from boxes or bags that are bound shut (or at least appear to be!). You can use a whole slew of props in your tricks, from the classic rabbit-producing top hat to totally new and original props. The costumes, sounds or music, props, and stage set will come together to create a style for your act.

Earning the trust of your audience is important when you are a magician—if your audience trusts you, they will watch you with awe. With that in mind, learn to speak in public and perform with confidence. Practice, patience, and a love of performing are necessary to succeed in this career.

Preparation

High School

Put on your own magic shows! Family and friends are your best audience. You can learn magic tricks from books or tapes, and you can even attend classes to learn the art of optical illusion. You can learn a lot by watching other magicians perform tricks, but you'll have to practice a lot on your own, too. Theater (drama club), art, math, science, and psychology are all related to this career.

College

While you don't need a college degree to be a magician, you will probably want to earn one as a backup plan. Classes in communication, public speaking, and theatre will be helpful for your budding magic career. You can also try working as a part-time magician while you're in college—make business cards and pass them out on campus and in town.

Possible Majors

Theater, art, music, education, communications, psychology, philosophy, science

Will I Be Rich?

If you are great at what you do and have a large following like David Copperfield or Penn and Teller, you may get rich. Otherwise, the money you make will depend on how often you perform and how much you charge. In the beginning, it may be a good idea to have another way to bring in some income until your magic career takes off. Regardless, you will be rich in passion and excitement if you love magic. You'll also get to travel a lot to perform in various locations; if you work in a circus, you'll be on the road most of the time.

Fun Facts

The Magician and the Parrot

A magician was working on a cruise ship in the Caribbean. The audience would be different each week, so the magician allowed himself to do the same tricks over and over again.

There was only one problem: The captain's parrot saw the shows every week and began to understand what the magician did in every trick. Once he understood that, he started shouting in the middle of the show.

"Look, it's not the same hat!" "Look, he's hiding the flowers under the table!" "Hey, why are all the cards the ace of spades?"

The magician was furious but couldn't do anything; it was the captain's parrot after all.

One day the ship had an accident and sank. The magician found himself on a piece of wood, in the middle of the ocean, and of course the parrot was by his side.

They stared at each other with hatred, but did not utter a word. This went on for several days.

After a week the parrot finally said, "Okay, I give up. What'd you do with the boat?"

[Source: www.basicjokes.com]

Quote

"If you're a magician, you'll never feel like you're working. It's all fun."

—Allan J. Sherer, magician

Related Careers

Actor, clown, teacher, mime, stunt double, stage technician, costume designer, comedian

MAKEUP ARTIST

The Basics

A makeup artist (also called a cosmetologist) applies makeup to people to create a desired effect. Makeup artists may apply makeup to male and female fashion models, actors, celebrities, musicians, news anchors, or dancers; they also apply makeup to people attending fancy events like proms and weddings. Makeup artists may work for themselves or at a salon, or they may have an agent who arranges and books appointments.

The right makeup for a person depends on many factors. Makeup artists take into consideration a person's coloring, their facial structure, the event the person will be attending, the kind of lights the person will be under, and the type of film a photographer is using. If the client is a model or an actress, the makeup artist usually discusses the desired look with a photographer or director. Even the time of day counts—believe it or not, different types of makeup look good during the day and at night. To top it off, makeup artists must choose from tons of different brands and colors of foundation, blush, powders, lipstick, and eye makeup to create the perfect look.

Sure, you'll have to be patient, creative, and detail-oriented to succeed as a makeup artist. But you'll also need to be able to work delicately with your hands. (You want people to trust you with their face, right?) You will need to have great communication skills as well—if you work on a person's face for hours, you'll need to keep the conversation alive. According to one Los Angeles makeup artist, "You get the greatest gossip out of people when you are working on their face!"

Preparation

High School

Read fashion and beauty magazines and practice applying makeup to your friends. To develop versatile skills, try a wide range of styles, from conservative to wild. Organize some photo sessions with your friends; if you apply their makeup and take pictures, you can keep a portfolio of your makeup work. Art courses will be your best bet in high school; painting will help you work with color and design, and photography will give you the skills to record your designs.

College

You probably won't find too much specialized training in this area in college, but you can learn a lot about theatrical makeup and costumes in your school's theater department.

Possible Majors
Costume design, theater

Training Programs

Through makeup artist training courses, you can learn how to apply makeup for films or special events like weddings, character makeup, photographic makeup, or you can even learn how to apply permanent makeup. Most programs offer hands-on experience, so you can practice your use of color and tone. Training programs can last anywhere from thirty-five hours up to over 600 hours.

Will I Be Rich?

If you have some star clients, you just might get rich from this career. If you are working on a film set, photo shoot, or music video, you can expect your days to be long and tedious. Some makeup artists claim to reapply makeup all day—up to ten hours—when they are on a shoot. Be prepared for mixed reactions at first—some people won't like the way you make them look, while others will be thrilled. Regardless, there's great satisfaction in making someone look glamorous and gorgeous!

Fun Fact

A Subtle Hint

"Whether you are sixteen or over sixty, remember, understatement is the rule of a fine makeup artist. Adjust your makeup to the light in which your wear it. Daylight reveals color; artificial light drains it."

—Helena Rubinstein (1870–1965),
cosmetician and founder of Helena Rubinstein Inc.,
a makeup manufacturer and distributor.
[Source: www.creativequotations.com]

Quote

"Sometimes when you look at someone after you have worked your magic, you can't believe how gorgeous they look! Then, when they see themselves in the mirror, and you see them liking what they see—you can't help but feel incredible!"

—Gina Brooke, makeup artist, Los Angeles

Related Careers

Artist, fashion designer, hairdresser, model, personal trainer, massage therapist, actor, costume designer

MARKET RESEARCHER

The Basics

Market researchers collect, organize, study, and make sense of the data and opinions they collect. This information helps businesses, political parties, and advertising agencies understand what people like and don't like. If you have ever filled out a questionnaire in a restaurant that asks about your meal, then you have taken part in a market research project. The purpose of the survey was to gather customer feedback. After reviewing the responses, the restaurant may change its menu and service to better serve its customers.

As a market researcher, you will measure the public's opinions on a variety of topics, including politics, books, food, drinks, music, name brands, and transportation. Aside from analyzing recent surveys, you will also review old surveys to find out whether the public's opinions have changed over time. You may collect information from surveys, personal or telephone interviews, or questionnaires, and you will use computer programs to analyze your data. Market researchers usually try to gather information from a target audience, or the segment of the population who is most likely to use the product or service you're researching. This could be any group of people, including those in a specific age group, neighborhood, or career.

What makes a successful market researcher? Great communication skills are the most important, since you will often interact with the public; but attention to detail and organization are crucial, too. And even though you may have your own strong opinions on a particular topic, you can't let them get in the way of gathering research and coming to fair conclusions.

Preparation

High School

You can conduct surveys in your own school. Create a questionnaire about students' interests in music, art, television, or just about anything. You may be able to use this information for a school newspaper article about current trends. If your high school offers statistics classes, take them! English and math classes will come in handy, too, since you will need to interpret and analyze results.

College

In college, you can learn a great deal about marketing and business. Outside of class, try to find part-time work with a market research company. Schools often survey their own students about their experiences on campus, and you may be able to help out. Apart from the business side of things, classes like sociology and psychology will also give you some insight into why people do what they do (or buy what they buy).

Possible Majors

Marketing, statistics, business administration, communications, economics, psychology, sociology

Will I Be Rich?

Working as a market researcher will probably pay your bills, but it won't make you a millionaire. Developing your own surveys or starting your own market research company can help bring in more dough, though. You probably won't have to work long or crazy hours, unless you are under a deadline and someone needs the information ASAP. Market research projects can range from fun and interesting to pretty darn dull. But knowing that your research helps businesses and politicians make improvements that benefit the public can bring great satisfaction.

Fun Facts

And You Call Them Your Friends?

Do you know the first and last names of the characters on the hit television show Friends? Out of 319 people surveyed, 41 percent knew all the names, 36 percent got some of the names partially correct, and 23 percent didn't know their names at all. (By the way, the names are Chandler Bing, Phoebe Buffay, Monica Geller, Ross Geller, Rachel Green, and Joey Tribbiani.)

What Is Cool?

What do you think makes a brand that you like cool? According to 150 kids surveyed, 30 percent agreed that what made a brand cool was that it was fun. Eighteen percent said discovery was important, and 17 percent said that if a brand was popular, it was cool. Other factors that kids considered were individuality (12 percent), humor (8 percent), rebellion (3 percent), and familiarity (3 percent).

[Source: www.reveries.com]

Related Careers

Taste tester, statistician, scientist, advertising executive, journalist, salesperson, creative director

MASSAGE THERAPIST

The Basics

Massage therapists soothe your aching muscles. They use a hands-on approach to ease pain, reduce tension, and improve flexibility and circulation. Studies have shown that massage can help people sleep better, maintain focus, and feel better overall. People of all ages and backgrounds appreciate a good massage; clients range from businesspeople and construction workers to pregnant women, athletes, dancers, and the elderly.

As a massage therapist, you will provide a safe, nurturing environment that helps people relax. You want your clients to feel instant peace and comfort when they arrive, so you might use soothing music, aromatherapy candles, and dim lighting. Some people might ask you to concentrate on a certain part of their body; otherwise, you will provide an overall massage, working on a person's back, arms, legs, feet, hands, head, neck, and shoulders. You may use lotions and oils as you knead, tap, stroke, and apply gentle pressure to muscles and tissues of the body. There are different types of massage, and you might specialize in one or be skilled in several. Swedish massage energizes and stimulates circulation with long, flowing strokes, while a Reiki massage (dating back to ancient Tibet) combines hands-on touch with visualization to improve a person's energy.

Your days will be a mixture of silence and conversation, as some clients will want to chat while others prefer to stay quiet. Going with the flow is a helpful trait for massage therapists, as you never know what your clients will want until they are on the massage table. Aside from a caring nature, you will need physical strength to work on people all day.

Preparation

High School

Take classes in anatomy and biology to learn about the body's tissues and muscle groups. Volunteer at a local hospital or community center to get experience interacting with people in a service situation. And hey, treat yourself to a massage—it's research!

College

A bachelor's degree isn't necessary but would be useful if you decide to pursue another career down the road. Courses in human anatomy, health, and rehabilitation will get you in touch with what's on the inside. And since you will be interacting with people all day, psychology and communication classes would also be a good choice.

Training Programs

A training program to become a massage therapist could take you three months to over a year. Most are full-time programs that prepare you for the state licensing exam. Classes cover a variety of massage techniques and include lots of hands-on experience. Many programs offer internships, too.

Will I Be Rich?

You can earn a decent living as a massage therapist, depending upon how many clients you see each day and whether or not you work for yourself. (If you work for yourself, you have a lot more freedom.) Interacting with people of all ages and backgrounds can be a highlight. And making people feel good is a rewarding way to spend your days.

Fun Facts

Sore Paws?

Some massage therapists choose to extend their practice and do massage for pets! Dogs, cats, even horses, all enjoy and can benefit from a gentle massage.

On-the-Job Massage

To relax the many people who are stressed out on the job, companies such as American Airlines, General Electric, and the United States Department of Justice offer massage breaks for their employees.

[Source: www.dispatch.com]

Quote

"A massage is a gift to the body. Helping people to let go of their worries, stress, and pain each day is a dream job! You go to sleep at night feeling as if you have helped people to make friends with their minds and bodies."

—Rita Comisky, licensed massage therapist, New York, New York

Related Careers

Yoga teacher, physical therapist, chiropractor, personal trainer, doctor, nurse, holistic doctor

MATHEMATICIAN

The Basics

Mathematicians spend their days working with numbers to solve problems. Those problems can relate to economics, engineering, or science. To work on those problems, mathematicians use computers, theories, and some very large, complex math formulas. In fact, some mathematicians may work on a single math question for months—even years—at a time!

There are two kinds of mathematicians. *Theoretical mathematicians* work to create new math principles. Their work may not have any obvious practical uses. It can often be about discovering mathematical relationships or other abstract values. That's what we call *pure* mathematics, and it helps advance the science of math. Most theoretical mathematicians are professors or students who are paid to work on important math problems.

Applied mathematicians are more concerned with solving practical problems that relate to everyday life. For example, they may want to figure out the aerodynamics of a new car, they may work for the government, trying to encode (or decode) very important military information, or they may work to analyze financial figures relating to the economy.

Whichever type of mathematician you want to be, expect to be challenged. Even the most brilliant math wizards get stifled. Considering how complicated some of the problems can be, many mathematicians fail more often than they succeed. As long as you're curious and willing to test your abilities, you can have what it takes to be successful.

Preparation

High School

It may come as no surprise that the best preparation for a career as a mathematician is to study hard in your math classes. Try to excel in your class, whether it is algebra, geometry, trigonometry, or pre-calculus. If you think solving equations is fun, you're on the right track. But to be a mathematician, you're going to have to use math that's much more advance than that! If you school has a math club, join it.

College

You'll need at least a college degree for even a low-level job as a mathematician. You should study a wide range of math skills, ranging from theory and statistics to topology and discrete mathematics (sounds intimidating, right?). You can stand out and make an impression on a future employer if you study something else, too. For example, you can earn a double major in mathematics and economics, engineering, or computer science. Familiarize yourself with computers, too, because advanced math calculations and models are performed on them.

Graduate School

Nearly 200 colleges offer PhD degrees in mathematics. To be a theoretical mathematician, you'll most likely need to get this advanced degree. An advanced nonmath degree can be useful, too. For example, computer science, engineering, physics, and statistics are all related to the field of mathematics.

Will I Be Rich?

Because of the amount of education they need, mathematicians are usually paid pretty well. To make the most money, however, mathematicians need to manage a whole team of mathematicians. That means personal and management skills can be crucial.

Fun Fact

No, Not That Kind of Pie

Pi (π) is an important number in mathematics. Most measurements involving circles require pi. However, it's a very strange number. Mathematicians call it irrational. That's because it never ends and never repeats, so you can't get an exact value for it. It starts at 3.1415926 . . . but goes on forever. People have been trying to get an exact value for it for 4,000 years! Recently, a supercomputer calculated its value to a billion digits, and it still didn't end!

Myth v. Reality

Myth: Mathematicians spend all day staring at numbers.

Reality: Mathematicians spend a lot of their day working with numbers, but they need interpersonal skills, too! Some math jobs require written reports, so English skills can be just as important.

Related Careers

Statistician, computer programmer, computer scientist, physicist, astronomer, engineer, professor, scientist

MILITARY PERSONNEL

Air Force • Army • Navy • Marine Corps • National Guard

The Basics

Military personnel are the brave souls who lead, organize, manage, and fight in our country's armed forces. They undergo intense training that requires discipline, physical and mental strength, and commitment to service.

To become a military service person, you will need to be willing to sweat and take orders from your superiors. Courage, discipline, motivation, and a desire to serve your country are also necessary characteristics. When disaster strikes, you will need to maintain your calm and act on behalf of your country. In addition, the rigors of your training and service require great physical and emotional strength.

If you join the *air force*, you can choose from over a hundred jobs that relate to air and space defense. You may train to be an airlift pilot, an astronaut, a bomber navigator, an aerial gunner, a communication and information officer, an air traffic controller, a special investigations officer, or an aerospace medicine specialist, to name a few.

In the *army*, you also have many career options. You may become an infantry soldier, a gunner, a tank crewman, an engineer, an intelligence officer, a troop commander, a doctor, a veterinarian, a dentist, a technician, a communications specialist, or a radio systems operator.

Those who serve in the *navy* operate a submarine or a vessel. Your naval career, however, is not limited to seafaring jobs. In fact, you may choose a career in photography, aviation, computers, engineering, recruiting, medicine, counseling, electronics, science, telecommunications, and technology—and those are just a few options.

If you join the *Marine Corps*, you may work on land, on sea, or in the air. You can choose from careers such as aviation electrician or operator and aircraft maintenance and repair person. In addition, some other options are: rifleman, machine gunner, tank crewman, field artillery radar operator, electronics intelligence interceptor, field radio operator, data programmer, public affairs representative, postal clerk, and aviation operations specialist.

If you choose to join the *National Guard*, you will serve your country on a part-time basis. In other words, you'll be able to hold another job outside of your commitment to the National Guard. You will still go through the same basic training that active military personnel go through. After it's over, though, you will train one weekend per month and for two weeks each year and be called upon when your country needs your help.

Preparation

High School

Talk to a recruiter about military school; it helps to speak with recruits who are in the military to get firsthand advice. Ask as many questions as you can about living conditions, what you will do on a daily basis, and anything else you would like to know, so you can make an informed decision. Joining a sports team in high school will help you to stay in shape and get a taste for being part of a team. A wide range of classes, including physical fitness, English, math, and science will come in handy for a military career.

College & ROTC Programs

While a college degree is not required to join the military, it will certainly help prepare you for your military experiences. College life, in many ways, is all about survival. You can major in ROTC (Reserve Officer's Training Corps) in college, which is a great way to prepare for the military. ROTC programs mix classroom learning with hands-on experience. The training that you receive in ROTC programs prepares you for leadership positions in the military. If you are chosen for an ROTC scholarship, you'll receive money for tuition and fees, plus a stipend! As a scholarship recipient, you'll have a required amount of service time after graduation.

Possible Majors

Army ROTC, air force ROTC, navy ROTC, Marine Corps ROTC, history, American history, military science

Military School

Another option for those who are interested in joining the military is to go to a four-year military academy. These schools are extremely competitive to get into, so you will need to do super well in high school to gain entry. If you are admitted, you will work incredibly hard for the next four years, dividing your time between classroom studies and hands-on experience. The federal military academies in the nation are the United States Military Academy (USMA), United States Coast Guard Academy (USCGA), United States Merchant Marine Academy (USMMA), United States Naval Academy (USNA), and United States Air Force Academy (USAFA).

Initial Requirements

You must have a high school degree or a GED and be between the ages of seventeen and thirty-five years old to join the armed services. In addition, you need to be a United States citizen who has a birth certificate and a clean police record. You will need to pass a written exam (The Armed Services Vocational Aptitude Battery) and satisfy some physical requirements, including having good vision and being in good shape overall. Once you meet all the necessary criteria, you will need to sign an enlistment contract that details how long you will be on active duty.

Basic Training

Basic training lasts from six to twelve weeks, depending on which division of the military you enter. You will be put to the test in regard to your physical and mental strength, and you will learn a great deal. After basic training, you may choose to pursue specialized training, which lasts from a few months to a year, or further your education by taking college courses. The armed services will pay up to three-quarters of your college costs.

Will I Be Rich?

The amount of money you make as a military service person will depend upon your title and experience. A major benefit of military service is that you receive lots of perks, including free room and board, medical and dental care, a clothing allowance, military supermarket and department store shopping privileges, thirty days of paid vacation a year, and travel opportunities. In addition, the intensity of training and service helps to develop close bonds with others in the military, who will become lifelong friends.

Fun Facts

You Call This Basic?

Army Basic Combat Training (nine weeks)

In a typical day, you'll practice physical activities including situps, push-ups, runs, and even throwing grenades, while learning about loyalty, honor, integrity, courage, and selfless service.

Navy Boot Camp (eight weeks)

In Great Lakes, Illinois, at the Naval Training Center, you will exercise six days a week, and participate in battle stations—which means that you will be put in one stressful situation after another for up to twelve hours!

Air Force Basic Military Training (six weeks)

Aside from the physical aspect of the training, you will learn about teamwork and self-reliance, as well as the history, customs, and laws pertaining to the air force.

Marine Corps Recruit Training (twelve weeks)

Expect to go through a mental and physical transformation as you learn the meaning of teamwork during this training. From five A.M. to nine P.M., you'll learn basic combat skills, leadership skills, and how to be responsible and courteous.

Related Careers

Engineer, scientist, journalist, computer technician, police officer, corrections officer, personal trainer, pilot, sailor, politician

MODEL

The Basics

Professional models pose for audiences at fashion shows and showrooms and for artists. They may display beauty products, clothes, jewelry, shoes, or just about any product a client wants to promote. They may also appear in ads for various products, services, or businesses on TV, in catalogs, newspapers, or magazines, or even on billboards. Models can be found striking a pose in the studio of a painter, sculptor, or photographer as well.

As a model, you can expect to interact with many different people. Your agent is the person who negotiates deals with clients; sets up appointments, called "go-sees;" and books your photo shoots or other modeling appointments. Agents also make sure that you receive your pay and help you come up with a financial plan to start saving your earnings; since models often have short careers during which they make a lot of money, financial planning is crucial. During photo shoots, you will work closely with photographers, makeup artists, clothing stylists, and hairstylists. When posing for an artist, you may interact with just the artist or with his or her assistants as well. Posing for a painter or sculptor generally requires sitting still for hours at a time.

Regardless of whether you are a petite-size model, a plus-size model, a bathing suit model, or a hand model, you will need to take good care of your looks. They're your biggest asset in this career. It also helps, though, if you're patient and easy to get along with, and—of course—photogenic.

Preparation

High School

Your education is just as important as your looks, and the more you know, the better you will do in this career. Courses in nutrition, physical education, and health will equip you with the knowledge to stay in great shape. Enter a modeling search or contest—modeling agencies often advertise them in fashion magazines. Sign up for any fashion-related courses at your school, as well as any local or school fashion shows. Keep copies of any modeling work you do so you can build up a portfolio.

College

Since it's tough to make a living in this career, it will be wise to earn a college degree while you model on the side.

Possible Majors

Fashion design, fashion merchandising, marketing, costume design, graphic design, advertising

Modeling School

There are some schools that offer training courses to prepare you for a career in modeling. They may cover anything from posture and skin care to accessorizing and career tips. Although the completion of modeling courses or programs is not required, it helps some models gain a professional edge and a better portfolio.

Will I Be Rich?

You will travel a lot, meet a lot of great people, and as long as you keep getting work, you could be rich, too! So what's the downside of being a model? It's a very competitive career. Not only will you compete with other models for work; you'll also be up against actors looking for modeling jobs, too. Working models are often away from family and friends, so expect to rely on email and telephones for communication with loved ones. There may be times when you don't get work, so it's important to have other skills to fall back on.

Fun Facts

Top 10 Female Modeling Agencies

1. Tie between DNA and IMG
3. Tie between Next and Women Supreme
5. Elite
6. 1 Management
7. Ford
8. Vision
9. T Management
10. NY Models

Top 10 Male Modeling Agencies

1. IMG
2. Wilhelmina
3. Tie between Ford and Elite Men
5. DNA
6. Tie between NY Models and Clear
8. Tie between Major and Karin Men
10. Boss

[Source: http://teentvmovies.about.com]

Quote

"You get to meet so many fun, talented people and travel the world! It does get lonely being away from your friends and family a lot, but there's always email, and the new friends you make while you travel become your family, too."
—Donna Puzio, Ford model, New York City

Related Careers

Actor, musician, artist, fashion designer, dancer, makeup artist, hairdresser, advertising executive, agent, costume designer

MUSEUM CURATOR

The Basics

A museum curator is the person who is responsible for setting up and running exhibits in a museum. A museum exhibit displays objects with historical or cultural importance. Those objects can be just about anything—art, dinosaur bones, even shoes—as long as they are significant for some reason. Most curators work in art museums and put together shows that include paintings, photography, sculptures, books, and other art forms. However, curators also work in historical museums and planetariums.

Running an exhibit takes a lot of work. For example, you may want to show people how an artist's paintings changed over the course of his or her life. Or perhaps you want to demonstrate how women's fashion changed in the last twenty years. You have to keep track of the inventory. You need to label everything and be sure that the information is accurate. The objects must be arranged in a pleasing and easy-to-follow style—that's part of your job, too. You also have to explain the exhibit with written materials or audio tracks so your guests can learn about the items on display. Basically, you have to design exhibits that will both excite and educate people.

You're in charge of the show. So every big problem—and every little issue—falls into your lap. You'll need to work with a large support staff to get everything done. And if funding for the museum or institution is weak, you also need to raise money. To do that, you can write grants, raise awareness of your cause, or hold fund-raising events. It's not easy, and it's usually not fun, but it's just one of the many necessary jobs of a curator.

Preparation

High School

Find a field that you love, whether it's dinosaurs or Salvador Dali. You will need an extensive knowledge of art and history to be a curator someday. Curators tend to lecture a lot; you can learn a lot by going to a lecture at a museum or university. Get the best grades you can because you'll need them.

College

If you can study art history or museum studies, that's great. But even a field like public relations can be a huge help. Specialize in your field; if you want to be a curator at a planetarium, for example, you can study astrophysics. Keep those grades up and try to get some practical experience. Most museums offer educational, volunteer, and internship opportunities. Those are good ways to find out more about museums and art, especially for your field. Check with local institutions to see how you can get involved.

Graduate School

Curators are scholars. And since graduate school is where you continue to learn, a graduate degree is essential if you want to be a curator. In fact, most national museums require a PhD (as well as at least five years of experience). Immerse yourself in your subject because this will be your life. Museum studies, museum education, curatorship, art history, or restoration science would all be terrific graduate degrees to earn.

Will I Be Rich?

Curators don't really get rich. Museums and libraries just don't have the money available to pay curators so much money. In fact, many curators get paid poorly for that very reason—at least considering the amount of work they do. But curators surround themselves with the beauty of art or history nearly all day long. Most folks would consider that life to be pretty rich.

Fun Fact

The Louvre in Paris, France, is the largest museum in the world. It holds the ultrafamous Mona Lisa, and its collection grows all the time. In 2002, the curator for the Louvre purchased five sketchbooks that belonged to the artist Adolphe William Bouguereau. During the bidding for the art, she claimed, "Musees Nationaux, Droit de preemption!" That means that no one else could own the sketchbooks because the national museum took priority.

[Source: www.artrenewal.org]

Related Careers

Artist, historian, critic, agent, editor, art dealer, art and antique restorer

MUSIC CONDUCTOR

The Basics

A music conductor is in charge of leading a group of musicians. Symphony orchestras, high school orchestras, and many types of instrumental bands follow the lead of a conductor. Surely you've seen a conductor waving his or her baton and hand about, signaling to the musicians. But what does it all mean?

During performances, conductors cue different sections of the orchestra as to when to begin playing and when to stop. They signal to musicians about the tempo and intensity—when the music should speed up, slow down, become louder and more powerful, or quiet down to a whisper. The conductor shapes or interprets a song and performance, and there are tons of different details a conductor can communicate to his or her players. The musicians will change their tone according to the conductor's directions. If all goes well, the ensemble will sound great together—that's one of the conductor's main goals. Conductors also may audition and select the musicians, direct rehearsals, and choose the songs to be performed.

A musical imagination, passion, and great communication skills (both verbal and physical!) are necessary for conductors. As a conductor, you must also remain calm under pressure, even when it seems like all the lights in the theater are beaming down on you. The ability to inspire your musicians and connect with them is important, too.

Preparation

High School

Start by playing a musical instrument. Take advantage of the music classes at your school, including band and chorus. In band rehearsals, watch your conductor or band leader; pay attention to his or her cues and what they mean. Using this knowledge, you can practice your conducting skills while listening to music at home.

College

During college, you'll have a chance to explore music on a deeper level, learning about music history and different musical theories. You can either take courses in the music department at your school, or you can enroll in a school dedicated to music, such as Juilliard. A sample of the classes you can choose from includes: musical theory, music interpretation, composition, and conducting. Get involved with music and theater performances at school, and volunteer to conduct the ensemble or assist the conductor.

Possible Majors

Music, music conducting, church music, music therapy, music education, musical theater, music management, music theory, music composition

Will I Be Rich?

As a music conductor, you will spend tons of time rehearsing with musicians. Going over the same part again and again can be really draining, but when you hear the final product, it's all worth it! Working as a music conductor is a great job for passionate music lovers. If you do it well, your career will be full of personal rewards. You may even receive fame and recognition, although the likelihood of striking it rich is pretty small.

Fun Facts

Leonard Bernstein

Music composer and conductor Leonard Bernstein (1918–1990) conducted the New York Philharmonic for the first time when he was twenty-one years old. He was filling in for Bruno Walter, who was sick. Bernstein's stardom began that night. His relationship with the New York Philharmonic lasted until his death in 1990.

Famous Conductors of the Nineteenth Century:

- Hans von Bulow (1830–1894)
- Hans Richter (1843–1916)
- Arthur Nikisch (1855–1922)
- Arturo Toscanini (1867–1957)
- Pierre Monteaux (1875–1964)

Famous Composers Who Were Also Conductors:

- Johann Sebastian Bach (1685–1750)
- Ludwig Sphor (1758–1859)
- Carl Maria von Weber (1786–1826)
- Felix Mendelsohn (1809–1847)
- Gustav Mahler (1860–1911)
- Richard Strauss (1864–1949)

Related Careers

Musician, rock star, teacher, professor, artist, actor, choreographer, director

MUSICIAN

The Basics

A musician is basically anyone who creates or performs music. Musicians play one or more of a ton of different instruments, including guitar, piano, drums, cello, flute, saxophone, trumpet, xylophone, harmonica, and even pails and toy keyboards. They play in rock groups, jazz bands, symphonies, rap groups, or really any type of ensemble—or they go solo. Some musicians are vocalists, too. But even though any gal who plays guitar can call herself a musician, unless she has made some money doing it, she isn't a professional. Professional musicians make a living from their music.

There are lots of ways to make a buck playing music. You can play live shows and go on tour, perform at weddings and parties, play instruments for studio recordings, and sell CDs of your music. You can also write or compose music or lyrics for other singers or musicians. Those who create operas, symphonies, and scores for movie and television are usually called *composers;* those who write songs for other musicians or bands to play are often called *songwriters;* and those who write the words to songs are called *lyricists.*

It takes a lot of passion, talent, and practice to be a professional musician, and that's not all. You'll have to be dedicated and patient, too—you may have to work at it for a while before the job offers flow in regularly. Unless you can find a steady gig as a musician, you'll have a lot of odd jobs in music. You'll need to learn to budget and save your money to enjoy this lifestyle. And enjoy it you will—musicians, like other types of artists, are usually thrilled to be able to earn a living doing what they love.

Preparation

High School

Sing, play an instrument, form a band . . . if you're an aspiring musician, you're probably already doing this stuff. If not, though, it's okay to start now. While some musicians train and practice from an early age, many discover their talents later in life. At any rate, practice is absolutely essential to the developing musician, so make sure you do it. Listen to different types of music to get an idea of what's out there. Try writing your own songs—and don't limit yourself by what you think is possible. Chorus, band, and other music classes are musts, too.

College

A college degree isn't a requirement for musicians, but it will certainly help you gain a deeper understanding of music. You can delve into your music studies at a music school or the music department of a college or university. Take advantage of courses in music theory and history and music composition. And of course, continue to take lessons in your instrument of choice. Play your music wherever you can—at school performances, at coffee shops, at parties—wherever. And keep practicing.

Possible Majors

Music, music history, music composition, music theory, music performance, music therapy, music education, musical theater

Will I Be Rich?

There are no guarantees that you'll strike it rich in this field. Despite the frustration that can accompany a musician's job (which includes possible rejections), most musicians are happy with their career choice. Playing, touring, and attending shows are really fun, and a lot of other people are envious of the freedom that musicians enjoy.

Fun Facts

Great Minds on Music

"Music is a moral law. It gives a soul to the universe, wings to the mind, flight to the imagination, a charm to sadness, gaiety and life to everything. It is the essence of order, and leads to all that is good, just and beautiful, of which it is the invisible, but nevertheless dazzling, passionate, and eternal form."

—Plato

"Without music life would be a mistake."

—Friedrich Nietzsche
[Source: www.oddmusic.com]

Quote

"As a musician you need to keep your objectivity, remember why you're an artist—not spend all your money on musical equipment—and live from your heart."

—Dan McBride, singer/songwriter

Related Careers

Rock star, music conductor, artist, dancer, choreographer, agent, music teacher, critic, director

NEWS ANCHOR

The Basics

News anchors are the personalities behind news television shows. They present news stories on local events as well as state, national, and worldwide events. In most cases, news teams, including journalists/reporters and editors, research and prepare the stories that news anchors share with the public.

As a news anchor, you will need to communicate with your audience and hold their attention. You may specialize in a specific field, such as business, foreign affairs, health, social events, sports, theater, or weather (meteorology). At times you may take on the role of a journalist, who researches and writes a story, or a news correspondent, who travels to the location of the story and covers the news from that site. In addition to those roles, you may also conduct interviews with famous politicians and celebrities. On set, you will interact with makeup artists, lighting technicians, and the camera crew, in addition to the other news anchors and reporters.

You will need to have a great presence, outstanding communication skills, and a pleasant voice to be a news anchor. A good personality and an outgoing nature will go far, too. You will need to remain calm under pressure, be knowledgeable, and have an interest in current and world events to succeed in this career.

Preparation

High School

It's important to gain experience speaking in public and presenting issues, so run for school office or join the debate team. Write news stories for your school newspaper. If you can get some airtime on public access television, you and your friends could act as a news crew. In the classroom, English classes will help fortify your writing skills; theater or drama classes might give you some confidence and performance pointers; and courses in history, geography, and science will give you a better idea of world events.

College

A college degree is highly recommended for this career. Join your college newspaper and write news stories. An internship for a local TV news broadcast or radio station will provide you with great hands-on experience. Classes in business, economics, English, journalism, political science, and writing will come in handy.

Will I Be Rich?

Expect your life to be hectic as a news anchor. You will work irregular hours, covering news stories and preparing for news broadcasts. In the event of a local, state, or national disaster, your work schedule will change to meet the news program's needs. You will have a lot of pressure to meet deadlines when it comes to stories you are covering. Being in the public eye has its stressful moments, but you can become somewhat of a celebrity, despite the fact that you won't strike it rich, like many entertainers. Luckily, you will get to work with intelligent people, meet interesting folks, and have fun on the set, too.

Fun Fact

News Anchor Boot Camp

At APTRA Anchor Academy in Malibu, California, ten aspiring news anchors go through a weekend of intensive training. Students work with professionals in broadcasting at Pepperdine University's TV studio. APTRA's Reporting Academy program takes place simultaneously, and both groups get to take home a tape of their work at the end of the weekend. (APTRA stands for the Associated Press of Television-Radio Association of California and Nevada, in case you were wondering.)

[Source: www.aptra.org]

Related Careers

Writer, editor, journalist, talk show host

NURSE

The Basics

Because a large part of a nurse's job is caring for the sick, they often work with people who are feeling not so great. But nurses are skilled in helping people relax and feel the best they can. They have a great deal of medical know-how, but they combine that knowledge with caretaking. A nurse might calm a child's fears or try to make a patient more comfortable. Nurses record patients' symptoms, note their reactions to medicines and procedures, and keep track of patients' progress. They help people of all ages and backgrounds to heal and to keep healthy.

As a nurse, you may work in a hospital, clinic, school, nursing home, or private practice. You will balance your time between assisting one or more doctors and attending to patients. If you're a *general nurse*, you will help doctors with routine tasks, from giving vaccination shots to drawing blood. You will check and record a patient's weight, heartbeat, and blood pressure, and answer any questions they may have. If you're a *surgical nurse*, you will assist during surgeries. If you're a *psychiatric nurse*, you will care for patients who have mental disorders. *Private nurses* either tend to a specific patient in a hospital or work in a patient's home. *Nurse practitioners* have more advanced education and are more like doctors. They can diagnose patients and write prescriptions.

You will need to be compassionate, caring, and energetic to be a nurse. Nurses must remain focused, even in unpleasant situations. Great listening skills, a good outlook, and an ability to make patients feel calm and comfortable is important, too.

Preparation

High School

A great way to get a feel for nursing is to volunteer in a hospital. If you don't mind the sights and smells of a hospital environment, you've passed your first test. Classes such as health, biology, chemistry, and physics will steer you down the right path—medicine involves a great deal of science.

College

If you plan to be a nurse, you will need to graduate from an approved nursing program. You can become a licensed practical nurse (LPN) in one year. The next level—a registered nurse (RN)—offers more responsibility and higher pay, but will take two to four years of education. Nursing programs are offered at vocational and technical schools, as well as junior and four-year colleges. (Four-year colleges will provide a wider range of opportunities for you down the road.) An internship will give you hands-on experience. All nurses are required to pass licensing exams before they go into practice.

Nursing, pre-med, psychology, sociology, nutrition, medical technology

Will I Be Rich?

Many nurses say that helping people is a reward in and of itself. You will earn decent money—though not nearly as much as doctors do. Expect to be on your feet a lot and to work long shifts. If you take a job in a hospital, you may work weekends and nights. Nurses are in contact with illness and disease, so they must try to keep themselves healthy. The job is often emotionally exhausting, but nurses come home knowing they've helped many people who needed them.

Fun Facts

Famous Nurses

Can you match the nurse with the correct title?

Nurses

1. Florence Nightingale

2. Clara Barton

3. Mary Eliza Mahoney

4. Mary Breckinridge

Titles

A. Founder of the American Red Cross

B. First African-American Nurse

C. Founder of the Frontier Nursing Service

D. Otherwise known as Lady of the Lamp

[Source: www.mynursingjourney.com]

Related Careers

Doctor, nutritionist, physical therapist, professor, paramedic, massage therapist, holistic doctor

Answer key: 1. D 2. A 3. B 4. C

NUTRITIONIST

The Basics

Nutritionists help people to maintain a healthy, balanced diet. People may come to nutritionists because they want to feel better; some want to improve the way they look; and some have a medical condition such as diabetes or high blood pressure that requires a certain diet. Many people consult nutritionists, including most Hollywood celebs! No matter what the case, nutritionists teach their clients healthy eating habits.

As a nutritionist, you will meet with clients to learn about their diet and overall health. You will then offer suggestions about the types of foods that would make a better diet (fewer cookies, more carrots!). Together, you'll come up with a healthy eating plan, and you'll teach your client how to prepare nutritious snacks and meals. If you work with a client who is ill or elderly, it's important to check with your client's doctor to make sure your food recommendations are okay. Most nutritionists believe "you are what you eat"—meaning people should eat what's good for them.

Aside from working for private clients, nutritionists often work for schools, hospitals, corporate cafeterias, prisons, nursing homes, and airline companies. There, they create healthy eating plans and oversee food purchasing and preparation in kitchens. Creativity and an ability to work well with others will prove helpful for this career. Since you will be helping to plan and create meals, great organizational skills will come in handy. If you love to cook, that's even better!

Preparation

High School

Eat healthy! Try to encourage your friends and family to eat that way, too. Read all you can about nutrition and exercise and learn to cook healthy meals. See if a local nutritionist needs any help after school. Take biology, psychology, and sociology classes to learn about the human body and mind; home economics, health class, and math will give you the practical skills to succeed in this career.

College

Gain some experience working with food; get an internship or part-time job with a health services organization, a kitchen, or a caterer. Take classes such as biology, chemistry, data analysis, microbiology, math, nutrition, psychology, and sociology.

Possible Majors

Nutrition, dietetics, health administration, home economics,
food service systems management, human development, food science

Will I Be Rich?

You will be rich in health and balanced living if nothing else, and you'll make some pretty good dough, too. Kitchen work can be hot and grueling; you'll probably be on your feet all day and working long hours. But if you consult with clients one-on-one, you may be in a more comfortable work environment with a more flexible schedule. Nutritionists usually meet lots of people. And since you are helping people to better themselves, job satisfaction is high.

Fun Facts

Great Moments in Food History

1904—Popcorn, hot dogs, ice-cream cones, and peanut butter were introduced at the St. Louis World's Fair.

1920—Seventy percent of the population baked their own bread.

1947—The first microwave oven is introduced; it's called the Radarange.

I'm Stuffed!

- *In America, an average family of four consumes almost 6,000 pounds of food per year.*

- *In Japan, the most popular pizza topping at Domino's is squid.*

- *Across the world, there are more than 15,000 varieties of rice.*

[Source: www.foodfunandfacts.com]

Quote

"It's unbelievable how much food and eating habits affect the way a person feels. After a month of eating healthy, balanced meals, my clients not only look different, but claim to have more energy and to feel great!"
—Paul Nison, Raw Food Nutritionist, New York City

Related Careers

Nurse, doctor, journalist, personal trainer, chef, yoga teacher, dietician, physical therapist

OCCUPATIONAL THERAPIST

The Basics

The goal of an occupational therapist is simple: to help people. The person can be anyone from a newborn baby who was born too weak to an elderly woman who needs to recover from a stroke. The types of help you can give differ as much as the types of people who you can help. All occupational therapists have one thing in common, however: They all find ways to help people live more independent, healthy, and happy lives.

To be an occupational therapist (OT), you need to have a passion for helping others. The people whom OTs work with can have many disabilities, such as blindness, mental illness, or a serious physical injury. Some OTs focus on one type of disability or one age group; other OTs do just about everything. They might work in a school, a hospital, or a patient's home.

You need to care for your patients by teaching them to cope with their problems. For example, you may need to train a child who has lost a leg how to walk. Or you may need to convince a quadriplegic—a person who can't move his or her limbs—that he or she can ski down a mountain if they work hard enough.

You need more than just a desire to help other people, however. You will need to have patience because many people take a long time to improve their condition or get better. (Some live with lifelong disabilities.) You will also need to have energy because your oomph will inspire your patients to stay positive and work hard for their goals. Finally, you'll need to have a good background in science or health because you'll be working with the human body.

Preparation

High School

It's never too early to start building up your scientific knowledge. Because you'll be dealing with many physical problems, you should learn anatomy and/or physiology. It also helps to learn about the way people act, so a psychology or human behavior class can put you in the right direction to be a highly skilled occupational therapist.

College

To become an occupational therapist, you need a special degree in occupational therapy. Fortunately, there are many OT programs in America. You can even learn to become at OT through the army! Occupational therapy programs are five years long, at which point you'll need some more experience to prove you're ready.

Occupational therapy

Additional Requirements: OT Exam and Internship

If you have a bachelor degree in occupational therapy, you don't need to enroll in graduate school. You do need to intern for at least six months, though. This gives you the practice you'll need to become a professional. In addition, you also have to pass a national OT exam. Once you've passed that, you can work anywhere in the country.

Will I Be Rich?

Professional occupational therapists will tell you that their job is the most rewarding job on Earth. The ability to put a smile on a kid's face or inspire someone who might otherwise feel sad or hopeless is priceless. When it comes to money, the pay is pretty good, and you can make extra money by working with patients one-on-one. If you're successful, you can open your own practice.

Fun Fact

Born Out of Necessity

Occupational therapy began after World War I when many injured men returned from the war. Occupational therapists helped them to recover, improving the spirits of the soldiers. After World War II, occupational therapists became very important and very much in demand.

Quote

"The most important trait you can have to be a terrific occupational therapist is a never-ending smile. If you can be happy around your patients, the joy is contagious. And happier people are healthier people!"

— *Jill Sherman, licensed occupational therapist*

Related Careers

Physical therapist, doctor, nurse, speech therapist, special education teacher, social worker, psychologist, sociologist

PALEONTOLOGIST

The Basics

Paleontologists earn their living searching for dinosaur bones, studying fossils, and coming up with theories about how animals once lived—and died. They're passionate about dinosaurs and science, and they usually enjoy taking adventures. That's because a big part of paleontology is working in "the field," which is where paleontologists search for dinosaur bones. That could be anywhere from the American West to Mongolia. Argentina and Africa are also good places to find important fossils.

For many paleontologists, going to the field is one of the most fun parts of their job. That's where they get the excitement of finding bones that once belonged to incredible creatures. But digging for hours in extremely remote places of the world can also be very hard work. Almost every paleontologist works in the field at some point (usually for a few weeks during the summer).

During the rest of the year, paleontologists spend most of their time in a museum or a university that has a dinosaur department. They work on computers, trying to figure out what their findings reveal. They use their data to create dinosaur family trees (called *systematics*) and theorize how dinosaurs existed. Paleontologists also try to use concrete data to prove historical facts, rather than relying on theories.

If you are patient, focused, and passionate about natural history, you might make a great paleontologist someday.

Preparation

High School

Besides taking classes in science, the best thing you can do in high school is to volunteer for your local museum. Once you know some people at the museum, it will become easier to ask for a summer job. You also get a much better idea of whether or not you like the work associated with paleontology.

College

Many paleontologists studied geology (the study of Earth) or biology (the study of life) in college. But the specific major doesn't matter as long as you have a good science background and a working knowledge of biology. A few classes in geology will help you when you get to graduate school—so you don't have to catch up. And again, volunteer wherever possible. The more contacts you can make before you're done with school, the better your chances will be to become a successful paleontologist.

Possible Majors

Geology, biology, archaeology

Graduate School

All paleontology programs in the United States are at the graduate level. In other words, there is no way around grad school if you want to become a paleontologist. Most people get their masters degree; you'll need a PhD if you want to teach at a university.

Will I Be Rich?

Most paleontologists don't make a ton of money. The exception would be if you get to become a curator in a big museum and become famous. If you get to be famous, then you can make extra money giving lectures or writing books. Even if you find a very rare dinosaur, it's illegal to sell it for money. Your passion has to be for dinosaurs, not dollar bills. Paleontology is becoming a more competitive field, so the number of available jobs is limited.

Fun Fact

Roy Chapman Andrews, one of the most famous paleontologists of all time, started his career in the early 1900s scrubbing floors at the American Museum of Natural History in New York, New York. Eventually, he traveled around the world, writing about his adventures and discoveries wherever he went. He helped inspire the movie character Indiana Jones and eventually became director of the museum he used to scrub floors for!

[Source: www.unmuseum.org]

Quote

"Most of the time in the field is spent walking around, staring at the ground, prospecting for eight hours. People don't think of that as glamorous. But when someone finds something really good, that's when everyone starts digging."

—Sunny Hwang, paleontologist

Related Careers

Archaeologist, scientist, historian, anthropologist, museum curator, art and antique restorer, professor

PARAMEDIC

The Basics

If you've ever been in an emergency situation, you were probably grateful to see the paramedic show up. A 911 operator dispatches paramedics to the scene of an emergency, where they must rely on their medical know-how and act fast to treat those injured. "It's a matter of life and death" is a phrase they live by each day on the job.

Paramedics basically serve as doctors-on-the-go, although they do not have a medical degree. Paramedics work in teams to administer first aid and get the patient to the hospital. Once they arrive, paramedics help transfer the patient inside and provide doctors and staff with details about the patient's situation, health, and what care he or she has received. As a paramedic, no two of your days will be alike. One day you'll attend to a three-car accident or the home of a person who is having a heart attack. On another, you might race to the scene of a crime to treat a person who has been hurt with a weapon or hurry off to a lake where a boat has capsized. You will often cooperate with police officers and firefighters.

Stress and anxiety are naturally part of this job. If tragedy scares you or you're the slightest bit squeamish, this may not be the field for you. You need to be a good decision maker and be skilled in emergency care and procedures. You will also need to be balanced and emotionally strong for this career, as well as physically strong—in some cases you will have to carry people or rescue them from dangerous situations.

Preparation

High School

Volunteer in a hospital or a health center that treats people in emergency situations. It will help you see what it's like to take care of people who need immediate medical attention. Take classes in health and psychology, and stay in shape through gym class and other forms of exercise.

College

Perhaps you want to work in health care but aren't sure which career you'd like to pursue. Exploring your options while in college can help you make a decision. Strictly speaking, though, a college degree is not a requirement for a paramedic.

Possible Majors

Pre-medicine, nursing, rehabilitation therapy

Training Programs

Paramedics receive the highest level of training under the general job title of Emergency Medical Technician (EMT). Students must have a high school diploma or GED in order to enter a training program. It's a long road to become a paramedic. Generally, 750 to 2,000 hours of classroom and on-the-job training are necessary. You will learn how to assess patients, give intravenous fluids, and tend to wounds before you get to the hospital. You will spend time in a hospital emergency room and on an ambulance. Regardless of your training, it's experience working as a paramedic that will be your greatest teacher.

Will I Be Rich?

Although this job is often stressful, as well as emotionally and physically challenging, it is also fulfilling. Saving lives is an exciting and rewarding part of your daily job. Expect to work long hours for not too much money. Advancement is possible, but you will need to give up your paramedic work in the field to become a manager or director of emergency services.

Fun Fact

Buckle Up

Federal safety officials claim that roughly 600 people are hurt in car accidents across the United States every hour! Paramedics are usually the first people to arrive at the site of an accident. They treat the victims and stabilize them, so they can be taken to a hospital and receive medical attention from doctors.

[Source: www.cnn.com]

Related Careers

Nurse, doctor, private health care worker, firefighter, police officer, holistic doctor, physical therapist

PARK RANGER

The Basics

Park rangers oversee the national, state, county, and city parks, as well as the many visitors to those parks. There are millions of acres of parks in this country, and it's the ranger's job to keep those areas safe, clean, and fun. Rangers have to enforce the park's rules, carry out possible rescue operations, teach visitors about wildlife, and perform dozens of other important duties. It's one of the few jobs that can take place almost entirely in the natural beauty of the American wilderness.

Safety is a major concern to rangers. They are trained in first aid and are prepared to rescue hurt or lost campers in the park. Another part of the job of a park ranger is policing the great outdoors. National park rangers make sure that people don't abuse the parks, and they have the right to arrest people who do. That takes confidence and an ability to take charge.

A park ranger is also an environmentalist. As a park ranger, you can protect the land in several ways. Not only do you guard the park from vandals but you also work to prevent forest fires, save wild animals, and keep pollution to a minimum. Educating visitors, a major part of being a ranger, also helps the environmental cause. If a student learns about conservation, fragile habitats, and the importance of the parks, he or she will be less likely to later injure the environment.

Preparation

High School

Go out and spend some quality time with Mother Nature. After all, if you become a park ranger, she may be your only colleague on many long shifts. Study everything you can about your surroundings, from the abundance of animals to the types of timber. Maintain good grades, and see if you can volunteer at a park. Helping to pick up trash may seem like dreary work, but it can set you in the right direction.

College

Some colleges have special degrees tailored specifically for parks and recreation. The courses in these colleges teach you about the particulars of working at a park. Having a degree in parks and recreation is obviously a great asset for being a ranger, but you don't absolutely need it. You can study a related field, such as botany—or even criminal justice. Feel free to study something you love, but get experience in the parks if you want to work in one someday. For example, a summer internship or job taking care of the park trails can be your first step to a successful career as a ranger.

Possible Majors

Parks and recreation, recreation management, botany, ecology, environmental engineering, forestry, forest engineering, forest resources, natural resources, biology, plant biology, wildlife management, zoology, criminology

Will I Be Rich?

Being a park ranger is generally a low-paying job. You have to start at the very low end of the salary range, and you can't advance too much. Top park administration officials earn a good living, but most rangers don't. But for the rangers who love spending their lives in the spectacular American parks, there may be no greater prize.

Fun Fact

It All Started Here

The United States of America established the first national park in the known universe. That was the world-famous Yellowstone National Park, and it was founded in 1872.

Related Careers

Police officer, environmentalist, botanist, crocodile hunter, farmer, fisherman, veterinarian, ecologist, biologist, tour guide, criminologist

PERSONAL TRAINER

The Basics

People who are serious about fitness often look to personal trainers. And personal trainers are serious about fitness! Their entire jobs revolve around helping people stay fit and healthy. Whether it's at the gym, in a park, or at a client's home, you will assess a client's level of physical fitness and create an exercise plan to improve it. Then you'll set short- and long-term exercise goals and encourage your client to achieve them.

As a personal trainer, you will work one-on-one with your client to explain specialized gym equipment, demonstrate exercises, and help perfect technique. You need to ensure your client is using proper form to prevent any injury. Stretching, weight lifting, and aerobic exercise may all be components of a personal training workout. But there's a mental aspect, too. Your client not only needs physical instruction but also a dose of support and motivation. You need to be a good coach and applaud even minor achievements. You may meet with your client every day, every week, or just every once in a while, depending on the arrangement. Track your clients' progress with reports on each exercise session. A plan that isn't working should be revised. And when your plan is a success, you and your client can make it a bit harder to achieve bigger results.

You will need to be outgoing, motivated, and sensitive to your client's abilities and level of fitness. Plus, you will need to be strong and in good health yourself to assist your clients all day. Since there's always new information regarding health and fitness, plan to attend seminars and workshops to keep up to date.

Preparation

High School

Get yourself to a gym or create your own workout program to do at home or in a park. Read fitness books and rent fitness videos from the library. Join a sports team or two, and learn as much as you can in health and gym classes.

College

A college degree isn't required to be a personal trainer, but it will certainly enhance your knowledge of health, physical education, and how the body works. Classes such as human anatomy, human physiology, first aid, sports nutrition, and fundamental sport skills will all come in handy. Get a part-time job at a local gym or sports facility. If possible, coach a children's sports team or volunteer at a nonprofit organization's recreation program.

Physical education, athletic training, sport and leisure studies, recreation, nutrition

Certification Programs

Personal training certification programs consist of hands-on training and lectures. You will learn about anatomy and how different exercises affect different parts of the body; you'll pick up some nutrition facts as well. Once you are certified, you need to renew your certification every two years. Personal trainers should also know CPR and first aid.

Will I Be Rich?

You'll be buff! And if you have a steady stream of clients who rely on you to keep them in shape, you will earn a nice sum. If you're a fitness nut and love working with people, a job as a personal trainer will keep you looking and feeling great even while you're at work.

Fun Facts

Couch Potatoes

- About 29 percent of Americans age 18 or older do not partake in leisure-time physical activity.

- Daily enrollment in physical education classes declined among high school students from 42 percent in 1991 to 29 percent in 1999.

- People with less than a twelfth grade education are more likely to be sedentary (meaning they sit down often and exercise rarely).

[Source: www.justmove.org]

Related Careers

Physical therapist, yoga teacher, coach, athlete, counselor, teacher, choreographer

PHILOSOPHER

The Basics

If you are wondering why you are reading this, what the meaning of a career is, and where the words on this page came from, then you may be a philosopher in training. In fact, most people, regardless of whether or not they have devoted their careers to philosophy, are philosophers in some way. If you question why things are the way they are and discuss or debate topics about life, friendship, and politics with your friends, you are already involved in intellectual debating, which is every philosopher's favorite pastime.

If you want to discuss philosophy all day with like-minded people, and read, research, and write about it in your downtime, then the life of a philosophy professor will suit you. (Since you can't really make a living by simply being a philosopher, teaching is a necessity.) As a philosophy professor, you will work in a college, spending between twelve and fifteen hours a week in class. You will set aside a number of hours each week to meet with students. The rest of your time will be devoted to researching and writing. To maintain your job as a professor, you will probably have to get your work published as well.

As a philosophy professor, you will need to be a great communicator and a great listener. It's important to understand what others have to say in order to respond properly in intellectual debates. A love of reading and learning is also necessary, since so much of your life will consist of sharing knowledge.

Preparation

High School

Sign up for the debate team. Discuss topics that are meaningful to you with friends. Study the teachings of famous philosophers throughout history, and try starting your own philosophy club. Classes in English, math, science, and psychology will help you prepare for your college courses.

College

In college, you'll take classes to help you prepare for your graduate degree in philosophy. Some new classes in your schedule may include ethics, logic, and metaphysics. Be sure to make time for intellectual debates with your professors and friends. The more that you express your viewpoint in the company of others and listen to what they have to say, the more you will begin to understand yourself.

Possible Majors

Philosophy, theology, classics, ancient studies, comparative literature, peace studies

Graduate School

It will take you between five and seven years to complete a PhD in philosophy; you will then write your dissertation. It's a good idea to try teaching at the college level while you are a graduate student—many graduate programs will arrange for you to teach freshman classes in philosophy.

Will I Be Rich?

If you write a breakthrough philosophy book, you may get rich—but don't count on it. Regardless, you will be rich in ideas, conversation, and knowledge. Professors often say that the highlight of their jobs is getting to work with intelligent, interesting people who love to learn. Philosophy students in particular tend to be a very bright, curious group.

Fun Facts

Throughout history, philosophers from all over the world have shared their thoughts with society:

"No great genius has ever existed without some touch of madness."—Aristotle

"The man of knowledge must be able not only to love his enemies but also to hate his friends."—Friedrich Nietzsche

"What difference does it make how much you have? What you do not have amounts to much more."—Seneca

"Whereof one cannot speak, thereof one must be silent."—Ludwig Wittgenstein

"The learner always begins by finding fault, but the scholar sees the positive merit in everything."—Georg Hegel

"Man is born free, and everywhere he is in chains."—Jean-Jacques Rousseau

"Poets utter great and wise things which they do not themselves understand."—Plato

"The unexamined life was not worth living."—Socrates

"That which is not good for the beehive cannot be good for the bees."—Marcus Aurelius

[Source: www.memorablequotations.com]

Related Careers
Writer, professor, teacher, politician, lawyer, scientist

PHYSICAL THERAPIST

The Basics

If you have ever had a sports-related injury or been in a car accident, you may have gone to see a physical therapist. They are the people who help you to get better when you have injured a part of your body. They may treat people in hospitals, health clinics, or private offices.

As a physical therapist, you may treat between eight and twelve patients a day. Each treatment can last from thirty minutes to an hour. When you treat a new patient, you will first examine his or her medical history and ask questions about the patient's pain or condition. You may also check in with the patient's regular doctor; if the patient has certain health conditions, you want to make sure the treatment doesn't put them at risk for further injury. You will test your patient's range of motion and strength in regard to the injury by asking the patient to do simple exercises. Then you may use machines, exercises, and massages to help build a person's flexibility and strength.

Some patients may become frustrated if they don't get better right away. You will need to be sensitive to your patients' feelings and motivate them to work hard and to keep up with the exercises you prescribe. You will also need to be good on your feet, as your days will be very active. You will bend and move about a lot, shifting patients into various positions, so you will need to be physically strong. If you love working with people, are patient and caring, and love science, this may be the career for you!

Preparation

High School

Why not volunteer in a physical therapist's office or in a health care facility that treats people who have been in accidents? It will be a great chance for you to get a feel for what the job entails before you choose this career. Take biology, chemistry, gym, math, and physics classes to help prepare for college.

College

Students who major in physical therapy spend their time between the classroom and the lab and may receive some supervised clinical experience, too. Your classes will likely include anatomy, physiology, biology, biomechanics, chemistry, human growth and development, nutrition, physics, and psychology.

Possible Majors

Physical therapy, athletic training, kinesiology, anatomy and physiology, rehabilitation services, occupational therapy

Obtaining Your License

After you graduate with a degree in physical therapy, you can't practice just yet. First you'll need to pass an exam to get your license.

Will I Be Rich?

Not only can you earn a decent living as a physical therapist but also you can help people to get better! Don't expect this job to be easy, though. It's physically demanding and tiring, so it helps if you are in good shape. One physical therapist said: "I take a lot of hot showers and spend time in the steam room to ease the stiffness I get from working with patients." In your downtime, expect to do a lot of paperwork, between filling out patient progress reports and insurance claims.

Fun Facts

All Better

Check out these world-class athletes who turned to physical therapy to help them heal:

- Eric Kramer: NFL quarterback, Chicago Bears

- Todd Zeile: infielder, Major League Baseball, New York Mets

- Peter Carruthers: Olympic silver medalist 1984 Pairs Ice Skating, U.S. National gold medalist 1981–1984

- Marla O'Hara: Professional Beach Volleyball champion

- Russell "Rusty" Rothenberg: U.S. National Men's Water-Ski Fly Champion & Record Holder Men's III

- Skip Hicks: NFL running back, Washington Redskins

[Source: www.athleticpt.com]

Related Careers

Coach, occupational therapist, personal trainer, speech therapy, yoga teacher, athlete

PILOT

The Basics

A pilot flies planes. But he or she also has many additional responsibilities. A *commercial pilot* oversees a flight crew (a *copilot* and a *flight engineer*); interacts with air traffic controllers; and watches the flight monitors, which show whether the plane has enough fuel and whether its engines and systems are working properly.

As a pilot, your work begins before you leave the ground. First you need to plan your flight and gain approval from air traffic control personnel. Your route, altitude, and the speed that you fly at depend a lot on weather and flight conditions. Next you'll make sure that everything in the plane, from the engines to the controls, works properly. Most pilots agree that takeoff and landing are the most difficult parts of the flight; after that, unless you hit torrential storms, you'll be in for a smooth flight. You can even put the plane on automatic pilot, which is an electronic device that flies the plane. Just be sure to keep your eyes on the flight monitor! Although you may feel all alone up there, you're not—air traffic control stations monitor your progress along the way, guiding you if you run into any problems.

Excellent vision and hearing, superior coordination skills, and the ability to remain calm under pressure are crucial for this job. "It's a huge responsibility," one pilot with Jet Blue airlines confessed. "People put their lives in your hands when they step on a plane. You need to make sure you get them to their destination safely."

Preparation

High School

In school, classes in computers, English, math, and science will help prepare you for this career. But outside of school, once you reach age sixteen or seventeen, you can take to the sky—private lessons are available in small private planes (like a Cessna) if you're able to pay the price. Of course, these planes are much smaller than a typical commercial airline, but you have to start somewhere.

College

Only two years of college are required to become a pilot, although most commercial pilots have a four-year college degree. Check out which colleges offer pilot training programs. If you decide to pursue another major, you may also be able to take flight courses and join a flight team.

Possible Majors

Aviation, air force ROTC, aerospace engineering

Pilot's License Requirements

To earn a commercial airline pilot's license you need to accumulate 250 hours of flying time, pass a written test given by the Federal Aviation Administration (FAA), and pass a practical test and a physical examination. You will receive a rating based on the type of plane you fly, such as a single-engine plane or a multi-engine plane.

If you want to be an airline captain, or chief pilot, you need to obtain another license, called a transport pilot's license. This will require a minimum of 1,500 hours of flight time, including night flying and instrument time. Most pilots begin their careers as flight engineers. This job requires 500 to 1000 hours of flying time. It can take anywhere from five to fifteen years to become a chief pilot, so buckle your seat belt for a long, safe ride!

Will I Be Rich?

Expect to spend time away from home on overnight layovers. The good news is that airlines will pay for your hotel, land transportation, and meals in between flights. Since flights take off and land at all hours of the day and night, it's unlikely that you'll work from nine to five. But the longer you've been flying, the more likely you are to end up with good flight assignments. As you gain experience, you will earn more money, too, so keep flying and racking up those flying hours!

Fun Fact

Think the island of Manhattan is big? The Dallas Fort Worth International Airport is bigger than the entire island, and it's also insanely busy each day with 2,300 flights.

[Source: www.dallascvb.com]

Related Careers

Flight attendant, race car driver, aerospace engineer, astronaut, air force pilot

PLUMBER

The Basics

It's easy to take plumbing for granted—from your home's toilets, sinks, showers, and bathtubs to the dishwasher, water heater, and washing machine. That is, until you need to call a plumber. Plumbers install, maintain, and repair pipes affecting these household fixtures and appliances. If drains clog (or worse!) plumbers can reach into their toolbox and fix them on the spot. Plumbers know the water system inside and out because they also install the pipes, fixtures, and appliances in new houses and offices or those that are under construction.

As a plumber, expect your phone to ring at all hours of the day and night. When a bathroom floods or a water heater bursts, your customers will need you to come to the rescue quickly. Reading blueprints will be part of your job if you are working on a new building, an addition to a home; these drawings map out the planned location of the pipes. Once you have the piping in place, you will install fixtures and appliances. Then you will connect the whole plumbing system to outside water or sewer lines. You're not finished until you check the plumbing system with pressure gauges. A pressure gauge indicates fluid pressure. A plumber is able to tell if the pressure measures just right or if the plumbing system needs an adjustment.

Physical strength, skill with tools, and great communication abilities are the traits of a good plumber. Generally, people will call on you to fix a messy situation—so tough skin is in order. It's important to do some investigating before you get down to work. Knowledge of exactly what to look for can save you a lot of time on the job. Plumbers should be patient, too, since larger problems may require many hours and lots of focus.

Preparation

High School

If you can find a plumber who will let you be his assistant, go for it! Take courses in math, since you'll need to write invoices and keep track of expenses. Shop class will build useful skills, too. You'll need to be adept at taking things apart and putting them back together.

College

Although not required, college can't hurt. If you have any related interests you might like to pursue, you can explore them during your undergraduate education.

Possible Majors

Environmental science, architectural engineering, physics, electrical engineering

Apprenticeship

It's no quick task to become a plumber. First you will need to complete an apprenticeship after you finish high school, where you will learn on the job by working alongside a skilled plumber. Make sure you're in good physical condition—you will be carrying heavy loads and squeezing into hard-to-reach places. An apprenticeship will teach you the basics behind using the right tools and installing pipes and fixtures. There's a lot to accomplish before your apprenticeship is over—expect to put in four to five years of on-the-job training plus more than one hundred hours of classroom training on local plumbing codes, regulations, and more. While there's no official national license needed to be a plumber, most states require plumbers to be licensed. You'll likely need to pass a detailed written exam.

Will I Be Rich?

Expect to be on call all the time. But since plumbers often get paid hourly, the more you work, the more you'll make. While the job can be dangerous—you'll handle specialized tools and pipes can get hot—there's some satisfaction in making sure your customer can take a nice, hot bath when the job is done. If you work for yourself, you can make a decent living.

Fun Fact

Plumber's Tip

If you hear a drip drop, make it stop! Did you know that a leaky faucet in your home can lead to 15 to 20 gallons of wasted water a day? If you fix a leaky faucet, you are saving up to 6,000 gallons a year.

[Source: www.plumbshop.com]

Related Careers

Electrician, engineer, construction worker, carpenter, landlord, architect

POLICE OFFICER

The Basics

A police officer has one of the most important jobs in the world: He or she must protect the lives and property of the people. Police officers have the ability to stop crimes from taking place, arrest criminals, and rescue people.

As a police officer, you can fill many roles: You can be a *beat cop* and keep the peace in a particular neighborhood on foot; or you can be a *patrol cop* riding around in a patrol car, and answering radio calls that come from a police precinct. On any given day, you can receive a call about a local robbery, a dispute, or people in need of help. If you're an *emergency service officer,* you will take part in dangerous encounters, such as hostage situations and rescue missions. Emergency service officers go through an extra year of police academy training to prepare for their risky job. Whichever role you pursue, you can expect to spend a few hours or more a week filling out paperwork.

As a police officer, you will need to be patient, fair, and trustworthy; you must have good negotiation and communication skills. You will need to be committed to truth and devoted to keeping the peace. According to a New York City police officer, 85 percent of a police officer's career is spent in service; only about 15 percent is spent fighting crime. In other words, most police officers spend their days and careers helping people rather than battling criminals.

Preparation

High School

If your high school offers criminal justice or law classes, take them! Self-defense courses will form a good foundation for more advanced training later. If your school doesn't offer any, check out if there's an after-school or community program that does. In addition, track and other sports will help you get in shape.

College

A necessary step on the road to being a police officer is police academy training; a college degree is not required. However, a two-year associate degree or a four-year bachelor degree will help you rise up in the ranks once you become an officer.

Possible Majors
Criminology, criminal law, pre-law, communications, psychology

Police Academy

After high school, you can take the Police Academy entrance exam. Once you pass the written exam and the background tests, including medical and psychological exams, you can begin your six- to nine-month full-time commitment at the police academy. You will learn everything about an officer's duty, procedures, tactics, self-defense, and law. You'll also take a really strenuous gym class to whip you into shape. Upon graduation, you're assigned to a police precinct or station house.

Will I Be Rich?

Your pay may not be impressive when you start out, but there is much room for promotion. After five years on the force, officers can become lieutenants by passing an exam. More exams passed and credits earned open up doors to becoming a captain or police chief. After twenty years on the job, an officer can retire and collect a pension, or salary. While the job is often dangerous, knowing that you are helping society makes it all worthwhile.

Fun Facts

All Dressed Up

- Police officers go to work and return home each day in street clothes. They have locker rooms at the precinct where they change into and out of their uniform.

- Officers pay for their own uniforms and are responsible for cleaning them. The polyester suit and bulletproof vest are not too comfortable in the summertime heat!

- The rig, or gun belt, weighs roughly thirty pounds!

- Police officers don't have to wear their hats indoors or while driving in a patrol car.

Quote

"As a police officer, I try to treat everyone the way I would want my mother or father treated—with respect and fairness. If you break the law, though, you need to be willing to pay the consequences."

—John D., New York City police officer

Related Careers

Detective, criminologist, corrections officer, FBI agent, sheriff, state trooper, bailiff, special agent

POLITICIAN

Mayor • congressperson • senator • governor • cabinet member
• president of the United States

The Basics

Politicians are the leaders of our government. They are the men and women who work to improve society by making decisions that affect its citizens. Their decisions can increase or decrease taxes, give or take away funding, or change laws. Politicians work for the government, and they must figure out the budgets: deciding where money comes from and where it goes. There's never enough money to spread it to all the people who want or need it. That's where the decision making comes in, and it's never easy. The role of the politician helps to shape the fabric of our nation.

Above all else, politicians need to have a strong passion for and knowledge of government. Politicians also need charisma, charm, and intelligence. (Good looks don't hurt, either.) As a politician you also ought to be able to work well with other people. No matter what your job in politics, you will have to work with—and rely on—other politicians to get things done. You must be able to speak confidently and clearly in public. What you say in speeches and debates and how you convey your meaning will influence people to vote for you—or the other guy. That's why it's crucial that you also listen to what the voters have to say.

In simple terms, politicians can make a big difference. As a politician, you need to take your job seriously. And you need to have moral integrity. That means always doing what you feel is right for everybody. There will always be people who oppose you, so you will have to fight for what you believe in. In many cases you will need to compromise. You shouldn't give up on your objectives, but you usually need to cooperate to accomplish something significant.

There are many different offices that a politician can hold. The country's voters have the right to elect most of them, though a few positions are appointed. Below is a list of the major positions a politician can hold:

A *mayor* is the person in charge of a city or incorporated village. He or she runs the budget for the town and serves as the leader of the governing body.

A *congressperson* is the man or woman who represents his or her district. There may be anywhere from one to fifty-three districts in a state, depending on the population. The citizens of each district elect their congressperson to a two-year term. The congressperson works in the legislative branch of the government, in the House of Representatives. He or she votes on laws that affect his or her state, as well as the country.

A *senator* represents the state that he or she lives in, also in the legislative branch. There are two senators for every state, and the state's citizens elect them to six-year terms. Together, the House and the U.S. Senate write bills, which can turn into laws. They don't sign the bills into law or enforce them, but they have to agree, at least a little bit, to write practical laws.

A *governor* is the leader of a state's executive branch. There is only one per state, and the state's citizens elect him or her to a four-year term. The governor gets to sign bills into law, and he or she is responsible for all the state agencies. Governors approve laws, but their primary job is to enforce the law.

Cabinet members are the top advisors to the president. Each member of the cabinet is in charge of a different section of the government, such as the health department, the treasury, or the environmental agency. The president appoints the cabinet members and can usually hire or fire whomever he or she wants at any time.

The *president of the United States* has the most powerful job in the nation. He (or she!) controls the executive branch of the federal government, chooses the members of the cabinet, and runs the country's military. Presidents serve four-year terms, but they can only serve twice.

Preparation

High School

Study hard in your history and social studies classes, as well as any others that relate to government in a major way. Get involved with your school's government. Run for class president, and you'll get a taste of elections and what it's like to run a government. You may not get to change major laws in society, but you will have some power as class president. You can also join your school's debate team and learn how to argue your point and win arguments with your words. A Model Congress or Model UN organization is also a fantastic way to understand the organizations of politics.

College

A political science major teaches you all about the government and how it works. History courses, too, can provide insight into our country's past—and future. There is no one topic of study you need to pursue to become a politician. There are, however, all kinds of other activities that you can do in college to prepare for a life in politics. Most colleges have political groups and societies. And there is usually a well-structured student government. If you know at this point that you want a career in politics, check out these opportunities. You'll know soon enough if you're made for politics.

Possible Majors

Political science, history, American history, pre-law

Will I Be Rich?

You don't become a politician to make money. It's not that kind of a job. In fact, most politicians will *need* money to win elections. They use it to kick-start their career and get their name known. Therefore, many politicians become rich *first,* such as the mayor of New York City, Michael Bloomberg. [Bloomberg earns a salary of $1 per year as New York City mayor!] High-level politicians, however, can make a decent living. The famous ones can even earn extra money by delivering paid speeches or writing books. But that's not the case with most politicians. Most hardworking politicians put in a lot of time. It's not a nine-to-five job.

Fun Fact

Nontraditional Presidential Career Paths

Politicians can come from all walks of life. They don't need to have been lawyers or businesspeople (though many were). Some of the United States presidents had some very unpolitical careers before they took charge of the nation. Andrew Johnson was a tailor. Lyndon B. Johnson was a schoolteacher. Jimmy Carter was a peanut farmer. And Ronald Reagan was a Hollywood actor.

Quote

"To be a politician, it's so important to be able to come up to the plate and give it your all. You can't spend only an hour a day and not go to all the meetings or places where people expect to see you at. You've got to go the extra mile all the time. You have to have this in your makeup. If you're not prepared to put yourself into it, you should try and do something else."

—Natalie Rogers, mayor, Ocean Beach, NY

Related Careers

Lobbyist, judge, lawyer, FBI agent, business executive

POSTAL WORKER

The Basics

Postal workers send, sort, process, and deliver mail. They are government employees, and they may work as window clerks, mail processors, distribution clerks, or as mail carriers. Since many postal workers often serve customers directly, they must be courteous and have good communication skills. In addition, they must pay close attention to detail and be able to work and read quickly; it's important to ensure that the right mail gets to the right recipients, despite the large quantities of mail processed and delivered each day.

If you are a *window clerk*, you will work in a post office, selling stamps and money orders and processing envelopes and packages. If your customers are sending valuable items through the mail, you will help them certify, insure, or register their mail.

As a *mail processor*, you will sort outgoing and incoming mail for delivery. Although machines do a lot of the sorting nowadays, you will still need to move around sacks and bundles of mail.

As a *mail carrier*, you will deliver mail to homes and businesses. You may either drive as you deliver mail or walk on foot from building to building. You'll also collect mail, money for CODs (cash on delivery), and receipts for registered and insured mail. After making your rounds, you will return to the post office to turn in collected mail, money, and receipts.

Preparation

High School

If you deliver newspapers, you'll start to get an idea of who lives where along your route; you'll remember which street numbers appear on which block, and so on. This type of geographical organization is important for those who will become mail carriers later on down the road. In school, your English courses will help you develop your reading skills. If you can take a speed reading course, more power to you.

College

You can learn more about what people send in the mail—letters, applications, business documents—in college. Earning your degree is not required for this job.

Possible Majors

Communications, English, creative writing, journalism, business administration

Postal Service Exam

You must be eighteen years old and a United States Citizen or legal resident in order to take the postal service exam. The postal exam measures your speed and accuracy at checking names and numbers. In addition to the written test, you will need to take a physical exam. If you plan to drive a mail truck, you will need to have a driver's license and a good driving record, too.

After you pass the written exam, you may have to wait up to two years for an available job with the postal service. Once you receive a job, you will undergo on-the-job training.

Will I Be Rich?

If you are a distribution clerk or a mail processor, you may have to sometimes work nights and weekends sorting mail. The job is often stressful, since you have tight deadlines—people need to get their mail on time! If you're a mail carrier, you'll be in the office in the morning and out and about during the afternoon. When the sun shines, you will be glad that you work outdoors most of the day, but when it's cold and icy outside, you may not be thrilled to walk or drive around delivering mail. All postal workers put in longer hours during holiday seasons because of the volume of cards and gifts being sent. You won't get rich being a postal worker, but knowing that you're part of the process that enables communication across the world can bring great satisfaction.

Fun Fact

Beware of Dog

Ever seen a movie where a postal worker is bitten by a dog? Well, it does happen sometimes, but not as often as it did during the 1980s! In the mid-1980s, over 7,000 mail carriers in the United States received dog bites in one year! In 2002, the number of mail carriers who were bitten dropped to just over 3,000. The reason for this decline? Postal workers were trained to respond in these situations, and a public education campaign encouraged owners to keep their dogs at bay.

[Source: www.infoplease.com]

Related Careers

Banker, bank teller, police officer, librarian, salesperson, sanitation worker, tour guide, hotel manager, park ranger, administrative assistant, bookkeeper

PRINCIPAL

The Basics

All of us know that you're sent to the principal's office when your behavior is out of line. But does the principal sit there all day just waiting to punish disobedient students? Of course not! The principal is just trying to make sure that everything runs smoothly, and enforcing the rules is one part of that process. Principals are in charge of elementary schools or secondary schools. They establish school rules and supervise teachers, school counselors, and everyone else who works in the school environment.

As a principal, your days will be busy! You will work closely with teachers; you will hire them, motivate them, and help them perform to the best of their abilities. You will check on how the students and teachers work together in the classroom; you'll evaluate educational materials such as textbooks; and you'll keep an eye on the progress of your students. You will interact with parents and members of the community, and you may also create after-school activities and summer school programs. In addition, you will prepare budgets and set goals for your school.

If you want to be a principal, you'll have to be good at speaking in public and making decisions. That means you have to have confidence—you are the leader of your school, and you want it to be the best school it can be. Since you never know what will come your way as a principal, it's important that you can also remain calm under pressure.

Preparation

High School

Run for class office to gain some leadership experience. Try out for the debate team, and participate in other school events that allow you to be social—like emceeing (hosting) a school production or joining the drama club. You'll need to learn how to work with kids, too; you can do this through babysitting, helping out in an after-school program, or even hanging out with little kids in your family.

College

If you major in education during college, you'll get some experience in the classroom as a student teacher and see how a school operates. You may also major in another subject area and obtain some education credits later on. Either way, you'll probably be doing some teaching before becoming a principal.

Possible Majors

Education, education administration, teacher education, special education, counseling

Graduate School

To become a principal at a public school, you need at least a master's degree. Many principals also have PhDs in education administration. If you earn your PhD, you'll probably be able to earn a higher salary as a principal. In most states you also need to be licensed as a school administrator before becoming a principal.

Will I Be Rich?

If you have a passion for education and would love to manage the daily activities of a school, then this is the career for you! You'll have to work hard and may travel to a lot of conferences. Although you will solve problems and listen to complaints, you will also motivate teachers and encourage students to play an active role in their education.

Fun Fact

The mission of PENCIL (Public Education Needs Civic Involvement in Learning) is to improve public schools by getting people and private industries involved in education. In PENCIL's Principal for a Day program, participants visit a school, meet with the principal, visit classrooms, and discuss education. Past participants include:

- Hillary Rodham Clinton
- David Remnick, the New Yorker
- Antonio "L.A." Reid, Arista Records
- Julianne Moore, actor
- Deborah Wright, governor

- Jerry Seinfeld, comedian/actor
- Suzanne Vega, musician
- Kenneth Cole, fashion designer
- Tiki Barber, New York Giants
- Kaity Tong, news reporter

[Source: www.pencil.org]

Quote:

"My favorite moment each day is when I walk through the halls before the students arrive at the school. It's silent and still. I like to think of it as the school's time for getting ready for the endless possibilities of the day ahead."
—Mr. Randolph, elementary school principal, Brooklyn, New York

Related Careers

Teacher, professor, college president, college dean, college administrator, guidance counselor, librarian

PRINTER

The Basics

Printers are the people who put ink on paper to make books, newspapers, magazines, pamphlets, greeting cards, posters, and all sorts of printed goods. Printers are the last people to take part in the publishing process. They prepare projects for printing by arranging the typeface and artwork. If a job requires more than black ink, printers set up the colors so that they will print accurately.

As a printer, you may fill one of many roles. You may meet with publishers and try to sell your printing services to them. If you're a *production manager* for a printing press, you must figure out how much a project will cost and oversee staff and deadlines. If you're a *plant manager,* you will make sure that the press is set up correctly for each project. You can also be a *printing press operator*. That's the person who is responsible for producing the final results. This job is all about attention to detail. One wrong move, and hundreds of pages print incorrectly. If you like to be the last link in a project, the job of a *binder* may be for you. A binder completes the printing project by putting together, or binding, books, magazines, or newspapers in numerical order.

If a career in printing appeals to you, you will need to be a good communicator and work well in a team environment. Math skills and attention to detail are necessary for laying out text and images to print. But most importantly—for all people involved in the printing process—is adherence to deadlines. All projects have to be completed on the proper date, even if that means working extra hours. You'll have to work well under pressure to succeed in this industry.

Preparation

High School

To gain some experience using a printing press, sign up for a printmaking course. If none are available at your high school, you may be able to take summer courses for younger students at a local college or art school. This will introduce you to laying type and using the press, as well as the different types of papers, inks, and other printing products that are available. In addition, take art and graphic design courses, and practice laying out your own designs on computer programs.

College

Continue taking courses in printmaking, graphic design, and computer science. Try to get an apprenticeship, working alongside a skilled worker, at a printing press. Due to advances in the printing industry, your work may call upon your knowledge of fields such as chemistry and electronics, so take a wide range of courses. Additional courses that will provide some useful background information are art history, advertising, and math.

Printmaking, art, graphic design

Will I Be Rich?

While you won't earn a fortune as a printer, you will have great satisfaction in producing wonderful printed materials. Working in a press room can be physically and mentally demanding, though, especially when the pressure is on to meet a deadline. You'll also need to use caution around potentially dangerous machinery. And since technology is always changing, you will need to take classes every so often to update your skills.

Fun Fact

Quick History Lesson

While Johannes Gutenberg is credited with developing the printing press back in the 1400s, significant advances were made in the field by William A. Lavelette, an African American inventor, in 1878. Lavelette's patented press produced type that was more legible than previous presses, so the final product was of much higher quality.

[Source: http://desktoppub.about.com]

Related Careers

Printmaker, artist, computer technician, graphic designer, publisher, writer, editor

PROFESSIONAL GAMBLER

The Basics

A professional gambler bets money with the hope of winning more money. The word *gamble* means "to take risks," which is exactly what a gambler does. While there's always a chance that a gambler will win money, there's a chance that he or she will lose money, too.

Anyone who is twenty-one or older can gamble, but a professional gambler makes a living placing bets. (Those who gamble once in a while recreationally are referred to as social gamblers.) The most well-known setting for gambling is the casino, where you can play card games such as poker or blackjack or insert coins into a slot machine and spin the lever. Gambling isn't limited to casinos, though. Horse races and games like jai alai are other outlets for professional gamblers. By betting money on a winning horse or a jai alai player, they can rake in the dough. Some gamblers play the lottery each day in the hopes of winning the jackpot, and some even make money calling BINGO!

Professional gambling isn't all about luck. In fact, most professional gamblers study statistics, and assess, or evaluate, the risk of winning or losing their money before placing a bet. You have to be willing to take risks to be a professional gambler, but you have to know when to exercise caution, too. All gamblers must keep things in perspective to avoid becoming obsessed with the prospect of winning—gambling can be addictive.

Preparation

High School

Math classes such as algebra, calculus, and statistics will come in handy, as will economics classes. Host racing events (placing bets with Monopoly money) or bingo games, and give cool prizes to the lucky winners.

College

While a college degree isn't a requirement, many classes will be useful for the budding professional gambler. Some recommended classes include statistics, probability, accounting, calculus, economics, risk management, decision theory, and game theory.

Possible Majors

Business administration, statistics, accounting, finance, risk management

Will I Be Rich?

The outcome of this career is a gamble—you can get rich or go broke. Gambling is full of ups and downs and can be very stressful at times. If you do well as a professional gambler and save some money (this is crucial), you may even be able to retire early and live off of your winnings. One thing is for sure—because of the excitement of gambling, you will collect a lot of great stories.

Fun Fact

The New York Lottery

The most money that a single person ever won in the New York State lottery was $128 million. On February 11, 2003, Phin Suy, who worked as a gardener in Central Park, won the New York's Mega Millions drawing. He received a lump sum check for $75,338,496!

[Source: www.nylottery.org]

Myth v. Reality

Myth: Stockbrokers are professional gamblers.

Reality: It's true. Each day stockbrokers bet other people's money on stocks with the hope of earning more money for their clients.

Quote

"You hit the lottery by being born. Everything you do in life after you are born is a gamble—winning and losing are what life is all about. Place your bets with care."

—Max Peters, professional gambler

Related Careers

Stockbroker, financier, financial analyst, accountant, real estate broker, salesman, statistician, actuary

PROFESSOR

The Basics

Professors teach students at colleges and universities around the world. In addition to teaching a range of classes in their field of study, they also continue to pursue their own personal projects. For example, a science professor will perform research and write about his or her findings; a photography professor will take pictures, perform research, and try to get his or her artwork published in books or shown in galleries. Teachers also have another very important role—to motivate and inspire students by way of their knowledge and passion.

As a professor, you may teach for up to fifteen or sixteen hours a week, but you'll do much more than that. You'll also design curriculum for your classes, correct assignments and tests, and prepare lectures. In addition, you'll conduct research, and you'll have office hours, so students can speak with you and ask questions. You'll have to work your way up to being a full-time professor, though. Along the way, you may hold one of many positions: *adjunct professor, lecturer, assistant professor,* or *associate professor.* Although these jobs are similar, a full professor has more responsibilities and is paid more. To become a professor, you must have your articles or books published, or otherwise achieve some level of success with your personal pursuits.

It's not easy keeping a classroom full of young adults interested in your subject matter; you have to work hard to make it fun and engaging. Discipline, passion, and creativity are all important traits for professors. Great professors are also confident speaking in public and know how to relate to their audience.

Preparation

High School

Arrange an informational interview with a professor at a nearby college. English, writing, and computer courses will help all future professors, but learning a lot in one subject area will bring you closer to being an expert. Take as many advanced placement courses as you can, especially in your favorite subject. Any opportunity you can find to be a teacher's assistant or student teacher (perhaps in private dance or music lessons) will help you develop some sense of what it takes to teach.

College

A great way to learn about a professor's career is to ask one—talk to your professors. You don't have to major in education to become a professor; instead, you can major in the subject area you'd like to teach in preparation for graduate coursework.

Graduate School

You will need a PhD to teach at many colleges, but some will hire you if you've earned only your master's degree. You'll work hard, perform a great deal of research, and come up with a final project or dissertation. This will make you an expert and prepare you for your career as a professor.

Will I Be Rich?

Unless you write a best-selling book, you won't become a millionaire by teaching. You will, however, be rich in knowledge! You can pretty much make your own hours outside of class time, so the schedule is often flexible. The amount of degrees you earn, years you teach, and your scholarly achievements are factors for promotion. The job can be stressful at times. But what other job will pay you to share what you love with students and spend time researching your favorite topics?

Fun Fact

The Nutty Professor

Eddie Murphy stars in this movie as Professor Sherman Klump, the freaky professor who invents a miracle formula that cuts him down to half his size. For Professor Klump, this is a good thing until he realizes that his skinnier self, who he calls Buddy Love, leaves as soon as his miracle formula wears off!

Quote

"Class by class, there's the chance to think anew about everything I'd thought I knew. Moreover, it's the perfect job for those who can't imagine the world without loud and continuous chitchat."

—Lee K. Abbot, author and professor of English and creative writing at Ohio State University

Related Careers

Teacher, writer, politician, college dean, college president, principal, artist, historian

PSYCHIATRIST

The Basics

You've probably seen psychiatrists portrayed on TV. They're usually sitting at their desks, listening attentively to their patient, who is lying on a comfy leather couch. This isn't too far off, but there's more to the job than just lending an ear. A psychiatrist analyzes the way people think, feel, and act. Psychiatrists diagnose different types of mental illness and treat them through counseling sessions and sometimes medication. A psychiatrist's patients may range from those who suffer from depression to those with eating disorders, addictions, or even split personalities.

Psychiatrists administer tests to their patients to learn more about their illnesses. Depending on their condition and progress, a psychiatrist prescribes a treatment. Sometimes they use psychotherapy to treat patients. This means that they meet with patients regularly to discuss how they think or feel and learn more about their thought processes. Psychiatrists also prescribe medication to help their patients get better. In severe cases, a psychiatrist may admit a patient to a hospital for medical attention. Psychiatrists may work in psychiatric hospitals, medical centers, community agencies, prisons, nursing homes, schools, or rehabilitation centers. Many psychiatrists also have a private practice, meaning they take on their own patients and set their own hours.

Aspiring psychiatrists should be great communicators with super listening skills. They should also be generous, compassionate, trustworthy, and sincere.

Preparation

High School

Reading case studies by psychiatrists is a great way to learn what a day in the life in this job is all about. You can also volunteer in a hospital or health care facility that treats patients with mental illnesses. Classes such as chemistry and psychology will be a big help for medical school down the road.

College

Continue to read as many psychiatrist case studies as you can. Sign up for classes such as psychology, communications, physiology, chemistry, and sociology to learn how people think and interact. Prepare for the MCAT exam, which you will need to take to get into medical school.

Possible Majors

Psychology, pre-medicine, mental health services

Medical School and Residency

Future psychiatrists spend up to seven years taking classes and completing a residency or internship. During the first two years, you will take a core of classes that includes behavioral science, biochemistry, chemistry, neuroscience, physiology, and psychiatry. During the next two years, you will study and work with mentally ill patients. Next, successful completion of a written exam can earn you a state license, and then you'll complete your residency.

Certification

After their training is complete, most psychiatrists take a voluntary examination given by the American Board of Psychiatry and Neurology to become a board-certified psychiatrist.

Will I Be Rich?

You'll earn a pretty nice salary as a psychiatrist, but expect to work long hours. When patients call on you for help, you need to be there for them, regardless of what time of day or night it is. You'll also need to keep up with advances in the field and new medications for mental and emotional illnesses.

Fun Facts

What About Bob?

If you want to see a funny flick that involves a psychiatrist trying to get some peace and quiet away from his patients, check out What About Bob? In the movie, Bob Wiley (played by Bill Murray) stalks the famous psychiatrist Dr. Leo Marvin (played by Richard Dreyfuss). Bob, a patient of Dr. Marvin, follows his doc to his holiday home, where he nags him to help him with his problems.

Myth v. Reality

Myth: Only weirdoes visit psychiatrists.

Reality: Anyone can develop depression or another mental illness. Psychiatrists treat all sorts of people. The good news is that whether a mental health condition is mild or serious, most of them are treatable by psychiatrists.

Related Careers

Psychologist, counselor, doctor, sociologist, social worker

PSYCHOLOGIST

The Basics

Psychologists study the mind and behavior. More specifically, they study how the inner workings of our brains and the world around us affect our behavior. They can use this information to help people better understand why they do certain things. Psychologists serve as counselors, researchers, or educators. They work in a variety of locations, including hospitals, clinics, nursing homes, courtrooms, research labs, businesses, and schools.

As a psychologist, you will work with a wide variety of patients, including some who are mentally or emotionally upset or unstable. You may work with patients who recently suffered an illness, such as cancer or a stroke, or people who are coping with a divorce or the death of a loved one. Generally, your days will consist of one-on-one meetings with patients; you will ask questions and try to learn more about them through their responses. You will help your patients understand why they act a certain way or what causes certain feelings. With your assistance and guidance, your patients can begin to make changes in their lives.

As a psychologist, you must be sensitive, compassionate, and patient. You must also have great listening and communication skills—you'll have to be able to inspire others to get through a crisis.

Preparation

High School

A high school psychology course is a great place to get a head start in this field. Use what you learn about a lot of famous psychologists and their theories as a springboard, and check out books by or about these psychologists at your local library. Courses in biology and sociology will boost your knowledge of life-forms and their interactions, while English classes will help develop your language skills.

College

Read as many case studies and books on psychology as you can. Sign up for a variety of psychology courses, from adolescent psychology to abnormal psychology, and ask your psychology professors about their careers. You'll probably also take classes in sociology, human development, biochemistry, communication disorders, and English, too. Apply yourself and work hard—graduate programs in psychology are difficult to get into.

Possible Majors

*Psychology, biopsychology, developmental psychology, experimental psychology,
clinical psychology, educational psychology, human development*

Graduate School

Expect a long road ahead if you plan to become a psychologist. You'll need to earn a PhD in psychology, and your coursework will take from five to seven years to complete. In addition, you'll need to write a dissertation (a long paper on an original topic) and become certified and licensed by your state.

As an alternative, you can earn a doctor of psychology degree. Your program will focus on clinical work, and no dissertation is required. If you want to work in a school, do research, or assist a psychologist, a master's in psychology might be enough.

Will I Be Rich?

If you work for yourself, you will set your own hours and make a great living. Keep in mind, however, that you will need to offer evening and weekend hours to accommodate your patients. If you work in a hospital, nursing home, or another health facility, you may work odd shifts, too. School psychologists, or those working at other institutions, usually work during the day. While this job can be intense and emotionally challenging, those who love working with people and have a desire to help them will find this job very fulfilling. The first few years are usually the toughest, so hang in there!

Fun Facts

Words of Wisdom from Dr. Joyce Brothers, Psychologist

- Trust your hunches. They're usually based on facts filed away just below the conscious level.

- The person interested in success has to learn to view failure as a healthy, inevitable part of the process of getting to the top.

- The best proof of love is trust.

- A strong, positive self-image is the best possible preparation for success.

[Source: www.brainyquote.com and www.lordly.com]

Related Careers

Sociologist, social worker, anthropologist, psychiatrist, counselor, doctor, biologist, special education teacher, professor

PUBLICIST

The Basics

A publicist lets the public know about a company, event, person, or product. Celebrities have publicists; so do many other people or companies who stand to gain money or popularity from publicity. Publicists write press releases, prepare press packets, and serve as spokespersons for their clients. They create an image and attract attention for the people they represent.

As a publicist, your day will consist of writing press releases and talking on the phone to media folks. Your goal is to secure positive publicity and exposure for your client and to answer questions the media has about your client. Since so much of your job deals with the public, you will need to be a confident and articulate speaker and writer. Your days will be hectic, and you will have to meet many deadlines. On the flip side, you'll probably attend a lot of parties and other social events, so you can chitchat, network, and develop contacts with new people.

You have to be very outgoing, creative, and energetic to succeed in this career. You also have to have tough skin. As one New York City publicist put it, "You need to be ready for anything, always. You never know when the media is going to ambush you. Always smile, speak clearly, and always promote your client!"

Preparation

High School

Use your time in high school to develop your writing and public speaking skills. English courses may offer a chance to speak in public or take part in debates. The debate team will offer a great opportunity to defend your position, which will come in very handy in this field. You can also run for a leadership position, like class president, or represent a classmate who is running for president with promotional materials, like posters.

College

A college degree in public relations will give you a fine foundation for this career. Classes you will want to take include advertising, communication, English, journalism, public relations, public speaking, and writing. Internships are especially important in this field because you'll need to build up your list of contacts. You may also need to call upon fellow classmates later in life, when they are prominent figures in their own careers. Make sure you keep in touch with them and remain friendly.

Possible Majors

Public relations, communications, business administration, journalism

Will I Be Rich?

Your paycheck will depend on your experience and your reputation in the field. If you represent people who are already famous or you make your clients famous, you'll certainly earn more money. At any rate, you will have a lot of fun and get to go to great parties when you're not at your office.

Fun Facts

Bad Publicity Is Still Publicity

- *Olympic skater Tonya Harding received a lot of attention when she plotted against her skating rival, Nancy Kerrigan, back in 1994.*

- *Lizzy Grubman was a publicist who got her own publicity! Back in 2001, she was arrested after injuring sixteen people with her car outside of a nightclub in the Hamptons. Her company, Lizzie Grubman Public Relations, still serves clients such as Britney Spears, Jay-Z, and N'Sync.*

Myth v. Reality

Myth: It's who you know.

Reality: Actually, it's true! If you know the right people, you will go a long way as a publicist. Knowing who to call when you have information to share is what will get your clients noticed!

Related Careers

Advertising executive, marketing executive, wedding planner, agent, journalist, writer, editor, rock star, actor, politician

PUBLISHER

The Basics

You may think of a publisher as a person who puts out books. But the truth is that publishers can create and distribute any sort of reading material from calendars or comic books to pamphlets or monthly magazines. They can even publish websites. If a document includes text, pictures, graphics, and/or data, a publisher combines them to create a neat, attractive package. He or she has to accomplish hundreds of small tasks to create this final product.

Publishers have to make all sorts of decisions regarding their materials. A publisher works with his or her team to choose the size and style of the font, the layout and look of the page, and the content of the product. The product needs to appeal to readers, so the publisher must decide which stories people will want to read. Even when the product is finished, the work isn't; you have to decide how best to market your materials. It's your job, ultimately, to find a way to make a profit.

If you're a publisher for a big publishing house, you may have a staff to help you put together the product. You may need to hire editors, writers, or designers to assemble a nice-looking, well-organized published product. You may need a sales staff, a marketing staff, and maybe some assistants, too. Therefore, you'll need to be a good communicator, and you'll need to be organized as well. It can take a great deal of determination, patience, and inspiration to be a publisher.

Preparation

High School

Believe it or not, you can be your own publisher in high school. Write some articles, and have your friends contribute, too. You can write about anything that interests you—sports, music, fashion, seventeenth-century Mongolian architecture, whatever. You can put this information together on a website or in a small printed or photocopied magazine. Work hard in all your English classes because language is the basis of publishing. Volunteer for your school newspaper or a local publication. You won't get to be the publisher, but you will get to see what he or she does.

College

Being a publisher requires artistic, editorial, and managerial know-how. So use your time in college to study all the angles. Take writing or journalism classes to become a better writer. Learn graphic design, so you can understand the techniques—and software used—for laying out art. Learn the business of running a business. That's what a publisher does. You can study management or finance for that side of publishing. Perhaps most importantly, get involved with a publication. Even if you have to intern, at least get your foot in the door.

English, English composition, English literature, creative writing, journalism, business administration, advertising, marketing

Will I Be Rich?

As a publisher, you may be in control of your own product. In that case, your finances are linked to the success of the product. Especially if you own your company, you can get rich or go broke depending on how good your publications are. If you posess good computer and people skills, plus a great eye for detail, design, and content, you can be extremely successful.

Fun Fact

Harry Potter Fever

The lucky publishing house for the Harry Potter *series is Scholastic. In June 2003, the fifth book in the* Harry Potter *series was published:* Harry Potter and the Order of the Phoenix. *Despite being nearly 900 pages long, the publishers at Scholastic predicted a great demand for the book. They ordered 8.5 million copies to be printed for its first run. That was the largest first printing for a book ever!*

[Source: www.nydailynews.com]

Related Careers

Writer, editor, graphic designer, journalist, printer, artist, illustrator, salesman, advertising executive, market researcher

RACE CAR DRIVER

The Basics

Race car drivers compete in races and drive their cars at high speeds—up to almost 200 miles per hour. This is a tough, demanding, and dangerous job. In addition to worrying about their own cars, race car drivers always have to watch out for other drivers to avoid crashing or falling behind. The competitive nature of the sport adds a great deal of stress to the race, too; every driver wants to come in first, of course.

As a race car driver, you will spend a lot of time exercising—you need to stay in excellent shape—and practicing on the track. Racing conditions are strenuous, so the more you prepare physically, mentally, and emotionally before each race, the better. You will also work with your crewmembers to keep your car in top condition. During a race, whenever you need gas, a tire replacement, or some other mechanical repair, you'll pull into the pit, where your crewmembers are waiting to service your car.

Aside from your responsibilities on the road, you will also have obligations to your sponsor (the person, company, or organization who supports you and your crewmembers financially). You will meet with your sponsors and give publicity interviews, and you may also do endorsements. When you endorse a product, such as a sneaker brand, you promote the product to help boost sales.

You will often work seven days a week, so passion for the sport is what will keep you going. You will need to remain calm under pressure and react quickly in dangerous situations. If you keep practicing, you just may make it to the Winston Cup Series, the most famous of all stock car circuits.

Preparation

High School

As soon as you get a driver's license and a car, keep a lookout for driving days at local racetracks. Sometimes you can drive your own car on the track on those days. The important thing is to race whenever you can, whether you drive a go-kart, your own car, or a race car. Time behind the wheel, or "seat time," as the pros call it, is how you improve your skills. Just remember to keep it safe and reserve your racing for the racetrack! Read up on racing in books and magazines, and check out the races in person if at all possible.

College

While you are busy doing all that racing, don't forget your studies! Racing is a huge business these days, and the more educated you are, the more likely you will be to make wise decisions regarding your career. In addition, you'll earn a degree that you can fall back on in case you are injured or decide to change careers.

Mechanical engineering, physics, applied physics, recreation management, athletic training, rehabilitation services

Racing Classes

Once you have some experience racing, it's time to take classes at a racing school. As long as you have the money and the desire, you will learn the basics about racing and car control.

Will I Be Rich?

If you have a good sponsor and win a lot of races, you can earn more than $100,000 dollars a year. Of course, there is a lot of risk involved, both physically and financially—you have to win to score the dough. You can make extra money on endorsements, too. For some, the thrill of racing is enough of a gift. Many race car drivers go on to become teachers and coaches for younger racers.

Fun Fact

Who Says Racing Is Just for Adults?

Seventeen-year-old Shelby Howard, IV, was the youngest driver to complete a full season on the ARCA Re/Max stock car racing series in 2002. Most of the other drivers were more than double his age, so it's no small feat that Shelby finished fifth among seventy-five other drivers. Shelby started racing at age nine; at twelve he became the mini cup national champion. Later that year, he began competing against adults. There's no doubt that Shelby has a long and eventful ride ahead of him!

[Source: http://abcnews.go.com]

Related Careers

Stunt double, athlete, pilot, mechanic, teacher, mechanical engineer, physicist

REAL ESTATE AGENT

The Basics

Real estate agents are essentially salespersons who help people find property that suits their needs. Some people are looking to buy a home, while others want to rent an apartment or building. Real estate agents also help people on the other end of the deal—those who wish to sell or rent their house, apartment, or building. *Residential agents* rent or sell homes and apartments; *commercial agents* rent buildings to businesses.

As a real estate agent, you will meet with people to find out what type of property they are looking for. After you determine how much your clients can afford to spend, you will search for available property that meets their criteria. You may even scope out the place before showing it to your clients. When you show the property, you will need to answer questions about the floor plan and the area's crime rate; when renting or selling residential property, you may also provide information about nearby schools and shopping centers. If a client decides to purchase the property, you'll help coordinate the signing of the papers and transfer of ownership, also known as the closing.

Real estate agents need to be well-informed, confident, and persuasive to win their customers' business. A professional, pleasant, even-tempered person makes people around them feel comfortable, and that's what you'll want to do; spending a great deal of money or selling property can make clients very nervous. You'll also have to be a good listener, sensitive to your clients' concerns, to understand what they are looking for.

Preparation

High School

Communication and presentation will be your most important weapons as a real estate agent. You can start building these skills in high school, with English, creative writing, psychology, theater, and debate classes. It's also crucial that you develop strong mathematical skills because you may be handling money and financial contracts when you close deals.

College

You can learn a great deal about real estate while in college, although a college degree isn't necessary. In addition to taking business and financial courses, you may get a chance to rent your own apartment. Nothing teaches you more about property than having to take care of your own. You may encounter a lot of the problems that potential buyers and renters ask about—bad plumbing, a leaky roof, or a broken lock—and you'll better understand their concerns.

Real estate, marketing, business administration, economics, finance

Real Estate License

You must be a high school graduate, at least eighteen years old, and pass a written test in order to earn your real estate license; in many states, you must also complete thirty to ninety hours of classroom instruction. You will need to renew your license each year, but you won't have to take another test unless you choose to work in a different state.

Will I Be Rich?

If you sell or rent a great deal of properties, you can earn a lot of money. Real estate agents are paid on commission (that's a percentage of the price that a house or property sells for) by real estate brokers. Commercial real estate agents might make more money on each deal, but their deals may be few and far between compared to residential brokers. If you're a real estate agent, you'll work odd hours, on evenings and on weekends because that's when most people are available to view potential property. If you love to work with people, you might enjoy helping them find their ideal home.

Fun Facts

Be Nosy!

Here are some important questions to ask when renting your first apartment:

- *Does anything need to be repaired?*
- *How old is the house?*
- *Where's the nearest [fill in the blank]?*
- *Is the neighborhood safe?*

Quote

"If you like working with people and getting to beautiful places, it's a great career."

—Sheila Blauner, real estate agent

Related Careers

Banker, lawyer, counselor, interior designer, real estate developer, salesperson, landlord, city planner

REAL ESTATE DEVELOPER

The Basics

A building is just a building until a real estate developer comes along. Real estate developers help a building take shape and turn it into a useful, functional place to live or do business in. They work with both old and new spaces—developing a completely new structure into twenty-one floors of beautiful, high-tech office space, for example, or fixing up an old factory and turning it into a cool new restaurant.

As a real estate developer, you look for good buys on land or buildings that you want to develop as your next new project. Since it's expensive to create or fix up a building, a real estate developer has to be a smart salesperson and convince other people—investors—to offer their money toward the project. You'll probably have to talk to banks or large companies to get the funds you'll need. While it is possible to use your own money, you'd need a lot of it—possibly millions of dollars!

Once the money is taken care of, you're responsible for seeing the project through to the end and taking care of every step along the way. Whether you're building or renovating, you have to deal with large-scale problems. For example, a building needs to be wired for plumbing, electricity, and telephones. All that responsibility falls on the shoulders of the real estate developer. It's a big job, but you get to be the person who makes it all happen. You'll need a wide range of talents to succeed at this job—from understanding finance, architecture, and engineering to staying calm when things go awry.

Preparation

High School

To be a successful real estate developer, you've got to know math. You don't have to take advanced calculus, but work hard in your math classes—especially any finance-oriented math. You may want to keep track of recent developments by reading the real estate section of your local newspaper.

College

Real estate and economics courses will help you establish a base knowledge of the business. Learn the trade by working for a developer, so you can get a grasp of the process. If you can intern or observe at a large real estate development company, you'll get to see how the developers create and renovate malls, office buildings, and houses.

Possible Majors

Real estate, finance, accounting, architecture, management

Additional Training

Special courses for real estate agents and brokers teach the basics of real estate. Even though you may never be an agent or broker, you'll learn to calculate mortgages and appraise the value of buildings, for example.

Will I Be Rich?

Successful real estate developers can earn a bundle. Even if you develop a property that isn't doing well, if you can wait it out, the property will usually be worth more than what you paid for it. Real estate values have always been rising, so there are ups and downs in the market in terms of people purchasing or renting property. If you can deal with the downs, you'll be just fine.

Fun Fact

A Wise Investment

Dutch settlers bought Manhattan from the Native Americans in 1626 for sixty guilders' worth of trinkets—roughly $24. According to Wall Street maven Peter Lynch, if the Indians had invested the $24 at 8 percent, they "would have built up a net worth of more than $20 trillion."

[Source: www.tlc.discovery.com]

Myth v. Reality

Myth: Real estate developing is easy.
Reality: It's a hard job with lots of aggravation. Finding good deals can be difficult and frustrating. Even Donald Trump went bankrupt for a few years!
Myth: Real estate developers sit behind a desk and tell people what to do.
Reality: Developers are always on the move, whether it's making presentations to banks or checking on their property.

Related Careers

Construction worker, architect, structural engineer, banker, real estate agent, city planner, landlord

RECORDING TECHNICIAN

The Basics

Recording technicians help musicians record and fine-tune their music. They work with all types of musicians, including jazz, rap, rock, and pop stars. Aside from their skill with equipment, recording technicians need to have a good ear and a lot of patience. Great communication and motivation skills, attention to detail, and of course, passion for music are necessary for this job.

Recording technicians operate a whole range of recording equipment, including microphones and mixing boards. At the beginning of the session, a technician's first job is to set up microphones that can be used for each singer or instrument. A band can either choose to record all their instruments at once or to record each instrument on a separate track. The recording technician manipulates the volume of each track with the mixing board, to make sure the guitar doesn't drown out the vocals, for example. The technician can also enhance a track by adding a desired effect, like a chorus or reverb.

After each recording, the technician plays it back in the control room to hear how it sounds. The technician, the musician, and the producer listen to a take to decide whether it's a keeper or needs some improvement. The song, or part of the song, is then rerecorded. In most cases, it takes multiple tries to get a song or track to sound just right. If there are no perfect takes, the recording technician can combine the good parts of each recording and mix them together to create the master version.

Preparation

High School

When you listen to music, pay attention to the role each instrument plays. Play an instrument in your school band. You'll see how the band conductor instructs certain instruments to raise or lower their volume or intensity; this is, in fact, similar to what a recording technician does when mixing a song. Find a local recording studio and volunteer to help out after school, and read music magazines to learn what's new in the music industry.

College or Technical School

Much of the technical training you need to be a recording technician is offered at colleges and universities; technical schools also offer the required training. Since a college degree is not a job requirement, either of these training options will work. Whatever path you take to be a recording technician, you'll need to get into the studio, through a job or internship, to really learn this trade.

Possible Majors

Recording arts technology, audio engineering, music, music history

Will I Be Rich?

You probably won't earn tons of dough as a recording technician, but you'll get to work with a lot of creative people, some of whom might be celebrities! Twelve-hour days are the norm during intense recording sessions, but you may work less when there are no musicians scheduled to come in. The work can be tedious, but you must remain focused. You will need to keep up with new technology and repair your equipment as needed to achieve the best sounds. If you love music and enjoy working behind the scenes to make the finished product, the job of a recording technician can be really satisfying.

Fun Facts

Beatle Mania

If you think that recording an album is an easy job, think again! It took roughly 129 days to record the classic Beatles album Sgt. Pepper's Lonely Hearts Club Band. *Below you'll find the number of the take that was used to create the master version of each song.*

"Sgt. Pepper's Lonely Heart Club Band": *take 10*

"Good Morning, Good Morning": *take 11*

"Lucy in the Sky with Diamonds": *take 8*

"Getting Better": *take 15*

"With a Little Help from My Friends": *take 11*

[Source: www.iamthebeatles.com]

Quote

"Listen to musicians—their ideas and their music. Grant them their freedom. It is the way to capture their true sound."

—James Flatto, recording technician

Related Careers

Musician, lyricist, rock star, music conductor, producer, stage technician

RECRUITER

The Basics

A recruiter has two jobs rolled into one. He or she helps people find jobs while helping companies fill job openings. Recruiters may work to fill entry-level positions, seeking out employees at college job fairs. Or he or she may work to fill high-level professional positions, like executives. A recruiter who works with high-end execs is sometimes also called a headhunter.

As a recruiter, you will interview people who are looking for jobs to find out more information about their skills, interests, and experience. You will then figure out if the person you interviewed would be a good fit for any available jobs. You'll set up job interviews for your clients and provide interview tips. If the interview goes well, congratulations—you've made an excellent match! But it's not quite over yet: You still have to work with both sides to figure out the finer details, like how much the employee will be paid.

However, if the job candidate and the employer are not a good fit, you will continue to work with the client until you help him or her find the right job.

If you want to be a recruiter, you need to have outstanding communication and negotiation skills. You also need to be patient, dedicated, incredibly organized, and committed to helping people. Did we mention that it helps if you're a caring and compassionate person, too? You may have to act as a shoulder to cry on.

Preparation

High School

The ability to work with and understand people and their behaviors is important for a recruiter; you can gain some knowledge in this area by taking psychology and sociology classes. You could also try to schedule a meeting with your guidance counselor to learn about different careers.

College

Some recruiters decide to focus on matching people with employers in just one job field. If this appeals to you, earn a degree in the field you wish to specialize in. You can specialize in almost any professional field, from computer science to education. The degree will make you a valuable resource because it will be easier for you to understand what each job entails.

Possible Majors

Business, communications, human resources management, psychology, counseling

Will I Be Rich?

You can make an above-average salary as a recruiter as long as you are a good matchmaker. Generally, your salary is dependent on the number of people that you place in jobs—the more people you place, the more money you earn. You will work long hours and have to do a lot of negotiating, but you will gain satisfaction from helping people find their dream jobs.

Fun Facts

Busy Bodies

A recruiter's job is not easy. He or she may review over 500 resumes a week and spend over ten hours a day on the phone talking to people about jobs!

Tips from a New York City Recruiter

- When you go on an interview, an employer wants to hire you! Hiring you means no more time spent interviewing. Walk into every interview knowing that the employer hopes you are the one for the job!

- Resumes don't get you hired. They may get you an interview, but resumes don't answer questions, solve problems, or have personalities! When you are on an interview, pretend that the employer has never seen your resume and let them get to know the real you—whatever cannot be communicated on a piece of paper.

Quote

"There's nothing more satisfying than helping people to find their dream jobs!"

—Arthur Flatto, recruiter, New York, New York

Related Careers

Career counselor, guidance counselor, agent, human resources manager, salesperson

REFEREE (OR UMPIRE)

The Basics

Referees—also known as umpires depending on the sport—are the people who make the calls in a sporting event. They watch the games and make decisions. For example, they might have to decide if a pass is out of bounds, if a pitch is a strike, or even if an athlete is cheating. Most work in groups, such as Major League Baseball umpires. Some work by themselves, such as boxing referees.

As a professional referee, you have to make split-second decisions that will affect the outcome of a game. Because of that, the stress level is high. You absolutely need to know every rule (no matter how obscure), and you need to have near-perfect eyesight and be relatively fit (referees often run around the field as much as the athletes!). You also need the ability to handle potentially angry athletes with your own fair degree of aggression.

You have probably seen referees in major events, such as NFL, NBA, NHL, or MLB games. To get to that high position, referees need to do a lot of training. Becoming a professional referee can be just as difficult as becoming a professional athlete. There are fewer positions available, and it can take many years to advance levels.

Preparation

High School

Most refereeing organizations require you to have at least a high school diploma. While you're in high school, get out there on the field, court, or rink. You should try to serve as a referee for a little league, summer camp, or even for your school. Even if the job is unpaid, you'll be getting some real experience—and maybe having some fun, too!

College

Although referees are not required to get a college degree, college is a great place to learn more about sports. Try to referee for one of your college's sports teams, and take the opportunity to learn more about other sports-related fields.

Possible Majors

Sports management, sport and leisure studies, athletic training, physical therapy, rehabilitation services

Additional Preparation

Different organizations have their own unique requirements. For example, Major League Baseball requires that their umpires attend a special umpiring school. You don't have to be in the school for very long, but that's generally where scouts can discover your talents. The premiere students at umpiring school get hired to work at the lowest level of professional baseball.

Will I Be Rich?

If you make it to the big time, you can do very well for yourself. Professional referees who make it to the top levels of sports are compensated for their devotion and talent. Those high-level professionals get lots of time off in a year, but may also spend months on the road. However, most referees spend their careers in the lower levels of professional sports making just enough to get by.

Fun Fact

Girls Can Play at That Game, Too

You may think of refereeing as a mostly male job. Don't tell that to Ria Cortesio, a female umpire in minor league baseball. Cortesio is the fifth woman to umpire a professional baseball game, and she hopes to be the first to make it to the major leagues. The first female umpire in a minor league game was Bernice Gera, in 1972. As of 2003, Pam Postema made it the furthest as a female baseball umpire; she umpired for thirteen years, including seven years at the AAA level (one level below the major leagues).

Related Careers

Athlete, coach, manager, judge

ROCK STAR

The Basics

Rock stars are rock 'n' roll musicians who have achieved ultimate fame. Any type of musician can become famous, but as far as rock stars go, Luciano Pavarotti, Celine Dion, and Dolly Parton won't cut it. Each person may have his or her own definition of what being a rock star really means. Most will agree, though, that in addition to the music, it has to do with image and attitude. Certain rock stars have been known to wear outrageous clothes, act wild, jump around, and smash their instruments onstage. Although this is an extreme example, rock stars tend to be trendsetters who inspire fashion and culture. They certainly inspire their fans!

Rock stars may perform solo, or they may be part of a band. Some write their own music, while others perform music by other songwriters. As a rock star, most of your time will be spent writing songs, practicing, recording tracks in the studio, playing gigs, and/or touring. Going on tour is considered one of the coolest and most fun aspects of this career, and it's no wonder—you get to travel all over the place and meet up with adoring fans from all over the globe.

It's not so easy to make it big, though—you'll need some help. Your agent will represent you and try to get good gigs and lots of press. Your manager will oversee your jobs, make sure you are paid, and keep your finances in order. Your record label gives you money to record your music and promotes your CDs and tours; in exchange, the label gets some of the sales profits. A lot of rock stars stay with one record label throughout their musical careers. But to have a long-lasting career, you'll need to be a motivated, dedicated, and passionate musician—and you'll need a strong stage presence, too.

Preparation

High School

Practice playing an instrument, try to write some of your own music, and join or start up your own band. You can record your songs easily with a tape recorder or a simple four-track recorder (it lets you lay down four separate tracks, and you can do it in the comfort of your own bedroom!). Music, chorus, and art classes at school will help you develop your talent and confidence.

College

Just in case you don't top the Billboard charts, you may want to earn a college degree to fall back on. Keep practicing and writing songs. Play in local bars, clubs, and at parties. Book shows for your band all over the place, so you can tour and try out life on the road. Try to take some music classes, too, like music criticism and twentieth-century music.

Will I Be Rich?

If you sign on with a big-time record label, you could make millions in record sales, touring, and endorsements. But until that happens, you may have to scrape by day to day and work a number of different jobs to stay afloat. Recording sessions, shows, and especially touring can be really exhausting, but they can also be totally exhilarating. If you yearn to be a rock star, you're not alone—this is the dream job for a whole lot of people. Although it's really tough to succeed, all the hard work pays off if you make it big.

Fun Fact

Rock Flick

If you think that Jack Black is just a funny man, think again! When Black's lifelong dream to become a rock star didn't come true, Black didn't give up. Instead, the comedian wrote songs that poked fun at rock and roll. If you want to learn more about Black's band, Tenacious D, *check out his movie* School of Rock.

Quote

"Long walks on the beach are fun and relaxing. When you're a musician, you tend to have more time to do those things. So pick up an instrument and practice every day. But get good grades, too, so nobody can accuse you of being a slacker."

—Evan Slamka of Marjorie Fair

Related Careers

Musician, music conductor, agent, recording technician, artist, producer, DJ, VJ, stage technician

SAILOR

The Basics

Sailors sail the seas in ships, working a centuries-old profession. Sailors can earn money as athletes, by winning high-profile sailing races. However, that's very difficult—and it costs a lot of money to race in tournaments competitively. Most sailors make their money from people who pay to ride on their sailboat. These people pay for different reasons. Some might want to learn how to sail or hear about the history of sailing. Others might want to go on a day trip or visit an exotic island. Some people just want to relax on a sailboat and enjoy a nice day on the waves and in the wind.

Anybody who works on a sailboat is a sailor. The *captain* is in charge of the boat, and he or she decides where to go and how to get there. The *first mate* runs the deck and is responsible for the safety of the crew. (Larger crews have more second, third, and even fourth mates.) Most sailboats have specialists; for example, the *engineer* fixes the mechanical parts of the boat, and the *bosun* (also known as a boatswain) maintains the rigging and the sails. *Cooks* prepare the crew's meals, and *deckhands* perform the many manual tasks that are needed for a smooth ride. (Of course, the term *sailor* can also apply to a naval officer, but we explain that career in our military personnel profile.)

You have to be in good physical shape to be a sailor. Sails can weigh a ton, and they're pulled up and down by hand. You also have to be able to live in a small space with several other people, sometimes for many days at a time. Oh, and you shouldn't get seasick easily! It's not always easy and it's not always fun, but there is nothing quite like the life of a sailor.

Preparation

High School

Many sailboats for hire accept volunteers. The best way to get a crew position on a boat someday is to volunteer there first. Volunteer spots fill up fast in the summer, so consider volunteering during off-peak times. If you're willing to help in the winter, then you'll learn a lot in a low-pressure situation.

College

Many colleges have a sailing team. Get experience on a team if you can. Depending on what you want to do on a sailboat, you might want to take carpentry or wood-building classes, or even a culinary course. Knowledge of history or science can help you if you end up working on an education-based sailboat. You don't actually have to know how to sail to be a sailor, but it sure helps!

Possible Majors

Athletic training, marine biology, tourism

Will I Be Rich?

You can make a lot of money if you win the top prizes in worldwide, famous racing contests. But otherwise, you will not be rich as a sailor. You get free food and a place to stay, and some deckhands don't even make more than that. The only person who makes a decent living on a sailboat with passengers is the captain.

Fun Fact

Around the World in 264 Days

In 1997, Australian David Dicks set the record for being the youngest person to sail around the world nonstop and alone. He left from western Australia on February 26, 1996 and returned 264 days later.

[Source: www.abc.net.au]

Quote

"The attraction to sailing for most is the ability to escape the monotony of a lot of jobs and do something off the beaten path. Most of them [sailors] love the outdoors and are highly motivated, independent people."

—Justin Riservato, sailor

Related Careers

Military personnel, fisherman, marine biologist, pilot, race car driver, tour guide, athlete

SALESPERSON

The Basics

A salesperson can sell everything from flat-screen TVs to Land Rovers to buildings and property. To sell products or services with any success, a salesperson needs to be knowledgeable about *what* they are selling and *who* they are trying to sell it to. He or she needs to understand what the customer is looking for and what other competition is out there. Therefore, a salesperson needs to be a great listener. Salespeople may work in stores, in an office, or they may visit customers in person.

As a salesperson, you will spend your days explaining the details of your products to customers, including the benefits of one brand or model over another. If you work in a jewelry store, you may help a customer pick out an engagement ring or a new chain for an antique pendant. Whatever it is you are selling, it's important that you know your stuff; customers tend to have a lot of questions. If you're selling art, you should know the language of art dealers; if you're selling gym memberships, it would help if you use the gym yourself. Aside from promoting and selling products, many salespeople close deals by writing up the sales slip and handling a customer's money. And just in case your customer is dissatisfied, you'll have to be well versed on the return policy for your products.

The best salespeople truly enjoy working with people and are super communicators. Customers can be crabby, exasperated, tired, and overdemanding. Come to work equipped with patience, courtesy, and an easygoing manner.

Preparation

High School

Take classes in math to get used to percentages and psychology to better understand how consumers think. Better yet, get a part-time job in a retail store you like. If that's too much to handle during the school year, take one just for the holidays or over the summer.

College

You can learn a lot about sales and business in college, but you don't need to major in one particular field. You can make the best use of your college years by learning to speak confidently and spontaneously to strangers and in public. You'll need to learn how to be persuasive, while remaining polite and professional.

Possible Majors
Marketing, finance, communications, business administration, psychology

On-the-Job Experience

The best way to prepare for a career in sales is to get as much sales experience as you can. At most stores, you can learn how to use a cash register, sell products effectively, and serve even the pickiest customers. Whether you work in an office or door-to-door, you must learn to effectively sell products and serve even the pickiest customers. More experience in sales can lead to more opportunities.

Will I Be Rich?

If you're a cosmetics salesperson, you probably won't make a fortune (though you'll have all the lipstick and perfume your heart desires). But if you sell expensive sports cars, you'll pull in some bucks, as long as you work on commission. (The commission system means you get to keep a percentage of the total price of any sale you make. Common in higher-priced sales environments, it rewards those who are good at the job.) The hours that you work will depend on what you're selling and in what type of store. Retail sales call for long hours during the bustling holiday shopping season. Many talented salespeople discover opportunities to move into management positions within the store or company, which can definitely increase your income.

Fun Facts

The ever-popular online auction site eBay.com proves that with something to sell and an Internet connection, all of us have the ability to be salespersons. Whether you have an old computer, a collector's edition of a sports magazine, or a brand-new shirt that just isn't your style, there's likely to be a willing customer on eBay. Be warned though: Browsing through eBay is like entering a huge department store—you may end up leaving with something that you didn't need! Sellers need to be over eighteen, so you may have to wait a few years—but many items are worth more over time!

Related Careers

Store manager, marketing executive, consultant, advertising executive, real estate agent, store owner, entrepreneur, market researcher

SCIENTIST

Astronomer • biochemist • biologist • botanist • chemist • flavorist • genetecist • geologist • marine biologist • meteorologist • pharmacist • physicist • zoologist

The Basics

Scientists are people who are passionate and curious about the world around them. They use their knowledge of science to make new discoveries and improve life. Some scientists search for new or better ways to keep our environment clean and safe. Other scientists team up with doctors to develop medicines or search for cures to life-threatening illnesses, such as cancer. Many scientists work for universities, where they also teach, or for the government.

There are many different types of scientists, but they all share curiosity, intensity, and perseverance. Scientists need to have excellent analytical and logical skills that enable them to solve difficult problems and overcome challenges. Great writing and oral communication skills are also essential, as scientists must communicate their findings with the rest of the world.

If you want to become a scientist, there are loads of options—way too many to describe here. Here is a sampling of scientists:

Astronomers study how the planets, stars, galaxies, and the universe have existed and changed over time. Astronomers observe and record changes in stars, planets, and galaxies that they see through enormous telescopes. They generally work for observatories, universities, and planetariums.

Biochemists spend their days in the lab, developing ways to solve biological problems at the molecular level. They examine the characteristics of cells in living organisms. Biochemists figure out how cells function and interact with one another to form complex organisms.

Biologists seek to develop solutions for problems in the plant and animal world, such as how to cut down on pollution. Biologists often work for federal government agencies, such as the Environmental Protection Agency (EPA), Centers for Disease Control and Prevention (CDC), and the Department of Agriculture. There are many specialties within biology, including botany and zoology.

Botanists study plant life. They classify and identify different types of plants and explore the relationships between them. Botanists may study how and where plants grow and how environmental elements, like sun and soil, affect plant growth. Botanists work in colleges, gardens, horticulture industries, farms, and swamps.

Chemists study the composition, structure, and properties of things that exist in the material world. In addition, chemists conduct experiments to learn how matter (solids, liquids, and gasses) reacts to other matter. They often work in laboratories conducting experiments. Many work for companies that create products, such as food, paper, plastics, and pharmaceuticals.

Flavorists use their knowledge of chemistry to create and improve the flavor and aroma of foods from ice cream to potato chips. Flavorists work for food processing companies and in ingredient supply companies. They also work for government agencies, like the Food and Drug Administration and the United States Department of Agriculture.

Geneticists study genes. Every living thing has genes, and they help determine who we will become. What genes cause a person to have brown hair, brown eyes, and a deep voice? It all has to do with our parents' genes, and their parents' genes, and so on. Why do certain genes cause illness or congenital defects? Some geneticists try to pinpoint what genes cause those problems and then research ways to prevent them. Other geneticists work on ways to improve plants and animals. Geneticists who help government agencies solve crimes use DNA testing to make sure that the right criminals are put behind bars.

Geologists study rocks. They analyze the formation of rocks, interpret data about rocks in labs, and spend lots of time outdoors studying rocks. They may study minerals found in the earth, ice, fossils, and the Earth's crust. Geologists may work for federal government agencies or determine the value of land for folks in the oil and gas industry.

Marine biologists study the ocean and the organisms that live there. They examine how marine organisms, such as algae, plankton, and shrimps, develop; how they relate to one another; the way in which they adapt to their environment; and how they interact with their environment. Marine biologists work for universities, aquariums, and private wildlife organizations.

Meteorologists report and forecast weather conditions and study weather patterns that occur over time. They may work as weather forecasters for TV news shows, or they may work at weather support stations for the military. (The military relies on weather predictions when they schedule missile launches and troop movements.) Some meteorologists work at sea, predicting the weather for ships, so they can plan their trips around the weather conditions. Other meteorologists work for airlines, predicting weather for pilots, so they can have smooth and safe flights.

Pharmacists prepare drugs or medicines that doctors prescribe to help patients. It's their job to give patients the right strength and dosage of any given medication. They also provide their customers with instructions on how and when to take the drug, as well as any possible side effects. Pharmacists work for drugstores and hospitals.

Physicists try to make sense of the universe, from tiny subatomic particles to entire galaxies. Physicists may develop ideas about what causes a certain phenomenon in nature and create tests to support their ideas. The study of black holes, for example, falls under the umbrella of physics. There are many different types of physicists, too, such as astrophysicists and nuclear physicists. Most physicists work for universities, where they spend their time teaching, conducting research in labs, and writing articles.

Zoologists study everything there is to know about animals. They explore animals' history, their physical appearance, their upbringing and development, and their natural environment. Zoologists may work for zoos, state park and wildlife departments, universities, and organizations that work to protect wildlife and the environment.

Preparation

High School

Take all the science courses your school offers, like biology, chemistry, and physics, to find out if you have a knack for science. Ask questions about the world you live in. Search for answers by experimenting and reading science books and journals. Investigate extracurricular stuff after school—there may be a geology class or nature club you could participate in. In addition to your science courses, pay attention in math class—you'll need really sharp math skills to excel in the applied sciences.

College

In order to be a scientist, a college degree (typically a bachelor of science) is necessary. The classes you take will be specific to your major. For example, astronomy majors will take classes in stellar and galactic astronomy, while physics majors take classes such as electromagnetic theory and thermodynamics.

Possible Majors

Astronomy, biochemistry, biology, botany, chemistry, genetics, geology, marine biology, pharmacy, physics, zoology

Graduate School/Career Preparation

Although you can find work as an assistant for many of the fields discussed above, you will need to get a master's degree as well as an MD or a PhD to become a full-fledged scientist. That means that after college you may be in school for an additional two to six years. Requirements for each specialty vary.

Will I Be Rich?

Expect to put in long hours either working in the field, in a lab, or a combination of both. Scientists often think about their work hours after they leave their jobs each day. Most, however, are passionate about their careers, so they don't mind the long hours they put in. You won't get a bundle of money in exchange for your hard work, either. But then again, money is not what a scientist is searching for.

Fun Facts

Stargazin'

Galileo, astronomer, mathematician, and physicist, was the first person to use the telescope for astronomy purposes. Through his telescope, Galileo discovered the four closest moons of the planet Jupiter—Ganymede, Io, Europe, and Callisto.

[Source: www.socialstudiesforkids.com]

Red Alert!

According to the research of Frank J. Turano, a molecular biologist, plants can tell when you touch them. Even pressing on a leaf gently can alert the plant to possible danger and trigger the release of amino acids. Why does this happen? It thinks you're a bug that's about to grab a bite to eat; the plant is actually getting stressed out.

[Source: www.ars.usda.gov]

Nature's Thermometer

If you are camping and need to know the temperature outside, listen for tree crickets. Setting your watch for fifteen seconds, count how many chirps the cricket makes. Then, add the number 37 to the number of chirps you counted. The total of those two numbers should provide you with the accurate temperature in degrees Fahrenheit!

[Source: http://home.nycap.rr.com]

Quotes

"When I was 12, I saw my first Jacques Cousteau film, and I knew I wanted to work with animals—especially dolphins. I decided to become a marine biologist so that I could study, work with, and protect the creatures of the sea.
—*Alyssa Zahorcak, marine biologist*

"Trust your instincts and do what ever makes you tick. If this does not make sense now, revisit this advice after a few years!"
—*Ivan Damjanov, MD, PhD, prof. at the U. of Kansas, School of Medicine*

Related Careers

Doctor, engineer, professor, teacher, writer, astrologer, fisherman, farmer, florist, park ranger, veterinarian, astronaut

SHOE DESIGNER

The Basics

Ever wonder who created the funky platform shoes you see in stores or the cool sneakers that come out season after season? Shoe designers are the creative forces behind the scenes. Since we wear their creations, shoe designers play a role in our everyday lives. They design flip-flops, work boots, practical shoes, high heels, hiking boots, ballet slippers, and even snowshoes.

How does a shoe become a shoe? Shoe designers begin with an idea or a vision. They then prepare sketches that capture their vision, using a computer or drawing materials. Designers who work for a design or manufacturing company must present their sketches to people who work in marketing, sales, and production. If the design pitch goes over well and the sketches are approved, a prototype, or sample, is made of the shoe. Once the sample exists, the designer makes last minute adjustments to the style, fabric, and color to make the shoe perfect. After a review of the final sample, the shoe moves on to production and then into stores.

If a shoe designer works independently, he or she has more freedom to create shoes for individual clients or small boutiques. One drawback to this option is that you may not have a steady income.

Aside from being creative, talented, and in the know about fashion, shoe designers need to be practical, too. They need to figure out who will buy the shoes, what their function will be (for school or for the prom?), and how much they will cost. Since styles can change rapidly and with each new season, shoe designers are always busy coming up with new ways for us to dress our feet.

Preparation

High School

If you want to design shoes, start taking notes. Examine the craft of different types of shoes—stitching, arch support, heel size, and subtle little details. Pay attention to how shoe styles shift to fit clothing styles, and start sketching your own original designs. Sign up for whatever courses in art and design your school offers to get a head start.

College

You will need a college degree for most entry-level design positions, so it'll be wise to apply to colleges and design schools. Design programs should offer classes such as shoe design, fashion illustration, accessories design, and fashion art and history. In addition, you'll learn about anatomy, kinesiology, physics, and engineering—each come into play when designing shoes. Try to nab an internship with a shoe designer or fashion designer, and start building a portfolio of your work.

Will I Be Rich?

If people love your designs, you may earn a lot of money as a shoe designer. If you're a creative person who loves fashion and is obsessed with shoes, you might want to look into this career option.

Fun Facts

Nike, Nike, Nike

Nike is the world's leading shoe company, with its shoes and products sold throughout the United States, as well as in about 140 other countries! Controlling almost half of the nation's athletic shoe industry, Nike creates and sells shoes for running, baseball, basketball, golf, wrestling, and volleyball. They also offer the Cole Haan line of casual and dress shoes.

[Source: www.hoovers.com]

What Do You Call Your Sneakers?

- *Court shoes*
- *Cross trainers*
- *Deck shoes*
- *Dogs*
- *Football boots*
- *Freestyle*
- *Gym shoes*
- *Hoop shoes*

- *Joggers*
- *Kicks*
- *Sneaks*
- *Track shoes*
- *Trainers*
- *Treads*
- *Tyres*

[Source: www.sneakers.pair.com]

Related Careers

Artist, fashion designer, interior designer, costume designer, creative director, engineer

SKI OR SNOWBOARD INSTRUCTOR

The Basics

If you love to ski or snowboard, there may not be a better job than this: Ski or snowboard instructors spend their days on the mountain, teaching other people the ropes on the slopes. The age of the instructor's student can range from age 3 to 103, and the skill level can be anywhere from just beginning to really, really incredible. You don't actually need to be a ski or snowboard expert to be an instructor. If you teach beginners, for example, you don't need high-level skills. Most mountains offer training for their instructors—even the great ones. You're never too good to stop learning yourself!

To be a helpful instructor, you need to like people. Some students may not "get it" at first, so you'll have to be patient and friendly while they learn. First-time instructors usually teach beginners or younger students, and they are often slow to learn. It can be frustrating, though there is less pressure when you work with younger students. You may work with individual students or with larger groups of more than ten people.

Because the winter is only a few months long, it can be difficult to be a full-time ski instructor. Many instructors work a second job during the year. However, if you have enough experience, you can actually travel to the southern hemisphere during America's summer to teach skiing nearly year-round!

Preparation

High School

Get on the mountain as often as you can during weekends and holidays. Even if you can only ski or snowboard five times a year, that may be enough to start a career as an instructor when you graduate. Ask if you can observe some classes. Watching a few lessons will help you figure out whether teaching others how to ski or snowboard is the job for you.

College

A college degree may not be necessary, but it certainly can come in handy. People from all over the world will look to you for help and advice, so interpersonal skills can improve your teaching abilities. A degree such as psychology can help you achieve this. Try to teach on nearby mountains during holiday periods. Mountains are often overrun at those times, so instructors are sometimes hired just to work those busy holiday weekends. It's a good way to get your foot in the door and your feet on the slopes.

Possible Majors

Education, psychology, sport and leisure studies, recreation management, communications

Certification

There is a national organization called the Professional Ski Instructors of America (PSIA). If you can get certified with PSIA, you can work at most mountains in the country. PSIA certification varies from state to state, and there are different levels of teaching ability. The more training you complete with PSIA, the more likely you are to get raises, a better class schedule, and a better resume.

Will I Be Rich?

There's a big range of salary, depending on your experience. You might start at about minimum wage or you can be comfortable if you are successful and work a lot. The bad news is that it is nearly impossible to get rich by teaching others to ski or snowboard. The good news is you get a free pass and often discounts on gear or equipment. For obsessive skiers and snowboarders, that's worth more than money.

Fun Fact

People Just Can't Get Enough of It

Snowboarding is still a very new sport. It was added to the Olympic Games for the first time in 1998 at Nagoya, Japan. (Canadian Ross Rebagliati won the first gold medal in the sport.) By 2000 it was the fastest-growing sport in America!

Quote

"The best part of being a ski instructor is seeing people take to the sport. Some students have never skied before or aren't athletic; to get them to enjoy the sport and fall in love with it is extremely gratifying."

—Matt Gorman, ski instructor, Taos Mountain

Related Careers

Teacher, athlete, coach, manager, personal trainer, park ranger, environmentalist

SOCIAL WORKER

The Basics

Social workers help people with their problems. Whether a person has difficulty with personal relationships, is sick, or is unemployed, a social worker can help find a solution. In addition, social workers connect people to helpful resources, such as health services or job opportunities.

As a social worker, you may work in a hospital, community center, school, court, social service agency, or private practice. You may help arrange an adoption, provide counseling for substance abuse, or counsel an entire family with domestic problems. It all depends on your specialty as a social worker. No matter what the case may be, you will meet with your clients to determine the problem and suggest possible solutions. Then, to see whether the plan is working, you will continue to follow up with your clients and check on their progress. In some cases, you will refer them to other specialists for help or rehabilitation.

Compassion, patience, persistence, and excellent communication skills go into the making of a great social worker. But there's more to it than that. You'll need to know everything there is to know about all types of assistance programs for people in need. This is crucial if you want to refer clients to services that will help them effectively.

Preparation

High School

If your high school offers psychology or sociology classes, sign up. It's also helpful to speak to a social worker—if your school has one, set up an appointment to learn more about the job. Volunteering at a community center is a great way to find out what it's like to work with the public.

College

A college degree in social work is your best bet if you want to be a social worker. Social sciences will play a big part in your studies. For example, you'll learn about how race, gender, and ethnicity may factor into social issues. You'll also learn about math-related subjects; statistics will help you understand the data in social studies, and economics will enable you to prescribe financial solutions.

Possible Majors

Social work, sociology, psychology, public policy analysis, public health, anthropology, political science

Graduate School

While it's not always necessary, in most instances you will need a master's of social work, or MSW, to practice. In graduate school, you will have a chance to work in the field and gain experience while being coached. People who wish to conduct research or teach in graduate MSW programs go on to get a doctorate of social work, or DSW.

Will I Be Rich?

You won't earn tons of cash as a social worker, but the satisfaction of helping people in need is priceless. Of course, the job requires a lot of hard work. It's emotionally demanding and you will spend long hours meeting with clients and completing paperwork. It takes a certain type of person to stay in this job—a persistent person with a positive attitude. One social worker told us, "Helping people is contagious; once you start, you want to keep going!"

Fun Fact

How It All Began

Social work in the United States began in settlement houses back in the 1880s. Settlement houses were places for immigrants to take classes to help them adapt to life in America and learn job skills. These settlement houses not only helped immigrants to find jobs, but also provided schooling for children and after-school programs for children whose parents worked. Although their function has changed in some respects, settlement houses still exit today, offering a wide range of programs for the communities that they serve.

[Source: www.socialworker.com]

Quote

"It's a tough profession that's not respected much in our society, but it's a very necessary one. You really can make a big difference in someone's life."

—Aviva Kam, MSW

Related Careers

Counselor, career counselor, psychologist, guidance counselor, sociologist, clergy member, psychiatrist, teacher, professor

SOCIOLOGIST

The Basics

Sociologists study groups of people in society. They are part scientist, part detective, investigating why a person functions the way they do as part of a particular group. Sociologists first seek to define the behavior of a particular group. They then attempt to answer many questions, including: How do people in this group affect or influence one another? What different roles do people play in this group? How does this group interact with other groups?

Sociology is a broad area of study, so you will probably focus your research on a smaller part of society. You may study social relationships within the family, the education system, politics, business organizations, religious groups, or racial or ethnic groups. A sociologist takes into account each person's age, gender, and race to learn how these characteristics might play into an individual's role in the group. Your research will have many benefits; it could help resolve conflicts and help lawmakers and administrators solve social problems.

As a sociologist, you will spend a lot of time researching, writing about your findings, and presenting them. That's why the ability to think, write, and speak in a clear and intelligent manner is essential. Curiosity, an open mind, and a love of working with people will help you through some difficult and lengthy research projects.

Preparation

High School

Statistics and math classes will come in handy, since you will be required to collect and interpret the results of your research as a sociologist. Computer classes and English classes will also be of use, since you will be writing a lot. Many high schools offer sociology classes, too; they can help you recognize behaviors in your family, between friends, and in your classes.

College

You'll need to earn a college degree to be eligible for most entry-level jobs in this field. As a sociology student, you will study society from many different angles. Your class schedule will include courses like social stratification, urban sociology, rural sociology, world population, and statistics.

Possible Majors

Sociology, psychology, political science, public policy, social work

Graduate School

You can teach at some colleges with just a master's degree in sociology. But you'll need to go all the way and get your PhD if you want to become a full-time professor or work for a research institution or government agency.

Will I Be Rich?

While it's not likely that you will be rich as a sociologist, you will have a wealth of knowledge and an understanding of how society functions. The workload can be heavy and the hours long; but if you're passionate about your research, it's a very rewarding job. The more advanced degrees you have in this field, the better chance you have of earning more money.

Fun Facts

It's Written in the Stars

Three of the most important and influential sociologists were all born under the birth sign of Taurus:

- Karl Marx was born May 5, 1818.
- Herbert Spencer was born April 27, 1820.
- Max Weber was born April 21, 1864.

[Source: The Secret Language of Birthdays by Gary Goldschneider and Joost Elffers]

Read Up

Check out some of these publications put out by the American Sociological Association to get a taste for current issues in sociology:

- Social Causes of Violence
- Hate Crime in America: What Do We Know?
- How Neighborhoods Matter: The Value of Investing at the Local Level
- The Immigration Experience for Families and Children
- Families, Youth, and Children's Well-Being
- Youth Violence: Children at Risk
- Welfare to Work: Opportunities and Pitfalls
- The Realities of Affirmative Action in Employment

[Source: www.asanet.org]

Myth v. Reality

Myth: Sociologists are very outgoing, social people.
Reality: Some sociologists are shy. They do interview people, but they also spend a lot of their time alone behind the scenes analyzing information and writing research reports.

Related Careers

Anthropologist, psychologist, researcher, social worker, professor, counselor, statistician, journalist, marketing executive, politician

SPECIAL EDUCATION TEACHER

The Basics

Special education teachers have the same purpose as regular teachers—to educate students in a variety of subjects. The difference is that special ed teachers work with students with particular needs. Some students may not be able to learn very well. Others may have emotional disabilities, meaning they could get angry or upset easily. Still others have physical disabilities such as blindness, which make the learning process more challenging. Special ed teachers need to be able to handle these challenges while staying cool and calm.

The job of a special education teacher is demanding, but also rewarding. Many students who have difficulty learning can become frustrated, and some can become moody or even violent. It's your job to try to calm the student and re-focus his or her attention on learning. It's not an easy job. Still, the power to help students with special needs learn, express their feelings, and gain confidence keeps some teachers around for a lifetime.

Special education can begin with students even less than a year old. A professional special ed teacher usually does this early intervention in the home. In fact, special education teachers may work at a student's home or a hospital in addition to regular or special ed schools. Since there are fewer kids than in a regular class, teachers can dedicate more time to forming strong, meaningful relationships with each student.

Preparation

High School

Volunteer at children's hospitals and special education schools. Each student in a special education program has unique individual circumstances, and you should become familiar with some of the different ways that students might act in the classroom. That way you'll be comfortable when you're placed in your own classroom.

College

You can get a special education degree in college, which will start you on the right track for a career in special ed. If you graduate with this degree, you'll be able to work for a few years full-time. To get a sense of the workload, observe special education schools or classrooms. Talk to the teachers there; they love to share advice.

Possible Majors

Special education, developmental psychology, psychology, social work, occupational therapy, education of the deaf, child development, communication disorders, elementary education

Graduate School

Just like with regular education, you need a master's degree to continue teaching in special ed. The special education programs are often more complicated—with more required classes and more work—but you'll be better prepared by the time you're done. You'll have to decide what level of special education you want to teach, as well as which subject(s).

Will I Be Rich?

Like most teachers, special ed teachers work very hard with not many chances to get rich. Their work is important and very respectable, and special ed teachers are in great demand. The money isn't bad, but few special ed teachers are in it for the cash. You can live well on the salary, especially as you get older. Don't forget about the summer vacations, either! You can make more money if you work as an administrator (like the principal). You can even open up your own school someday!

Fun Fact

Making a Difference

Annie Sullivan was Helen Keller's teacher; she taught the deaf, blind, and mute girl to talk, read, and write. Helen Keller later said in a 1925 speech, "It is because my teacher learned about me and broke through the dark, silent imprisonment which held me that I am able to work for myself and for others."

[Source: www.lionsclubs.org]

Quote

"The best part of the job is seeing your students happy and having fun. It's truly wonderful to watch them getting excited about learning. You're always amazed at how smart kids are and how much you can learn from them. "

—Beth Cornwell, special education teacher, New York City

Related Careers

Teacher, physical therapist, occupational therapist, psychologist, social worker, sociologist, speech therapist

SPECIAL AGENT

The Basics

You've probably seen James Bond or Austin Powers in movies and wondered whether it's really possible to do what these guys do—chase down villains and solve mysteries. While these movies are fiction, the role of the special agent is not. Allow us to explain: A special agent, in the most general sense, is a spy or someone who secretly watches or investigates others. A special agent makes sure that government secrets remain secret and tries to obtain government secrets from other countries. The general goal is to protect whatever country they are working for and reduce the threat of foreign attacks.

As a special agent who works in and for the United States, you will work for federal and civilian intelligence agencies, such as the Central Intelligence Agency (CIA), the Federal Bureau of Investigation (FBI), the National Security Agency (NSA), the Defense Intelligence Agency, and the Department of Homeland Security. If you work for the CIA's clandestine service, you will travel overseas gathering and analyzing information about foreign countries and their respective citizens. If you work as a special agent for the FBI, you will work in the U.S. to catch law-breakers and protect the citizens. Your secret missions will require all sorts of skills and talent. Along the way, you could be asked to do almost anything, from finding a missing person to finding your way out of a dangerous situation. The job of a special agent can be risky and serious—not quite like the jokes and antics you see in a lot of special agent movies.

Good special agents are intelligent investigators and problem solvers. They are courageous and stealthy, and they work well under pressure. In cases where special agents must work undercover, good acting skills are important, too. In order to work as a special agent, you'll have to love adventure and dangerous challenges.

Preparation

High School

Problem-solving skills are important for a special agent, so pay attention in math and sign up for logic or statistics. History and other related classes, like government or law, will give you a head start; you will need to be savvy about the world you live in if you are going to try to uncover foreign government secrets. You may use a lot of computer programs and electronic gadgets in your line of work, so start building up your technological knowledge. In addition, staying in shape and maintaining a healthy lifestyle will physically prepare you to handle tough situations.

College

A college degree and excellent grades are necessary to become a special agent. A wide array of courses on the United States and foreign relations, including foreign languages, international affairs, international business, international economics, political science, pre-law, and government will best prepare you for this career.

International relations, international studies, international business, international economics, political science, pre-law, army ROTC, air force ROTC, navy ROTC, Marine Corps ROTC, criminology, psychology

Additional Preparation

If the life of a CIA clandestine service officer appeals to you, you will need to be a U.S. citizen under the age of thirty-five. Military experience is a plus, as is a major in international economics or international business. In addition, it helps if you earn a related graduate degree or are fluent in a foreign language. You'll need to pass medical, psychological, and polygraph (lie detector) exams, as well as an intense background check.

If you wish to join the FBI as a special agent, you will need to be a U.S. citizen between the age of twenty-three and thirty-seven; have a valid driver's license and a college degree; pass a polygraph exam, a drug test, and a color vision test; and have great eye sight. It is necessary to be in great shape, too. In addition, the FBI's extensive background checks can take up to four months.

Will I Be Rich?

You probably won't get rich as a special agent, but you can earn a comfortable living. Expect to work odd hours and be on call all the time—your life will never be short on adventure!

Fun Facts

Spy Flicks

- *The* James Bond: 007 *series (1962)*
- The Bionic Woman *(1975)*
- *The* Austin Powers *series (1997)*
- Face/Off *(1997)*
- *The* Spy Kids *series (2001)*

Related Careers

Detective, police officer, criminologist, corrections officer, military officer, FBI agent

SPEECH THERAPIST

The Basics

Speech therapists diagnose and treat a variety of speech, voice, and language disorders. Some people are born with these disorders; some develop them; and some get them after suffering from a brain injury, emotional problem, hearing loss, or stroke. A speech therapist's goal is to help patients to develop or recover communication skills so that they can better communicate in school, at work, and in their daily lives.

Speech therapists treat a wide variety of disorders. Some patients have harsh voices or inappropriate pitch (that means they speak too low or too high). Others have trouble speaking or understanding language, and some even have a hard time swallowing. These are all people who can be treated by a speech therapist. As a speech therapist, you administer tests to your patients to determine what communication problems exist. Next you will create a treatment plan that is specific to your patient's needs and keep detailed records of his or her progress. In situations in which an illness plays a role, you may join forces with a doctor to create a treatment plan. You will also meet with your patient's family to explain what to expect, and in some cases, how they can play a role in the patient's progress.

Compassion, patience, and commitment are important traits for speech therapists to have. In addition, excellent communication skills are required to work with patients and their families.

Preparation

High School

Volunteer at a hospital or health care facility that handles patients with speech and language impairments. The sooner you are exposed to people with speech and language problems, the better. Learn sign language so you can better communicate with the hearing-impaired. Take classes in anatomy, biology, psychology, English, and foreign languages.

College

Try to get an internship with a speech therapist in a private office, a hospital, or a health care facility. Learning on the job will give you a great opportunity to see what this career is all about. Sign up for classes in speech pathology, phonetics, psychology, speech and language development, and speech and hearing processes and disorders.

Possible Majors

Speech pathology, American Sign Language, communication disorders, linguistics, special education

Graduate School

If you plan to become a speech therapist, you'll have to swing by grad school and get a master's degree in speech pathology. In addition, you'll need to acquire up to 375 hours of supervised clinical experience, which means that you will work under the guidance of a speech therapist. You will also need to pass a national exam and put in at least nine months of post-graduate professional experience to get a license.

Will I Be Rich?

The demanding job of a speech therapist requires a great deal of patience and focus. Your schedule and the amount of hours you work will depend on whether you work in a hospital, school, or private office. You're likely to earn more money if you have your own private practice, but working as a speech therapist in any of these environments can make you rich in satisfaction.

Fun Facts

Did You Know?

You'd never be able to tell that someone like James Earl Jones, who is known for his distinctive voice, stuttered before undergoing treatment with a speech therapist. The following people have also shown us that a speech disorder is no barrier to success:

- Ludwig van Beethoven, German composer
- Joseph Biden, United States senator
- Lewis Carroll, author
- Bill Clinton, United States President
- Winston Churchill, former prime minister of Great Britain
- Walter Cronkite, journalist
- Kirk Douglas, actor
- Ron Harper, professional athlete (NBA)
- Stephen Hawking, astrophysicist
- Florence Henderson, actress
- Helen Keller, author
- Bob Love, professional athlete (NBA)
- Marlee Matlin, actress
- Marilyn Monroe, actress
- Curtis Pride, professional athlete (MLB)
- Carly Simon, singer
- Richard Thomas, actor
- John Updike, author
- Heather Whitestone, former Miss America
- Frank Wolf, United States congressman

[Source: http://ericec.org]

Related Careers

Audiologist, counselor, physical therapist, psychologist, speech pathologist, occupational therapist, special education teacher, sign language interpreter

STAGE TECHNICIAN

The Basics

Stage technicians (also called *stagehands*) create the stage setup for plays, conventions, or concerts. The job involves setting up the physical stage, as well as setting up the lighting and sound systems. There are many different types of stages, and each one has its own unique features. If the stage is for a rock concert, a technician may need all day to set up and then take down the stage. If the stage is for a Broadway play, it may take weeks to set up the perfect stage design. The rock concert may require special effects; the Broadway show may need specific props.

The work is laborious and may require lifting, pushing, pulling, and climbing. But it is also artistic because stage technicians are concerned with the visual aspect of the stage. They have to worry if the curtain is straight, if the lights create any unwanted shadows, or if the speakers are in the right places. Some stagehands have to appropriately position the props.

To be a good stage technician, you should be ready to work hard and sometimes operate on very little sleep. (Some events begin early in the morning and end very late at night.) It helps to have a specialty in electronics, carpentry, rigging, or mechanics because they all play a role in being a stage technician.

Preparation

High School

Get involved in student productions—student plays, talent shows, and anything that gives you familiarity with the stage. Learn from more experienced students and teachers. People should be willing to help you if you show that you're genuinely interested. Ask questions and do some reading on your favorite part of design or technology: lighting, sound, or video.

College

Look for a college with a good theater program. There are some schools that focus on this line of work. Unfortunately, most theater programs at universities have majors only for performers or designers (costume, lighting, or scenery). Even if you can't find a technician program, you can probably work for the theater department to get hands-on experience. Most universities are filled with student groups that produce theater, dance, opera, comedy, talent shows, or musical performances. If you're willing to put in the time, it should be easy to get involved. Ask questions and learn from others.

Possible Majors

Stage design, theater, theatrical lighting, art, music, recording arts technology, video art

Will I Be Rich?

Unless you own your own production company, it's not really possible to strike it rich. However, the work is rarely boring and occasionally done outdoors, which is nice. You get to work backstage at cool shows and concerts, and you may get to meet some stars. You probably won't have to spend money on a gym membership because the work should give you plenty of exercise!

Fun Fact

In Demand

The work of a stagehand is evolving with the times. Due to constantly changing technology, younger people are having better chances of doing well. Video projectors, wireless computers, and digital sound and lighting consoles (programs) are just a few of the areas of expertise that require extensive computer knowledge.

Myth v. Reality

Myth: Stage technicians just move around heavy objects
Reality: Many stage technicians are intelligent and creative. Their opinions are usually considered in decision-making processes. The experience of a stagehand can be invaluable to a good design or creative team (i.e., the set designer and director).

Quote

"You can get to see many shows free while working as a stagehand. I've seen many rock shows, operas, ballets, and national touring acts all for free! And sometimes (if you're *really* lucky) you can meet the members of some of these groups."

—David Plevan, production manager, PoliticalProductions.com

Related Careers

Carpenter, electrician, engineer, lighting/sound designers, audio engineer, musician, music conductor, rock star, artist, dancer, choreographer, set designer

STOCKBROKER

The Basics

A stockbroker buys and sells stocks on the stock market for his or her clients. The client can be one person who hopes to make a few extra bucks, or it can be a large organization that is investing millions of dollars. In either case, the broker is in charge of the deal, which includes the transfer of money and ownership of a stock certificate. (A stock is a representation of a part of a company. For example, if a company has a million stocks, each stock is worth one-millionth of the company.)

Stockbrokers interact with their clients, whether it's on the phone, online, or in person. In many cases they will have to give their clients advice on what stocks are a good investment. That means knowing which companies or corporations are most likely to be successful and make money. That also means knowing when is a good time to buy a stock and when is a good time to sell it. Because you'll be dealing with other people's money—and sometimes lots of it—being a stockbroker can be very stressful.

You'll have to know and understand the stock market very well to be a stockbroker. You may have to explain terms and practices to your clients, in addition to giving investment advice. And you should have a good working knowledge of economics and all the major corporations in the country.

Preparation

High School

It's never too early to start studying the stock market. Watch the financial news and read the *Wall Street Journal*. Keep your fingers on the pulse of the American economy because you'll be living in it as a stockbroker. If you can, visit the stock exchange in person. That's where you get to see the traders exchanging the stocks that the stockbrokers brokered.

College

No particular college degree is required to be a stockbroker, but there are many classes that can help you prepare for the career. Business, finance, and economics relate to the stock market. You'll also need to be familiar with buying and selling, so getting a job as a business salesperson can be a big help for your career.

Possible Majors
Business administration, finance, risk management

Licensing Exams

You need a special license to be an official stockbroker. To get that license you need to pass a test called the General Securities Registered Representative Examination. Depending on the state you work in, you may also have to pass another test called the Uniform Securities Agents State Law Examination. (Whew!) You also need to work for a few months at a brokerage firm. All of this is needed to prove that you know your stockbrokering stuff.

Will I Be Rich?

Stockbrokers have the potential to make a great deal of money. If you're ambitious and have a good sense of economics, you can literally make millions of dollars for other clients; if you do, you can expect to get a nice chunk of change, too.

Fun Fact

Here One Minute, Gone the Next

The Great Depression began when the stock market crashed on October 29, 1929 (called Black Tuesday). In the span of a few hours, thousands of incredibly rich people became completely broke! The Depression lasted until the 1940s.

Myth v. Reality

Myth: You will get rich if you work in the stock market.

Reality: You *can* get rich, but it can be difficult to acquire a pool of clients. And if you don't have many clients, you won't broker many trades, and you won't make much money at all!

Related Careers

Real estate agent, salesperson, financial analyst, banker, financier, accountant, investment banker

STORE OWNER

The Basics

A store owner is his or her own boss. They get to run their own businesses, selling stuff from accordions to ziti—and everything in between. Some store owners sell soap, others focus on food, and others trade toys. You can sell just about anything you want, as long as there are customers who want to buy your goods.

The life of a store owner can be fun and exciting, but it isn't easy. You need to work very hard because you'll be the person responsible for the store. No one will care about the store as much as you do, and there is tons of work to be done beyond working the cash register. You have to hire employees you can trust, order correct supplies from vendors, file necessary papers, and crunch numbers for accounting. There are thousands of mini jobs for a store owner.

Before you become a store owner, however, you need money, skills, and a drive to build your own business. But most of all, you need to have a love for the business that you go into. You'll live, breathe, and sleep whatever field you've chosen, so a passion for it is crucial. No detail is too small for a store owner, and yet he or she has to make huge decisions, too.

Preparation

High School

There is no greater experience for running a store than working in one. If it's possible, get a summer job or after-school job working at a successful store; it doesn't matter what it sells. Learn the ropes and ask questions. Imagine how you would run your own store, which things you'd do differently or the same to solve problems. Customer skills are important, so practice being social and polite.

College

While you're in college, go out and get real-world experience. If you haven't worked for other people, you may not know how to work for yourself. Focus on the field you like by reading about it or visiting those types of stores. Also, running a business involves English, math, and even science and history. So get a diverse education. You never know how other classes may help you in the future; if you can build a website, for example, you may improve your sales.

Possible Majors

Business administration, accounting, entrepreneurship, management

Graduate School

It may be pointless to attend more school if you aren't sure you like the field. But if you're sure of your goals, a business degree will help you run a store. At this point, though, be sure you've had some actual experience working in stores. Don't start a business unless you've worked for one!

Will I Be Rich?

There are some store owners who make millions of dollars. And there are other store owners who spend every penny they have trying to make their store succeed. So while you can get rich, it doesn't come easy. The amount of money you make is often in proportion to the work you put into it. You always have to seek out customers.

Fun Fact

Would You Like Fries with That?

In 1954, Ray Kroc, the founder of McDonald's, spent his entire savings to start his food business. He believed in the idea of fast food and moved out west to pursue his dream. His first store opened in Des Moines, Illinois, in 1954. Fifty years later his company had more than 25,000 McDonald's restaurants!

Myth v. Reality

Myth: It's great working for yourself!

Reality: Yes, working for yourself can be great, but it also means a lot of extra work. It's not automatic. The most successful businesspeople are the ones who discipline themselves the best.

Quote

"Don't be afraid to open your own store. There are a lot of hard challenges, and it is easier to get a job for someone else. You must push through the fear toward the more difficult, more winding road. The end result is often worth it."

—Adam Weitraub, owner of Toyscape, a Chicago toy store

Related Careers

Entrepreneur, landlord, salesperson

STUNT DOUBLE

The Basics

If you think your favorite actors perform all of the crazy stunts you see them do in the movies, think again. In most cases, professionally-trained stunt performers take the risks that keep you on the edge of your seat. Stunt doubles take the place of actors to perform dangerous scenes in movies, television shows, and commercials.

As a stunt double, you will work on a number of different movies and shows, much like an actor. You may have an agent who books jobs on movie sets and TV shows for you. On the set, you will work with a stunt double coordinator, who schedules the stunt doubles and the scenes in which they are involved. You will also work closely with actors and with any other stunt doubles involved in the project. For some movies, stunt doubles and stunt coordinators spend weeks perfecting a stunt scene before they film it.

A stunt double's job is mostly physical. You'll have to be in great shape and have a lot of training and experience to flawlessly perform stunts. Stunt double coordinators may seek out stunt doubles who are experienced martial artists, rock climbers, race car drivers, or even dancers. It's important to be an expert in at least one physical activity, but being versatile certainly helps. You will need to be courageous, adventurous, and adaptable to enjoy this line of work. It also takes a lot of discipline and physical and mental strength to perfect a stunt, so persistence and dedication are necessary.

Preparation

High School

Apart from gym class, you can seek out other physical activities—gymnastics, sports, and cheerleading, for example. Outside of class, you can take martial arts classes, such as karate or kickboxing, or you can take some dance classes. Since you'll be pretending to be another actor during your stunts, it's a good idea to take a few acting classes.

College

You don't need a college degree to develop amazing physical talents, but there are many outlets for physical activity on a college campus. In addition, you can learn more about film, TV, and acting.

Possible Majors

Theater, drama, musical theater, dance, radio and television, sport and leisure studies, athletic training

Stunt School

You will also have the option to attend classes in which you can learn how to become a stunt double. These classes will teach you to perform crazy stunts, while giving you a basic education about the film industry. In some cases, an internship on a movie set or a TV show can lead to your finding work as a stunt double.

Will I Be Rich?

It's possible to earn a lot of money performing dangerous stunts, but you will often put your own safety at risk in order to do it. As a stunt double, you will generally work on a freelance basis; if you work on a television show, you may sign a long-term contract. Due to the high risk of injury involved, most people don't stay in this field for very long. Lots of stunt doubles eventually become coaches and trainers for future stunt doubles.

Fun Facts

America's Legendary Daredevil

Evel Knievel was not a stunt double, but performing stunts was his claim to fame. In high school and in the military, he excelled in ice hockey, track and field, ski jumping, and pole vaulting. In 1962, he formed Evel Knievel's Motorcycle Daredevils; in this troupe, Kneivel performed a lot of wild stunts, like jumping over live rattlesnakes and riding through rings of fire. Later, he even cleared up to nineteen cars with his motorcycle and jumped across rivers and canyons. His success did not come without injury, though; during his career, Knievel broke thirty-five bones and suffered a brain concussion.

Actors Who Use Stunt Doubles:

- *Harrison Ford in* Raiders of the Lost Ark *(1981)*
- *Sandra Bullock in* Speed *(1994)*
- *Keanu Reeves in* The Matrix *(1999)*
- *Brendan Fraser in* The Mummy *(1999)*
- *Pierce Bronson in* Die Another Day *(2002)*
- *Cameron Diaz, Drew Barrymore, and Lucy Liu in* Charlie's Angels: Full Throttle *(2003)*

Related Careers

Actor, coach, agent, personal trainer, athlete, dancer, choreographer, stunt double coordinator, race car driver

TALK SHOW HOST

The Basics

If you love to talk and enjoy being the center of attention, you just may have what it takes to be a talk show host. Talk show hosts may work in radio or appear on television. They interview guests or take calls from listeners and may cover a wide range of topics, from current events to controversial issues. Talk show hosts who interview celebrities generally focus on their guest's career and recent projects.

Each day, you'll spend hours at the television or radio station preparing for your show. You may prepare questions, perform research for future shows, attend station meetings, and make sure your guests are comfortable before you go on the air. If you're a TV talk show host, you'll spend some time in wardrobe, having your hair and makeup done before the show starts.

To become a talk show host, you'll need great interviewing skills, a clear and interesting speaking voice, a dynamic personality, and a good sense of humor. Since you never know what to expect, you will need to be cool under pressure and be able to go with the flow; you'll want your guests to remain focused and comfortable throughout the show. Compassion, sensitivity, and lots of energy are traits that you will need when interviewing people.

Preparation

High School

You can gain some major experience speaking in public while in high school. Join the debate team, try out for the school play, run for class office, or try all three. At home, try recording your own talk show with a video camera or tape recorder. A good talk show host knows a lot about plenty of different things to be able to converse with a wide variety of guests; study hard to ensure that you receive a well-rounded education.

College

Classes that involve public speaking and acting will help you develop confidence in yourself. Better yet, take advantage of the opportunities your campus offers: You can host your own radio show, report for the campus TV station, start a public access talk show, or join the drama club.

Possible Majors

Journalism, radio and television, theater, communications, public relations

Will I Be Rich?

If your show receives good ratings (meaning that a lot of people tune in), and the station you work for likes your show, too, there is a chance that you can strike it rich. Some TV talk show hosts earn millions of dollars! Of course, you'll need to make sure you continue to feature interesting guests and topics to keep the viewers coming back, and that could require a lot of work. If your TV show is successful, you'll have a wealth of clothing; if you appear on TV each day, you'll need a large and varied wardrobe. Fans notice every detail.

Fun Facts

Did You Know?

Jerry Springer is a lawyer and politician. At the age of thirty-three, he was mayor of Cincinnati.

All of us know Oprah Winfrey for her compassionate top-rated talk show and her televised book club, but did you know that in 1971 at age seventeen, she was crowned Miss Fire Prevention in Nashville? It's true. And in 1973, while a sophomore at Tennessee State University, she became the first African American woman news anchor for a news show in Nashville.

[Source: www.time.com]

Related Careers

Actor, journalist/reporter, producer, editor, news anchor, disc jockey, VJ

TASTE TESTER

The Basics

Ever try to convince a friend why one brand of cola tastes better than another? If so, you may have what it takes to be a taste tester. Taste testers taste food and provide an opinion as to which food tastes, smells, and looks better. They may note if one brand is better than another brand or if they sense that an ingredient, such as sugar or salt, is missing or added. Taste testers evaluate a wide range of products including soda, chocolate, cookies, potato chips, fried chicken, wine, root beer, and coffee, to name a few. Taste testers can be any age and from any background—except when it comes to taste testing alcoholic beverages (then they must be over twenty-one). Survey or research companies who conduct taste tests for food or beverage companies generally hire taste testers.

As a taste tester, you will pay attention to the taste, texture, smell, and appearance of foods, beverages, and also ingredients. You will provide either verbal or written comments about the foods you taste, depending on what the survey asks for. Sometimes you will compare a variety of samples from one company; other times you will compare food from one company with food from a competing company. The opinions you provide about foods and beverages will help companies perfect their products.

In order to be a taste tester you need to have a great sense of taste, smell, sight, and be free of food allergies. You will need to pinpoint exactly why you like or dislike something or why it is better or worse than another brand. Therefore, you should be articulate and detail-oriented.

Preparation

High School

Conduct your own taste tests in your home or at school. All you need to do is find a few people who are willing to participate and then mix up a variety of cookies, crackers, juice—whatever. Ask your participants which samples they like the best and why. In addition, make sure to sprinkle your schedule with classes in health, nutrition, and science.

College

While you can get a job as a taste tester without a college degree, earning a degree will give you more options in the job market. You can take classes related to research, such as marketing and statistics, and those related to human behavior, like sociology and psychology. If you're interested in nutrition, sign up for classes such as biology, chemistry, data analysis, nutritional therapy, physics, and physiology.

Food science, dietetics, culinary arts, bioengineering, hospitality, nutrition, writing, marketing

Will I Be Rich?

If you work for a survey or research company and have a steady taste tester job, you can earn a decent living. If anything, you won't go hungry! If you participate in taste tests for a variety of companies, you may want to find a full-or part-time job since the money you make from taste tests will vary. You will have a lot of fun as a taste tester, and you will help food companies produce the best products.

Fun Facts

Pets Know Best

Your pet can be a taste tester, too! It's true—dogs are used to taste test dog food, and cats are used to taste test cat food. If a group of cats or dogs smell food and walk away, chances are that the food isn't too appealing. If a group of cats or dogs devour food, however, it's a good sign that the food will be a big seller.

Drink This

Popular taste-testing themes include regular coffee vs. decaffeinated coffee, whole milk vs. 2 percent milk, Pepsi vs. Coke (the infamous Pepsi Challenge), and believe it or not, water. Many water companies hold taste tests to demonstrate the fact that they are using new technology to improve the water's flavor. In addition to the flavor of the water, its clarity and odor may also be considered.

Related Careers

Critic, chef, caterer, nutritionist, restaurateur, waiter/waitress, wedding planner

TEACHER

The Basics

Teachers have one of the most important jobs in the world. Their job is to educate students, including those who might not be the slightest bit interested in learning. The students can be any age, and the subject matter can be one of many possible subjects—or all of them. Teachers can work in public or private schools, primary or secondary.

In addition to what you see teachers do in the classroom, teachers spend time planning lessons and grading homework and tests. For ten months a year, the work rarely ends. Fortunately, teachers have the summers off (though they can teach classes in summer school for extra pay). That time off can be very important, as teachers need to experience life themselves; learning to do other things makes them better teachers back in the classroom.

To be a good teacher, you need be outgoing, confident, creative, patient, and open minded. You need to work well with others—both adults and children—and you should have good communication skills so you can listen and explain effectively. Your goal as a teacher is to see your students mature in terms of what they know and how they act. It's your job to help them discover their own talents and unique personalities. You never know who could be a budding Albert Einstein.

Preparation

High School

If you're serious about being a teacher in high school, start teaching! You can be a big brother or big sister in a peer-tutoring group. Help out with a sports team during school, or work as a camp counselor in the summer. Be well versed in all the major subjects, and be sure to take foreign language classes. Spend time with kids, even if it means babysitting on Saturday nights.

College

An education degree in college allows you to teach for a few years. If you want to continue teaching after that point, you will need a master's degree. You don't have to study education, though. You can study what you love, whether it's art, history, or science, for example. Later on, you can learn how to teach what you know. Outside of school, volunteer at any organization that helps kids.

Possible Majors

Education, elementary education, special education, teaching English as a second language, art education, music education

Graduate School

You need a master's degree to be a permanent teacher. Many teachers work toward their master's degree while they teach at a school. Others focus on graduate school full-time, which can take around two years. This is the point where you'll decide what you want to teach—which subject and which grade level (K–5, or 6–12).

Will I Be Rich?

The teaching experience is rich and rewarding; many teachers will say that the satisfaction you get from helping children can't be matched by money. However, when it comes to money, it's not usually great. You can live on it, and you usually get paid more with more experience. The free time is a big plus; few other professions have as much vacation time, and that can be priceless.

Fun Fact

Teachers Needed!

Teachers' jobs are not only incredibly important, they're also almost always in demand. There are currently more than three million teachers in America for more than fifty million students. As the student population grows, more teachers will be needed. Some people estimate that schools will need to hire 200,000 teachers every year!

[Source: www.ericfacility.net]

Myth v. Reality

Myth: Some kids can't learn.
Reality: Every student is able to learn; it's your job to find the way!
Myth: Every kid learns the same way.
Reality: That's not true! That's why you have to change your approach for every individual.

Related Careers

Guidance counselor, principal, professor, child care worker, social worker, test developer

TEST DEVELOPER

The Basics

You're probably pretty familiar with tests by now. Most likely, you take them all the time in your classes and sometimes for special reasons (to get into a certain school, for example). Well, somebody has to create those tests. In most cases, that will be your teacher. But for the statewide and national exams, there are special test developers who write the test and put it together. Test developers are the people who try to assess a student's abilities in a fair, logical, and consistent way. This sounds a lot easier than it actually is.

Testing is currently a controversial subject in America. Teachers are spending more time than ever preparing students for standardized tests. Some people think this means that students simply learn material to pass tests instead of learning why material is important. But testing serves a useful purpose; how else would anyone know if students are learning? A well-designed exam can also help show if a teacher is doing his or her job right. The real trick is to design a test with questions that accurately measure a student's knowledge of a subject.

To be a good test developer, you need great analytical skills. That means thinking critically so you can find any possible problems with every single question on an exam. Every question a test developer writes goes through a lengthy proofing and testing stage. For example, a question gets field-tested by students, checked for accuracy and bias, and edited for clarity. You can be involved in any of those stages. Tests have such importance for students today that a devoted and dedicated test developer can make a difference in thousands of students' lives.

Preparation

High School

Standardized tests become more commonplace in high school. You'll have to take the PSAT and SAT, and you might have high school exit exams, too. Study hard for these exams; analyze the released tests, and try to understand why the test developers chose their questions. A course can teach you a lot about these tests. Talk to your teachers about how they constructed their exams, and try to develop your own test—even for nonschool-related subjects.

College

A test developer will need to be well versed in many different subjects. For example, to get the most possible work, you could be knowledgeable in math, biology, and physics. In other words, while you're in college, don't choose too narrow a study. Major in anything you like, but broaden your horizons. If you end up working on tests, a range of skills will help you more than any one specialty.

Possible Majors

Mathematics, computer and information science, English, biology, physics

Will I Be Rich?

Many test developers get paid per each question they write. If you can write a lot in a short amount of time, you can make a good living. But beware: It can take a lot of time to come up with even a single good question. The work can be frustrating at times, though its importance can't be denied.

Fun Fact

The Birth of Test Preparation

For many years, ETS, the company that creates the SAT, swore that you could not prepare for their exam. Their employees said that studying for it didn't help much at all. Well, they were wrong! In the 1980s, The Princeton Review found that students can significantly raise their scores if they know how the test works. ETS was forced to change the way they developed their tests.

Myth v. Reality

Myth: Tests measure a student's intelligence
Reality: Tests only measure a student's ability to take tests and their knowledge of the material. No test you take in school measures intelligence.
Myth: It's unfair that students have to take so many tests.
Reality: It can be frustrating to take many tests. But it's the most tangible way to show what you know. You should look at exams as opportunities to show off your knowledge.

Related Careers

Teacher, professor, writer, editor, mathematician, computer technician

TOUR GUIDE

The Basics

Tour guides educate groups of people about where they are and what they're looking at—from neighborhoods, museums, and historical sites to parks and other locations. They can lead their tour group on foot, walking around the site, or on a vehicle like a bus, to cover a wider tour area. Tour guides share cool information about artwork, monuments, shopping, notable historical events—whatever information is relevant to the tour topic.

As a tour guide, you will be a navigator, teacher, historian, manager, caregiver, and in some cases, a travel agent, too. You will escort your group, look after them, and share information with them about their surroundings. If you work for a museum, they may instruct you as to what to say to visitors, but in most cases, you will need to perform your own research in order to prepare your lectures. If you work for a small company or run your own tour company, you may be able to design the tour from scratch. That way, you can personalize your tour by providing obscure trivia and other hard-to-find facts.

A career as a tour guide demands a lot, including a gift for speaking in front of large groups and the ability to remain calm and in control under all circumstances. In addition, tour guides need to be organized, responsible, and punctual. It helps if you are in great shape, too, since you will probably be walking a lot! Above all, you have to know your stuff—your tour group will usually pay money for your time and expertise.

Preparation

High School

As a tour guide, you'll need to call upon your knowledge in many different areas, but history, art history, drama, debating, and English will probably be most useful. Take first aid classes and CPR training, too, in case of an emergency en route. Read up on famous sites and locales to figure out which ones interest you the most. If you want to lead local tours, you can start by visiting local tourist offices and libraries. Gather information about hot spots and attractions such as museums and haunted houses, and go for a test run with a couple of friends.

College

While a college degree isn't required to be a tour guide, a history or art history major will give you a real edge in this career. If you wish to lead tours outside of the United States, you can study a foreign language and study abroad for a semester as well. Many tour companies hire college students to lead local and national tours during summer and winter vacations, so it may be easy to gain some experience.

Will I Be Rich?

If you work full-time, year-round as a tour guide, you can pull in a decent salary. You can make a little extra from tips, too, if you know what you're talking about. Although you may end up working twelve-hour-plus days and living a hectic, always-on-the-go life, your transportation, meals, and accommodations are usually taken care of. Most tour guides work as freelancers for a number of different tour companies in order to work throughout the year.

Fun Facts

Things You Might Learn from a Tour Guide:

- Strawberry Fields in New York City's Central Park consists of two and a half acres filled with 125,000 strawberry plants in honor of the former Beatle John Lennon.

- The Golden Gate Bridge in San Francisco is one of the strongest bridges ever built. Supposedly, it can withstand winds of over one hundred miles an hour. The bridge is a rusty red color because the architect, Irving Morrow, thought it would look nicer against the setting sun than a black or gray bridge.

- Gustave Eiffel, a French engineer, designed the Eiffel Tower in Paris, France. The Eiffel Tower was completed in 1889 for the Paris world exhibition. It took 132 workers and fifty engineers two years to build it.

    [Source: www.parisdigest.com and www.theinsider.com]

Related Careers

Flight attendant, hotel manager, translator, travel agent, teacher

TRAIN OR SUBWAY ENGINEER

The Basics

A train engineer drives trains from one station to another. The engineer may drive a *freight train*, which transports all sorts of cargo. The engineer may drive a *passenger train*, which transports people from place to place. Most trains run on diesel fuel, but some locomotives are electric. The engineer is responsible for just about everything that affects their vehicle—not just whether it arrives on time.

Engineers must use their technical knowledge to ensure that their locomotive is safe and prepared for service, even before the train rolls out of the station. Engineers use the train's controls to speed up or slow down the locomotive around curves and straightaways. They must follow railroad rules and orders from traffic control. They also keep on eye on gauges, making sure that (among other things) the train's speed, air pressure, and battery charge are all at appropriate levels. There are many small details that affect a train's performance, such as the number of cars or what's in them. As an engineer, you have to be aware of all of these factors.

Because train transportation goes on twenty-four hours a day, many engineers work odd hours. If you drive a freight train, you may find work whenever cargo needs to be shipped. Work on a passenger service affords a more predictable schedule. People who drive streetcar or passenger trains are often called operators. They generally don't work for the railroads, but instead for a city's mass transit system. The work is similar, though.

Preparation

High School

You can't be an engineer until you're twenty-one years old. But don't let that stop you now! Visit your local railroad station. If you show enthusiasm and interest, you might get a tour of the locomotive train yard. Better yet, a summer job working on the railroad can start you on the right track to becoming an engineer!

College

You don't need a college degree to become a subway engineer, but earning one could work to your advantage. You can learn about other types of engineering, such as mechanical engineering, as well as other topics that you will use on the job, such as physics and communication.

Possible Majors

Physics, electrical engineering, mechanical engineering, engineering, physics, automotive engineering

Additional Training

To become a train engineer, you need to enroll in a special training program for engineers. That's where you'll learn all about running a locomotive; you'll even get to practice on a simulator! Depending on where you want to work, this program may come with the job. You'll need to show you know the rules of the railroad, such as what train signals mean. Plus, you must pass a test showing you have good eyesight and hearing. For a streetcar or subway operator, you'll need to prove you know all the safety and emergency measures. There may also be other hoops to jump through, depending on your employer.

Will I Be Rich?

Because train engineers are one of the most skilled workers in the railroad industry, they get paid well for their work. Passenger train engineers usually get paid more than freight train engineers. It's not really possible to become a millionaire as an engineer, but driving a train is like a dream come true for locomotive fans.

Fun Facts

East Meets West

The railroads totally changed America. Once the railroad system was set up, people were able to send goods all around the country. An important date in American history is May 10, 1869. That's when railroad tracks from the west coast connected with the tracks from the east coast. The lines met in Promontory, Utah, and travelers were then able to take a train from New York to San Francisco.

Related Careers

Bus driver, taxi driver, pilot, auto mechanic, engineer, mathematician

TRANSLATOR

The Basics

Translators play a vital role in society, bridging the gap between different cultures and languages. Also known as interpreters, translators spend their days translating documents, speeches, and conversations from one language to another. This means that translators must be able to write and speak fluently in at least two languages, although many translators know several. Some translators know two languages as a result of their cultural backgrounds, while others study foreign languages in school.

Sure, most of us know a few words in another language; some of us can hold conversations in Spanish, French, Italian, or German, just from having taken these language courses in high school. But becoming a translator is no easy task. Translators don't just spit out the textbook meaning of a sentence in another language—they must also translate the tone and intonation of the speaker (the *way* they say it). If you translate books, articles, and legal documents, you will find that the proper translation can make the difference between a beautifully written story and a dry tale, or between clear legal instructions and a confusing muddled mess.

Translators may find work in a number of different companies and organizations. They may work for international businesses, law offices, colleges and universities, courts, and even in the United Nations. If you want to be a successful translator, you'll have to know about the subject matter of the material you're translating. For example, it would be difficult to translate legal documents without being familiar with legal lingo in both languages. Multilingual people with great communication skills and an ability to focus on detail can excel in this field.

Preparation

High School

The most important classes in school will be English and foreign languages—take as many as possible. If you hope to translate books and documents, practice by translating newspaper and magazine articles from one language to another. If you want to become an interpreter, listen to foreign language radio stations, and see how many words you can translate. If your high school has clubs for each foreign language offered at school, sign up.

College

While you will probably focus on one additional language in college, it's a good idea to take classes in other languages, too. Learn about the culture in the country or countries where your new language is spoken. Anthropology, sociology, history, and political science may also give you some insight into foreign cultures. If possible, travel abroad for a semester in a non-English speaking foreign country.

Possible Majors

Spanish, Arabic, Chinese, French, German, Hebrew, Italian, classics, Japanese, Korean, linguistics, modern Greek, Portuguese, Russian, any other language

Career Preparation

To obtain a job as a translator, you may have to translate some documents, present an oral translation, or answer questions about the country where the language is spoken. You will usually complete a training course once you are hired, and you may need to pass an exam to become certified.

Will I Be Rich?

Most interpreters work on a freelance basis and receive hourly pay, while some work in full-time positions for organizations such as the United Nations. You may get to travel frequently as a translator. Those who translate text are often paid per word, so the bigger the book, the bigger the financial reward.

Fun Facts

Bet You Didn't Know. . .

There are almost 3,000 different languages and more than 7,000 dialects spoken in the world. Dialects are different versions of a language specific to a certain region; pronunciation, vocabulary, and definitions of words may differ from languages. Over 1,000 different languages are spoken in Africa. Somalia is a rare exception in Africa; everyone in Somalia speaks the same language—Somali.

The World's Top Five Most Widely-Spoken Languages

1. Chinese (Mandarin)
2. English
3. Hindustani
4. Spanish
5. Russian

[Source: www.factmonster.com]

Related Careers

Professor, teacher, linguist, writer, editor, publisher, printer

TRAVEL AGENT

The Basics

Travel agents make traveling easier for vacationers and businesspeople by helping them make travel arrangements. They help book and purchase plane tickets, hotel rooms, rental cars, and anything else that travelers may need. In addition, when people aren't sure where to go, travel agents help them find the perfect destination.

As a travel agent, you will work closely with your customers to help them find accommodations that suit their interests and are also within their budget. In addition, you'll provide your customers with information on weather conditions, tourist attractions, restaurants, and hot spots that they can visit on their trip. For customers who are traveling to foreign countries, you'll let them know if they need a visa in addition to their passport, and you can provide information on how to obtain these forms of identification. You will also make sure they know what type of currency they'll need to use on their travels and what the current exchange rate is.

In order to provide reliable information about where to go, when to go, and what to do while they are there, you will need to perform some additional research and even travel yourself. This may sound like an easy job, but it carries a lot of responsibility. Giving someone the wrong flight information or sending them to an awful hotel will not be good for your business. Travel agents need to be superorganized, patient, and good with people.

Preparation

High School

Travel and explore—other neighborhoods, towns, states, and even countries. This will start to give you an idea of all the options that are out there. The more places you get to experience firsthand, the better you will be able to advise travel customers in the future. Foreign language classes will allow you to communicate with people at airlines, hotels, and cruise lines across the globe. Of course, it's important to know your geography, too.

College

College courses such as accounting, communications, geography, marketing, and foreign languages can provide you with some very useful information, though a degree is not required. Still, many schools have programs in travel and tourism, and the degree will give you an edge (as will a part-time job at a travel agency).

Possible Majors

Travel and tourism, hospitality, communications, recreation management

Vocational Schools

After you earn your high school diploma, you may elect to go to a vocational school and take either a six- to twelve-week full-time travel agent program or an evening and weekend program. These programs cover the basics of the travel industry, and you'll pick up a lot of useful skills and tips.

Will I Be Rich?

You may work long days and spend many hours in front of a computer screen, but the job does have its perks. Despite the fact that you won't get rich quick at this job, you will be entitled to travel discounts! To someone who loves to travel, this is an excellent benefit, and it can actually save them a lot of money.

Fun Facts

Exotic Destinations

- The Galapagos Islands *consist of thirteen major islands off the coast of Ecuador. If you want to see wildlife, such as iguanas, birds, and giant tortoises up close, this is the place to visit!*

- Turtle Island, Figi, *is a beautiful, romantic paradiselike island full of picture-perfect beaches.*

- Phuket, Thailand, *surrounded by the Andaman Sea, is a beautiful tropical island in Southeast Asia.*

- Christmas Island, *a tiny island in the Indian Ocean, is Australian territory, although it is closer to Java, Indonesia. This magical island is full of wildlife, a rich rain forest, and beautiful beaches.*

- Phi Phi Islands, Thailand, *surrounded by cliffs and hidden bays and beaches, is the perfect spot for scuba divers and fishers.*

Related Careers

Tour guide, flight attendant, real estate agent, pilot, wedding planner, train or subway engineer

VETERINARIAN

The Basics

If you love animals and want to keep them happy and healthy, you may wish to become a veterinarian. Veterinarians, or vets, diagnose and treat animals that are sick; they also make sure healthy animals stay that way. They give animals shots to keep them free of diseases such as rabies. When animals are sick or injured, vets give them medicine, perform surgery, or treat their wounds. Vets also provide pet owners with tips about what to feed pets and how to train and care for them.

When an animal is sick, you will first speak with its owner or caretaker to find out what the problem is. Then it's your turn to examine the animal, make a diagnosis, and create a plan of action for treatment. You will use a variety of medical equipment, like stethoscopes, and surgical instruments to treat animals. You may work in an animal hospital, a private practice, or a lab. Some vets treat dogs, cats, birds, and other pets, while other veterinarians treat farm animals, such as pigs, sheep, horses, and cows. There are also vets who treat and care specifically for zoo animals. If you care for farm or zoo animals, you will need to travel to your patients to treat them.

If you're a vet, you should adore animals and feel comfortable handling and treating them. You must also be able to communicate with their owners or caretakers. Compassion, dedication, and patience go a long way with finicky animals and nervous owners.

Preparation

High School

Volunteer in a local animal hospital or animal shelter. You can learn a lot by being around animals and caring for them. Also, try to set up an informational interview with a veterinarian, and ask questions about his or her day to day experiences. Biology, anatomy, chemistry, and other science courses will be most helpful later on down the road.

College

Sign up for pre-veterinary courses, such as chemistry, biology, genetics, math, physics, and animal sciences to help you get into a veterinary school. Experience working with animals, especially in a vet clinic, is usually available through internships.

Possible Majors

Pre—veterinary medicine, biology, chemistry, agriculture, animal science, pharmacology, wildlife management

Required Testing

In order to apply to veterinary school, you will need to take the Graduate Record Examination (GRE), the Veterinary College Admission Test (VCAT), or the Medical College Admission Test (MCAT), depending on what each school you apply to requires. Be sure to study hard—veterinarian schools are hard to get into.

Graduate School

You will need to earn a Doctor of Veterinary Medicine and obtain a license from the state you plan to work in to become a veterinarian. Your graduate and doctorate coursework will include mostly science classes and hands-on experience diagnosing and treating animals and performing surgery on them. After four years of classes, you will need to complete a three-year residency and then pass the veterinary medicine licensing exam.

Will I Be Rich?

Not only will you be rich in joy knowing that you are helping to save animals, but you'll also earn a great living. While the job is demanding and often requires you to be on call at all hours, it's a job that leaves most vets feeling satisfied at the end of the day.

Fun Facts

Be Your Pet's Best Friend

- Although your cat may go wild for raw fish, meat, or liver, you should keep him or her away from these raw foods. They may have parasites and bacteria that could be harmful.

- If you are a chocolate junkie, be sure to keep your sweet tooth to yourself. Chocolate is a known poison for dogs.

[Source: www.eastsideanimalhospital.com]

Quote:

"It's wonderfully fulfilling to help animals that are in pain or suffering get better. Seeing the joy that healthy pets bring to a family makes this the greatest job in the world."

—Dr. George L. Cameron, Cameron Animal Hospital, New Jersey

Related Careers

Biologist, chemist, doctor, zoologist, crocodile hunter, animal trainer

VIDEO GAME DEVELOPER

The Basics

If you have a passion for video games, you might want to design video games for a living. Most video games require a team of people, so a game developer can have many different jobs. Artists invent the game environments and create the characters. Designers use creativity and planning to make the game work the way it's supposed to. Programmers write the computer code that gives the machine instructions about what to do. Producers track the project and make sure it's on time and within budget. Each person employs a specific skill to make the game work.

A game for a major video game system may require a team of twenty-five to seventy people. And even with many people working on a game (sometimes working very long hours) it may take as long as three years to finish a video game. Developing a video game from a vision to an actual working product can be a *huge* project.

Depending on your role as a video game developer, you will need certain talents. For example, a texture artist should be familiar with animation or 3D-model building software. A tester makes sure that the game works and plays without any unexpected bugs. Being creative and having many different computer skills will give you the best advantage.

Preparation

High School

Play video games. That's important because you need a sense of what has already been done and what video gamers expect from a new game. You need to know what you like and what you don't like, and what is fun and what isn't. You can only learn that by playing games yourself. But that doesn't mean school isn't important! Take as many computer classes as you can. Don't underestimate any school subject because you never know what you'll need to create a realistic and innovative game. For example, you will need to know your history to develop a good World War II shooter game.

College

Art is the biggest part of most video games, so try to learn some computer art programs. Study physics and math, too. As games get more advanced, they use physics to imitate reality. For example, a developer who has studied physics knows that if a car flies up in the air, its tires fly off. Computer science is a great subject to study for aspiring programmers. Some colleges even have computer game design classes! And some video game companies offer internships to college students. An internship will give you a look at the people that publish, market, and create the games!

Video game design, computer and information science, computer graphics

Will I Be Rich?

It depends on who you're working for and how successful your project is. Many developers earn royalties on their video games. That means if your video game is really popular, you can make more money. Successful developers go on to start their own companies, which can bring in a lot of money.

Fun Fact

Pong

Most people consider Pong to be the first video game. Ralph Baer, a TV engineer, developed the game in 1972. The game was a computer version of ping pong, with a dot going from one side of the screen to the other. Games sure have come a long way since then!

Myth v. Reality

Myth: Designing games is fun and easy!
Reality: It can be fun, but it's a lot of hard work. Some game designers work twelve to fifteen hours a day!
Myth: You get to play video games all day.
Reality: You get to play the game at the end of the project to make sure it works the right way.

Quote

"Making video games takes time, focus, and determination. A project can potentially take up years of your life. If you're successful at it, you're doing everything you can to make the game as good as possible."
—*Daniel Suarez, senior producer,* Vivendi Universal Games

Related Careers

Computer technician, programmer, web producer, developer, mathematician, engineer, scientist, graphic designer, illustrator, artist

VJ

The Basics

A television VJ, or video jockey, announces upcoming music videos, interviews hot new or established music stars, and basically serves as a role model of sorts for teens and young adults. Sound like the ideal job? If you answered yes, you are not alone! Young people all over the world dream of being VJs for music programs like those on MTV. In addition, video jockeys can also work in clubs or at concerts, just like DJs. But instead of mixing up sounds for a crowd, they're mixing up video images that are projected on the wall.

As a VJ, you will need to be hip, fashionable, and supercool. But since hip, fashionable, and supercool mean different things to different people, the most important thing you will need to be as a VJ is yourself. Your job will be to connect with music fans and provide a fresh perspective on topics relating to music and popular culture. Since your job will revolve around music, a deep-rooted passion for music and an understanding of trends in the music industry are necessary for this career!

Since you will spend a lot of time in front of a camera as a television VJ, you will need to be able to stay calm, keep cool, and put on a really good show. While on the air, you may interact with special guests or a studio audience, so your communication skills will be in constant use. A cool, original style and a great personality will be your best assets as an aspiring VJ, but school and street smarts and tons of energy are also essential.

Preparation

High School

Take advantage of any opportunity to be onstage or on camera—play an instrument, sing, act, and dance in school productions; or take lessons in any of these disciplines. Keep up with popular music, and check out VJs on TV for some pointers. Work on developing your own style, but make sure you remain true to yourself. If you dream of being a TV star, keep your eyes peeled for news about VJ searches like those held by MTV.

College

You don't need a college degree to be a VJ. In fact, most television VJs are between the ages of sixteen and twenty-five, so some aren't even old enough to be in college! But since not many VJs have long-lasting careers in this field, it'd be smart to secure a college degree. Continue to play music, act, sing, and dance, and work as a DJ (disc jockey) for your college radio station. You can also take video art classes and produce your own music videos of local bands or performers or create videos for use in clubs.

Possible Majors

Music, art, dance, theater, musical theater, voice, music education, music management, journalism, radio and television

Will I Be Rich?

There are a lot of perks to being a VJ on a major network. You'll most likely have tons of fans, a cool wardrobe, lots of CDs, and free tickets to loads of concerts, parties, and other events. Although you may find work as a VJ on another music network, MTV will probably get you the greatest amount of exposure. This job involves a lot of time rehearsing and preparing for your show, as well as makeup and hairstyling sessions before going on the air. If you work as a VJ in nightclubs, you'll probably make less money and acquire less fame, but you'll have a live audience and the freedom to VJ as you please.

Fun Fact

VJs come and go faster than you can say "music video." How many past and present MTV VJs have you seen in action?

- Nina Blackwood
- Eddi Brokoli
- Downtown Julie Brown
- Juliya C
- Jesse Camp
- Adam Curry
- Carson Daly
- Anusha Dandekar
- Dewi
- DJ Clue
- Damien Fahey
- Mark Goodman
- Nadia Hutagalung
- Kennedy
- La La
- Benji and Joel Madden
- Jenny McCarthy
- Matt Pinfield
- Quddus
- Sarah Sechan
- Shanty
- Jim Shearer
- Jesse (Snider)
- Martha Quinn

Related Careers

DJ, actor, musician, news anchor, rock star, writer

VOLUNTEER

The Basics

Volunteers help with projects or tasks without receiving any pay. Why do they do it? To help people live better lives. In every town, city, and country, volunteers make a difference by donating their time to an important cause. Volunteers can choose to improve conditions overseas in a foreign country or in their own community. People of all ages and backgrounds choose to be volunteers.

As a volunteer, you may help with a number of different projects. You may build houses, assist farmers, or work in a soup kitchen or shelter. You can work at a hospital or administer health care to those who are ill but can't afford treatment. You can teach in classrooms or help develop programming for underprivileged students. For some jobs, you may need special skills or experience; for others, all you need are commitment, dedication, and a lot of love for humanity.

Life as a volunteer isn't glamorous. In fact, it may be unlike anything you've ever done before. Many programs send volunteers overseas to places like Africa, Asia, Central and South America, Eastern and Central Europe, and the Middle East. If you commit to helping out in a foreign country, you may need to learn new languages and familiarize yourself with new cultures. You may have to adjust to different living conditions. During your period of service, you may share an apartment with other volunteers or live with a family in another country. Although some volunteers may experience culture shock when they help out overseas, the experience is almost always incredibly fulfilling and educational.

Preparation

High School

It's never too soon to start volunteering. If there's a local hospital, school, shelter, or community project for which you would like to volunteer, go for it. There is always a cause that needs volunteers. You can volunteer your time at school, too—as a tutor or as an organizer of a food drive or another charitable project.

College

Whether or not you need a college degree to volunteer depends on where you plan to offer your services. The Peace Corps, for example, generally requires its volunteers to have a college degree. In college, you can pursue a major that you can use in your work as a volunteer, such as anthropology, teaching, pre-medicine, or a foreign language. Since most people cannot afford to volunteer forever, your college degree will help you obtain a paying job later. Be sure to check out volunteer opportunities throughout the school year and during semester breaks.

Possible Majors

Public policy, anthropology, education, economics, foreign languages, nutrition, political science, pre-med, pre-law, peace studies

Additional Requirements

Some volunteer programs will require that you undergo training or that you have a college degree in order to participate. Contact a program's coordinator if you have any questions before signing up.

Will I Be Rich?

Nope. You won't actually receive any pay for the work you do, although some volunteer programs do provide some sort of compensation. Many programs pay for your food, housing, and transportation. In addition, you may receive some money for your service, which is sometimes applied to help pay for student loans. Although being a volunteer won't help you to pay your bills, the experience will leave you spiritually and emotionally wealthy. In addition, the friendships you build with other volunteers and those that you help can last forever.

Fun Fact

Travel Light

If you're traveling overseas as a volunteer, it's best that you don't bring much, since you'll have to carry it everywhere. You may want to bring, among other things, a flashlight, a travel clock, a good book to read, a waterproof watch, a dictionary for whatever language you will need to speak, and some U.S. postage stamps.

Quote

"Two years in the Peace Corps will change your life. It's the most valuable education you will ever receive."

—M. Markowitz, Peace Corps volunteer, Africa

Related Careers

Anthropologist, doctor, teacher, professor, sociologist, scientist, philosopher, social worker

WAITER

The Basics

A waiter's main responsibilities are to serve and satisfy a restaurant's patrons. And it's not an easy job. Despite the physical stress of being on your feet all day, waiters (the good ones, anyway) must maintain a pleasant attitude. They must also remember many things at once and keep track of all of their customers at any given time. Waiters have to be on their best behavior—their tip depends on it!

Waiters may greet, seat, take food and drink orders, and serve customers. They may also set up tables for customers—providing napkins, plates, glasses, and clean up after them, too. Some restaurants have staff, including busboys and hosts, to help waiters clean up and set tables, as well as seat guests. As a waiter, you'll have to memorize and describe many menu items and specials to be able to explain options to your customers. If you wait tables in a small café, customers will expect speedy service; if you work in an elegant restaurant, customers usually want more time to enjoy their dining experience. If you work in a fancy restaurant, you may make wine suggestions or fill customers in on how certain dishes are prepared.

A friendly personality, pleasant appearance, and great memory serve you well as a waiter. Folks will not only expect you to get their orders and requests right, they will also expect service with a smile. Be prepared to socialize! In addition to talking about the menu, your customers may want to strike up a conversation about something else. Patience is also a crucial trait for a good waiter, since not every customer is a pleasure to deal with.

Preparation

High School

Experience waiting on tables is preferred by restaurants, so try to get a part-time job at a local coffee shop or diner. You will get to meet a lot of folks, earn some money, and have fun, too! Work on improving your memory; some restaurants actually test job applicants to see if they'll be able to remember their menu items. In school, pay attention in English (for communication with customers) and math (you wouldn't want to make any mistakes on patrons' checks). If you have a strong passion in another subject area, study hard. You never know when you will leave the world of waiting tables for your next career!

College

Restaurant employers won't require you to be a college graduate. Still, if you plan to move on to another line of work in the near future, college is highly recommended.

Possible Majors

Culinary arts, hospitality, or any major that suits your interest (if the waiting tables gig is only temporary)

Will I Be Rich?

Expect to be on your feet a lot! Life as a waiter can be hectic. During any given shift, you may take orders, deliver orders, and bring checks to various customers, all at the same time. Many waiters work part-time to earn extra money while pursuing other careers. While you're not likely to earn a lot of money per hour, you can earn a lot in tips; the more expensive the fare on the menu, the more tip money you will likely earn.

Fun Facts

Sweet Tooth, Sweet Tip

If you love when a waiter gives you a piece of candy with your bill, you're not alone! In a study in which waiters served customers a piece of candy with their bill, the customers tipped over 2.7 percent more!

[Source: www.howstuffworks.com]

Stars Who Waited Tables Before They Became Stars

- Kevin Bacon
- Colin Farrell
- Rebecca Gayheart
- Edward Norton
- Brad Pitt
- Frank Sinatra
- Mira Sorvino
- Bruce Willis

Myth v. Reality

Myth: If you are rude to a waiter, he or she will spit in your food.

Reality: While this is possible, it's highly unlikely, considering that kitchens in restaurants are full of watchful eyes. So chances are that the only saliva that will touch your food is your own. Relax and enjoy your meal!

Related Careers

Caterer, chef, baker, restaurateur, flight attendant, hotel manager, tour guide, administrative assistant

WEBSITE DESIGNER AND WEBMASTER

The Basics

For years, the newspaper was the king of the media. People waited for papers to show up at their front step every morning. Radio and television would later supply news more directly. Then the Internet changed everything. The World Wide Web provided a place where people could have immediate access to information and also interact with it. The Internet combines text, graphics, sound, and video into one powerful medium. That's where web designers and webmasters come in!

A *web designer* comes up with the plan for a website. He or she is often hired by a person, company, or organization that would like to make their information available to web surfers. The site has to serve a specific purpose. There are millions of websites on the Internet; why would someone visit one site? For starters, the site has to be well organized, so the person navigating the web page knows where and how to access the information. If it's not efficient, it won't be useful. The site has to be eye-catching and user-friendly, too. If it's not attractive, surfers may not stick around.

A web designer may work with a *webmaster*—the person who maintains the web site. Webmasters are concerned with the technical parts of the website. They make sure that the site functions properly all the time. Both web designers and webmasters need to know how to program in a computer language. (You can design a website by using an easy web design program, but your options will be limited.) In fact, they should be well versed in all sorts of technology. On top of all that, they'll have to be creative and come up with innovative design ideas. For some, the combination of creativity and technical understanding is a match made in Internet heaven.

Preparation

High School

Web designers and webmasters need to be intimately familiar with computer systems and software. So get started! There is so much to learn that it's almost essential to start early. If your school has a computer club, join it and learn from your peers. Design and maintain your own web pages. Make one for your school sports team, for your parents, or for your sibling's school projects. You'll learn from experience.

College

You don't need to study a particular field to be a web designer or webmaster. However, because so much computer knowledge is demanded in the profession, a computer science or programming degree goes a long way. Design is useful too, for obvious reasons. Frankly, any field of study is acceptable, so long as you gain hands-on technical experience. You should even be able to take web design classes at a big university.

Possible Majors

Computer and information science, information technology, computer science, computer engineering

Will I Be Rich?

If you can come up with a good idea for your own website, you could earn a pretty good profit. Designing or maintaining websites for other employers generally pays the bills (though without much hope of real wealth). If you can combine all the elements of a website—planning, designing, and programming—you'll make yourself more desirable to other companies. And then you'll earn better and steadier work.

Fun Fact

Growing Options for Site-seeing

In August 2003, the search engine Google.com found more than 3,083,324,652 web pages on the Internet. That means web designers had to plan and design more than 3 billion different web pages. (And webmasters have to monitor them!) That number is expected to grow, too. Soon there will be more individual web pages than there are people in the world!

Related Careers

Web producer, computer programmer, computer technician, computer scientist, engineer, graphic designer, mathematician, statistician, artist, illustrator

WEB PRODUCER

The Basics

Web producers oversee websites. They are responsible for developing and organizing content (information, articles, pictures, etc.) that appears on a website. Web producers may also work with web designers and computer programmers to create and improve websites that not only communicate important information, but also have cool graphics and a great design.

As a web producer, you will schedule projects for your company's websites and make sure your team meets their deadlines. You may be adding new interactive tools for site visitors, publishing new articles, or posting product descriptions. If anything goes wrong, you fix the problem. A working knowledge of HTML, or Hyper Text Markup Language, is necessary for web producers. (HTML is the common language for publishing on the World Wide Web.) You will also need some editing skills, since you will oversee the text that goes up on the site. Web designers create the graphics and computer programmers will develop the actual code behind the features on the site. It's helpful, though, if you understand the basics of design and programming so you can communicate with your colleagues to get the job done right.

Web producers are detail oriented, organized, and creative. They are able to multitask, while still meeting deadlines. In order to be happy in this career, you will also have to love working with computers and web applications.

Preparation

High School

Surf the web whenever you can. What makes a site fun and cool to use? Ask yourself how you would improve a site that you really like. Take computer classes—learn HTML and some graphics programs. Art and graphic design classes will help develop your visual sensibilities, and English and writing classes will improve your communication skills.

College

Use your college years to explore all the different components that go into web design, including computer science, advertising, marketing, English, and computer programming. Design and maintain your own website(s) if you haven't done so yet. You can make a site for a friend's band or create an online poetry zine.

Possible Majors

Computer and information science, English, English literature, English composition, advertising, journalism, marketing

Will I Be Rich?

If you can deal with the hectic pace and managing multiple projects at once, you can earn a pretty nice living. You can expect to work long hours whenever you are trying to get a new feature on the site up and running within a deadline. Fortunately, you get to see the fruits of your labors published on the web. Since web technology is continuously advancing, you will learn a lot on the job.

Fun Facts

Web Lingo

- Banners *are advertisements on a website that stretch across a page, just like a printed banner.*

- Clipart *is a graphic file that you either buy or download off the Web.*

- A domain *is part of the DNS, or domain name server. Domain names may be .com, .net, .org, .edu, .fr, .uk. The domain name often reflects the type of business or organization that the website represents.*

- *If your website receives a lot of hits, you have reason to celebrate. A* hit *is the unit of measurement Web folks use to keep track of how many people visit a website.*

- A home page *is a website's main page. That's generally where a visitor can find out exactly what's on a site and have access to other pages within the site.*

Related Careers

Computer programmer, computer technician, writer, editor, web designer, advertising executive

WEDDING PLANNER

The Basics

Your main job as a wedding planner will be to help couples plan the best wedding possible within their price range. You will make sure that everything is taken care of at all times, so the couple can relax and have a blast without worrying about anything going wrong. After all, they want to remember their wedding day as the happiest day of their lives—not the embarrassing day when the musicians were late, the food was cold, and the flowers were wilted!

The degree to which a wedding planner actually plans a wedding depends on how much help the bride and groom are looking for. For example, a couple may hire you a year in advance to do everything from finding a gown for the bride to booking flights and hotels for their honeymoon. Another couple may hire you just to plan the wedding party; in this case, you will find the right location and take care of the food, flowers, and music, and possibly the photographer and videographer as well.

Most wedding planners are very outgoing, as excellent social skills are needed to communicate and make arrangements with tons of different people. You must also be able to handle stress well in this profession, and when something goes wrong, you'll need to have a backup plan. In addition, you'll need some excellent business and math skills to be able to negotiate and manage your couple's budget—not an easy task! Your career will depend largely on your reputation, so you want to be sure that each wedding you plan is a success.

Preparation

High School

Join your school's party-planning committee to help plan school dances, bake sales, and other fun events. You can also try organizing these events on your own at school or in the community. Math courses will help prepare you to manage budgets; English will improve your communication skills; and art courses will help sharpen your eye.

College

There are many college courses that will help prepare you for this field, but a degree isn't necessary. Apart from taking basic business classes, you can learn more about the other aspects of wedding preparation—flowers, food, music, and even sociology and psychology.

Possible Majors

Hospitality, communications, business administration, public relations, culinary arts, recreation management, fashion design

Will I Be Rich?

You can earn a lot as a wedding planner; even if you don't, think of all the great parties you'll get to attend. Expect to put in long hours, running around doing ten things at once. A lot of pressure comes with the territory because each couple wants their wedding to be perfect. But if you love to see a plan come together, you will get great satisfaction from planning successful weddings.

Fun Facts

Wedding Cake Rituals Through Time

- Getting hit over the head with a wedding cake doesn't sound like too much fun—especially if you're the bride! Ancient Romans broke cake over the head of the bride as a symbol of fertility.

- The last thing a bride needs on her big day is a case of dandruff. Back in the day, though, many cultures showered a bride's head with wheat, flour, or cake and ate the crumbs for good luck.

- Ever wonder why a wedding cake has so many levels? Rumor has it that in medieval times, wedding guests brought their own small cakes. They were stacked up on a table, and the bride and groom would try to kiss over the tower of cakes. At some point, a baker (who probably couldn't stand looking at the messy medley of cakes) merged them all together with frosting, giving us a layered wedding cake.

[Source: www.bridalassociationofamerica.com]

Related Careers

Publicist, caterer, chef, hotel manager, travel agent, florist

WRITER

The Basics

Writers take thoughts, facts, and ideas and turn them into written text. While all of us learn how to write in school, not all of us become writers—a writer needs to have a special way with words to keep a reader's interest. Writers compose works of fiction and nonfiction for books, newspapers, magazines, journals, brochures, advertisements, or websites.

There are tons of different types of jobs for writers. Screenwriters write for television and film. Novelists write novels, ranging from love stories to mysteries to science fiction. Fiction writers, on one hand, can also write poetry, short stories, or plays. Nonfiction writers, on the other hand, may write magazine and newspaper articles that cover a variety of topics, including health issues, famous celebrities, and scientific discoveries. They also write reviews, instruction manuals, text and slogans for ads and commercials, and guidebooks like this one.

As a writer, you will work with an editor, who will read over and fine-tune your writing. On the one hand, you write for a newspaper or magazine, your editor will often assign writing topics for you; if you write fiction, on the other hand, you will be able to choose your topic. It may be more difficult to get your work published as a fiction author, though—you'll have to convince a publisher to put your writing in print! Many writers hire agents to promote and sell their work to publishers and film companies. Even with the help of an agent, though, you'll need talent, dedication, and perseverance to make it as a writer.

Preparation

High School

Write for the school newspaper and yearbook, and work on your own writing outside of class. Keep a daily journal. Take classes in creative writing, poetry, and literature. Take great care when you write reports for your other classes—this is good practice for writing nonfiction. A typing class wouldn't hurt either, since you'll need to type professional assignments.

College

In college, you'll be able to narrow your focus and concentrate on your favorite type of writing. Write articles, reviews, or stories for your school or local newspaper, and get involved in any creative writing publications the school puts out. An internship in publishing is a great way to get your foot in the door and get a taste for writing under strict deadlines.

Possible Majors

Creative writing, English, English composition, English literature, journalism, music, playwriting and screenwriting, theater

Will I Be Rich?

Top novelists can really rake in the cash, but most writers aren't loaded. Many work on a freelance basis, writing from home for various publications. While this may not provide a steady income, it allows for a great deal of freedom in your schedule. Other writers work for newspapers or magazines and earn a pretty decent salary. Whatever the case, writing usually involves deadlines, and this can be stressful. Sometimes it's hard to rush inspiration! The end product often makes all the trouble worth it.

Fun Facts

Persistence

- Ernest Hemingway tried forty-four different endings for A Farewell to Arms before settling on one that he thought worked well enough.

- F. Scott Fitzgerald's first novel, This Side of Paradise, was rejected two times by Charles Scribner's Sons publishers. When he rewrote and submitted it to the publisher the third time around, it was accepted for publication!

[Source: www.pbs.org]

Quote

"Don't be afraid to fail—especially not in a first draft. Writing fiction is taking risks and then rewriting and rewriting and rewriting what doesn't work."

—David Linker, writer

Related Careers

Editor, journalist, artist, director, producer, actor, professor, teacher

YOGA TEACHER

The Basics

The term yoga refers to a series of stretches and breathing techniques. The word *yoga* means union or connection in Sanskrit, the classical language of ancient India. Since yoga was first practiced centuries ago in India, the names of yoga poses are often in Sanskrit.

When you practice yoga, you connect your body movements with your breathing. This helps you to relax and focus, stay fit, and even increase your flexibility. People of all ages and backgrounds do yoga. Athletes and people recovering from injuries also practice yoga for its healing qualities.

As a yoga teacher, you will spend a lot of time teaching people how to breathe while they are stretching. Since you will interact with a wide range of people in your classes, good communication skills will come in handy. Aside from being attentive, inviting, and knowledgeable about the body, a yoga teacher should be thoughtful and patient. Your days will be pretty active and physical as a yoga teacher, so a healthy lifestyle, including sufficient sleep and a healthy diet, is highly recommended.

Preparation

High School

If your high school offers yoga for gym class, take it! If not, try to set up a weekly or biweekly yoga class after school or check out a yoga video with some friends.

College

You don't need a college degree to be a yoga teacher. But if you plan to pursue another career while teaching, as many yoga teachers do, you may need to go to college. To learn more about yoga, sign up for classes such as biology, community health, human anatomy, human development, first aid, kinesiology (the mechanics of movement), exercise, physiology, and rehabilitation.

Possible Majors

Health administration, human development, human anatomy, kinesiology, physical education, Sanskrit/yoga studies

Training Certification Programs

You'll also need to be certified to teach yoga. Some teacher training programs are full-time programs that last for a month or two, while others are part-time programs that may take anywhere from three months to over a year to complete. During the program, you will study anatomy/physiology, injury management, meditation, Sanskrit, spotting techniques, teaching methodology, breathing exercises, and yogic philosophy (the philosophy of yoga). In addition, you'll have to develop your own yoga practice. Most programs require you to pass an oral and/or written exam to graduate.

Will I Be Rich?

You won't make millions teaching yoga, but you will be spiritually wealthy and you'll have a great time, too! You can work full-time at one yoga studio or health club teaching a few classes a day, or you can teach at multiple studios. Most yoga teachers also teach private classes, which is a great way to supplement your income.

Fun Facts

Madonna, Sting, Cameron Diaz, Jerry Seinfeld, Gwyneth Paltrow, Sarah Jessica Parker, and Willem Dafoe are yogis! (A yogi is someone who practices yoga regularly.)

There are over 908 yoga poses, or asanas. Dharma Mittra, a yogi with a studio in New York City, demonstrated all 908 poses in his famous poster. (He also photographed himself in all of the poses!)

Myth v. Reality

Myth: Yoga teachers can twist their bodies into pretzel shapes.

Reality: Not all yoga teachers are flexible rubber-band people! In fact, physical flexibility is not a requirement for doing yoga.

Quote

"There is no way I could have played as long as I did without yoga. My friends and teammates think I made a deal with the devil. But it was yoga that made my training complete."

—Kareem Abdul-Jabbar, former NBA basketball star

[Source: www.bikramyoga.com/press/press0a.htm]

Related Careers

Artist, Ayurvedic practitioner, dancer, health administration, massage therapist, physical education, physical therapist, rehabilitation services, reflexologist

ZOOKEEPER

The Basics

Zookeepers take care of the animals in the zoo. They feed the animals, groom and bathe them, and keep their living quarters clean and tidy. Zookeepers also keep an eye on the animals' health and happiness, making sure they have a chance to exercise and play. When an animal moves from one home to another, a zookeeper sees to it that it is comfortable in its new home. If one of the animals is acting abnormally, a zookeeper alerts the veterinarian, who can then examine the animal.

As a zookeeper, you may care for lots of different animals, or you may care for a specific breed of animals—it depends on the size of the zoo. You will spend your days caring for the animals and bonding with them, and you'll also answer any questions visitors may have about the animals. An important part of your job is making sure that visitors don't feed or tease the animals. You will have the most contact with the animals, and their well-being depends upon you.

To succeed as a zookeeper, you'll need more than just a love of animals; you also need to have a deep understanding of their behavior and feel comfortable handling them. A zookeeper needs to know what he or she is doing to avoid injury—it can be dangerous cleaning a lion's or bear's cage. Since some of the animals are bigger and stronger than you are, you'll also need to possess a lot of physical strength to handle them properly.

Preparation

High School

Volunteer at a local zoo or at an animal hospital. The more experience you have working with animals, the better. Visit your local zoo often, too, and ask the zookeeper whatever questions you may have about their job. Classes in biology, chemistry, and other sciences will help you prepare for science courses in college.

College

A college degree is necessary to be a zookeeper. But while you are in college studying about animals, be sure to volunteer or get an internship at a zoo, farm, or animal hospital. What you learn in courses in anatomy, biology, chemistry, ecology, genetics, nutrition, and zoology will provide the background knowledge, but you need to interact with animals, too. Some zoos require that their keepers pass written or oral exams, and all zoos have strict physical requirements for their zookeepers, so be sure to stay in good shape.

Animal science, biology, pre-veterinary medicine, wildlife management, zoology, marine biology, conservation biology

Graduate School:

Although your four-year degree will get you in the door as an animal keeper, you'll need an advanced degree and additional training to hold the more coveted positions, like senior keeper, director, or curator.

Will I Be Rich?

A zookeeper's pay isn't outrageous, but money isn't what most zookeepers are after. A true love of working with animals brings people to this career, and most find it very rewarding. Apart from the physical demands of the job, a sick animal in your care will also demand your attention—expect to put in some extra time to make sure the animal is comfortable. If you work at a large zoo, you can advance to senior or head zookeeper over time.

Fun Facts

Young Zookeepers

Lots of zoos have zoo teen programs as well as apprenticeship programs that allow teens to spend time working at the zoo! Check out the following teen programs:

- *Seneca Park Zoo: Rochester, NY*
- *Smithsonian National Zoological Park: Washington, D.C.*
- *San Francisco Zoo: San Francisco, CA*
- *Buffalo Zoo: Buffalo, NY*

That's a Lot of Leaves

Although a diet of grass, leaves, twigs, and fruit may not sound like much to eat, it suits the African elephant just fine! It's hard to believe that the world's largest land animal, the African elephant, is a vegetarian, but it's true!

Related Careers

Farmer, veterinarian, crocodile hunter, park ranger, zoologist, scientist, environmentalist

INDEXES

ALPHABETICAL INDEX

INDEX BY CAREER TYPE

Education and Related Fields

Entertainment

Fine Art, Fashion, and Design

Math, Science, and Technology

Other

Publicity and Planning

Real Estate, Tourism, and Transportation

Retail and Customer Service

Social Sciences and Service

Sports and Fitness

ABOUT THE AUTHORS

A few months prior to embarking on this project, **Jodi Weiss** left her career in publishing to pursue her very own dream careers. She is currently a freelance author, an adjunct literature and creative writing professor at a number of New York City colleges and universities, and a yoga teacher. Jodi's own career journey is far from over; in fact, at present, she is gearing up to move into her next career as a literary agent!

Russell Kahn has been an über utility-man for The Princeton Review for more than four years, developing several book series, editing many books, and writing a couple of the most fun ones. Although the New York native doesn't play for the Yankees, he loves his job anyway.

Notes

Notes

Notes

Graduate School Entrance Tests

Business School
Is an MBA in your future? If so, you'll need to take the GMAT. The GMAT is a computer-based test offered year round, on most days of the week. October and November are the most popular months for testing appointments. Most business schools require you to have a few years of work experience before you apply, but that doesn't mean you should put off taking the GMAT. Scores are valid for up to five years, so you should take the test while you're still in college and in the test-taking frame of mind.

Law School
If you want to be able to call yourself an "esquire", you'll need to take the LSAT. Most students take the LSAT in the fall of their senior year—either the October or the December administration. The test is also offered in February and in June. The June test is the only afternoon administration – so if your brain doesn't start functioning until the P.M., this might be the one for you. Just make sure to take it in June of your junior year if you want to meet the application deadlines.

Medical School
The MCAT is offered twice each year, in April and in August. It's a beastly eight-hour exam, but it's a necessary evil if you want to become a doctor. Since you'll need to be familiar with the physics, chemistry, and biology tested on the exam, you'll probably want to wait until April of your junior year to take the test— that's when most students take the MCAT. If you wait until August to give it a shot, you'll still be able to meet application deadlines, but you won't have time to take it again if you're not satisfied with your results.

Other Graduate and Ph.D. Programs
For any other graduate or Ph.D. program, be it art history or biochemical engineering, you'll need to take the GRE General Test. This is another computer-based test, and, like the GMAT, it's offered year-round on most days of the week. The most popular test dates are in late summer and in the fall. Take the test no later than October or November before you plan to enter graduate school to ensure that you meet all application deadlines (and the all-important financial aid deadlines) and to leave yourself some room to take it again if you're not satisfied with your scores.

Understanding the Tests

MCAT

Structure and Format

The Medical College Admission Test (MCAT) is a six-hour paper-and-pencil exam that can take up to eight or nine hours to administer.

The MCAT consists of four scored sections that always appear in the same order:

1. Physical Sciences: 100 minutes; 77 physics and general chemistry questions

2. Verbal Reasoning: 85 minutes; 60 questions based on nine passages

3. Writing Sample: two 30-minute essays

4. Biological Sciences: 100 minutes; 77 biology and organic chemistry questions

Scoring

The Physical Sciences, Biological Sciences, and Verbal Reasoning sections are each scored on a scale of 1 to 15, with 8 as the average score. These scores will be added together to form your Total Score. The Writing Sample is scored from J (lowest) to T (highest), with O as the average score.

Test Dates

The MCAT is offered twice each year—in April and August.

Registration

The MCAT is administered and scored by the MCAT Program Office under the direction of the AAMC. To request a registration packet, you can write to the MCAT Program Office,
P.O. Box 4056, Iowa City, Iowa 52243
or call 319-337-1357.

GRE

Structure and Format

The Graduate Record Examinations (GRE) General Test is a multiple-choice test for applicants to graduate school that is taken on computer. It is a computer-adaptive test (CAT), consisting of three sections.

- One 30-minute, 30-question "Verbal Ability" (vocabulary and reading) section

- One 45-minute, 28-question "Quantitative Ability" (math) section

- An Analytical Writing Assessment, consisting of two essay tasks

    o One 45-minute "Analysis of an Issue" task

    o One 30-minute "Analysis of an Argument" task

The GRE is a computer-adaptive test, which means that it uses your performance on previous questions to determine which question you will be asked next. The software calculates your score based on the number of questions you answer correctly, the difficulty of the questions you answer, and the number of questions you complete. Questions that appear early in the test impact your score to a greater degree than do those that come toward the end of the exam.

Scoring

You will receive a Verbal score and a Math score, each ranging from 200 to 800, as well as an Analytic Writing Assessment (AWA) score ranging from 0 to 6.

Test Dates

The GRE is offered year-round in testing centers, by appointment.

Registration

To register for the GRE, call 1-800-GRE-CALL or register online at www.GRE.org.

Understanding the Tests

LSAT

Structure and Format
The Law School Admission Test (LSAT) is a four-hour exam comprised of five 35-minute multiple-choice test sections of approximately 25 questions each, plus an essay:

- Reading Comprehension (1 section)
- Analytical Reasoning (1 section)
- Logical Reasoning (2 sections)
- Experimental Section (1 section)

Scoring
- Four of the five multiple-choice sections count toward your final LSAT score
- The fifth multiple-choice section is an experimental section used solely to test new questions for future exams
- Correct responses count equally and no points are deducted
  for incorrect or blank responses
- Test takers get a final, scaled score between 120 and 180
- The essay is not scored, and is rarely used to evaluate your candidacy by admissions officers

Test Dates
The LSAT is offered four times each year—in February, June, October, and December.

Registration
To register for the LSAT, visit www.LSAC.org to order a registration book or to register online.

GMAT

Structure and Format
The Graduate Management Admission Test (GMAT) is a multiple-choice test for applicants to business school that is taken on computer. It is a computer-adaptive test (CAT), consisting of three sections:

- Two 30-minute essays to be written on the computer: Analysis of an Argument and Analysis of an Issue
- One 75-minute, 37-question Math section: Problem Solving and Data Sufficiency
- One 75-minute, 41-question Verbal section: Sentence Corrections, Critical Reasoning, and Reading Comprehension

The GMAT is a computer-adaptive test, which means that it uses your performance on previous questions to determine which question you will be asked next. The software calculates your score based on the number of questions you answer correctly, the difficulty of the questions you answer, and the number of questions you complete. Questions that appear early in the test impact your score to a greater degree than do those that come toward the end of the exam.

Scoring
You will receive a composite score ranging from 200 to 800 in 10-point increments, in addition to a Verbal score and a Math score, each ranging from 0 to 60. You will also receive an Analytic Writing Assessment (AWA) score ranging from 0 to 6.

Test Dates
The GMAT is offered year-round in testing centers, by appointment.

Registration
To register for the GMAT, call 1-800-GMAT-NOW or register online at www.MBA.com.

Dispelling the Myths about Test Preparation and Admissions

MYTH: If you have a solid GPA, your test score isn't as important for getting into a college or graduate school.

FACT: While it is true that admissions committees consider several factors in their admissions decisions, including test scores, GPA, work or extra-curricular experience, and letters of recommendation, it is not always true that committees will overlook your test scores if you are strong in other areas. Particularly for large programs with many applicants, standardized tests are often the first factor that admissions committees use to evaluate prospective students.

MYTH: Standardized exams test your basic skills or innate ability; therefore your score cannot be significantly improved through studying.

FACT: Nothing could be farther from the truth. You can benefit tremendously from exposure to actual tests and expert insight into the test writers' habits and the most commonly used tricks.

MYTH: There are lots of skills you can learn to help you improve your math score, but you can't really improve your verbal score.

FACT: The single best way to improve your verbal score is to improve your vocabulary. Question types in the verbal reasoning sections of standardized tests all rely upon your understanding of the words in the questions and answer choices. If you know what the words mean, you'll be able to answer the questions quickly and accurately. Improving your critical reading skills is also very important.

MYTH: Standardized exams measure your intelligence.

FACT: While test scores definitely matter, they do NOT test your intelligence. The scores you achieve reflect only how prepared you were to take that particular exam and how good a test taker you are.

Hyperlearning *MCAT Prep Course*

The Princeton Review Difference
Nearly 40% of all MCAT test takers take the exam twice due to inadequate preparation the first time. **Do not be one of them.**

Our Approach to Mastering the MCAT
You will need to conquer both the verbal and the science portions of the MCAT to get your best score. But it might surprise you to learn that the Verbal Reasoning and Writing Sample are the most important sub-sections on the test. That is why we dedicate twice as much class time to these sections as does any other national course! We will help you to develop superlative reading and writing skills so you will be ready to write well crafted, concise essay responses. And of course, we will also help you to develop a thorough understanding of the basic science concepts and problem-solving techniques that you will need to ace the MCAT.

Total Preparation: 41 Class Sessions
With 41 class sessions, our MCAT course ensures that you will be prepared and confident by the time you take the test.

The Most Practice Materials
You will receive more than 3,000 pages of practice materials and 1,300 pages of supplemental materials, and all are yours to keep. Rest assured that our material is always fresh. Each year we write a new set of practice passages to reflect the style and content of the most recent tests. You will also take five full-length practice MCATs under actual testing conditions, so you can build your test-taking stamina and get used to the time constraints.

Specialist Instructors
Your course will be led by a team of between two and five instructors—each an expert in his or her specific subjects. Our instructors are carefully screened and undergo a rigorous national training program. In fact, the quality of our instructors is a major reason students recommend our course to their friends.

Get the Score You Want
We guarantee you will be completely satisfied with your MCAT score!* Our students boast an average MCAT score improvement of ten points.**

*If you attend all class sessions, complete all tests and homework, finish the entire course, take the MCAT at the next administration and do not void your test, and you still are not satisfied with your score, we will work with you again at no additional cost for one of the next two MCAT administrations.

**Independently verified by International Communications Research.

ClassSize-8 *Classroom Courses for the GRE, LSAT, and GMAT*

Small Classes

We know students learn better in smaller classes. With no more than eight students in a Princeton Review class, your instructor knows who you are, and works closely with you to identify your strengths and weaknesses. You will be as prepared as possible. When it comes to your future, you shouldn't be lost in a crowd of students.

Guaranteed Satisfaction

A prep course is a big investment—in terms of both time and money. At The Princeton Review, your investment will pay off. Our LSAT students improve by an average of 7 points, our GRE students improve by an average of 212 points, and our GMAT students boast an average score improvement of 92.5 points—the best score improvement in the industry.* We guarantee that you will be satisfied with your results. If you're not, we'll work with you again for free.**

Expert Instructors

Princeton Review instructors are energetic and smart—they've all scored in the 95th percentile or higher on standardized tests. Our instructors will make your experience engaging and effective.

Free Extra Help

We want you to get your best possible score on the test. If you need extra help on a particular topic, your instructor is happy to meet with you outside of class to make sure you are comfortable with the material—at no extra charge!

Online Lessons, Tests, and Drills

Princeton Review *ClassSize-8* Courses are the only classroom courses that have online lessons designed to support each class session. You can practice concepts you learn in class, spend some extra time on topics that you find challenging, or prepare for an upcoming class. And you'll have access as soon as you enroll, so you can get a head start on your test preparation.

The Most Comprehensive, Up-to-Date Materials

Our research and development team studies the tests year-round to stay on top of trends and to make sure you learn what you need to get your best score.

*Independently verified by International Communications Research (ICR).
**Some restrictions apply.

Online *and* LiveOnline *Courses for the GRE, LSAT, and GMAT*

The Best of Both Worlds
We've combined our high-quality, comprehensive test preparation with a convenient, multimedia format that works around your schedule and your needs.

Online *and* LiveOnline *Courses*
Lively, Engaging Lessons
If you think taking an online course means staring at a screen and struggling to pay attention, think again. Our lessons are engaging and interactive – you'll never just read blocks of text or passively watch video clips. Princeton Review online courses feature animation, audio, interactive lessons, and self-directed navigation.

Customized, Focused Practice
The course software will discover your personal strengths and weaknesses. It will help you to prioritize and focus on the areas that are most important to your success. Of course, you'll have access to dozens of hours' worth of lessons and drills covering all areas of the test, so you can practice as much or as little as you choose.

Help at your Fingertips
Even though you'll be working on your own, you won't be left to fend for yourself. We're ready to help at any time of the day or night: you can chat online with a live Coach, check our Frequently Asked Questions database, or talk to other students in our discussion groups.

LiveOnline *Course*
Extra Features
In addition to self-directed online lessons, practice tests, drills, and more, you'll participate in five live class sessions and three extra help sessions given in real time over the Internet. You'll get the live interaction of a classroom course from the comfort of your own home.

ExpressOnline *Course*
The Best in Quick Prep
If your test is less than a month away, or you just want an introduction to our legendary strategies, this mini-course may be the right choice for you. Our multimedia lessons will walk you through basic test-taking strategies to give you the edge you need on test day.

1-2-1 *Private Tutoring*

The Ultimate in Personalized Attention

If you're too busy for a classroom course, prefer learning at your kitchen table, or simply want your instructor's undivided attention,
1-2-1 Private Tutoring may be for you.

Focused on You

In larger classrooms, there is always one student who monopolizes the instructor's attention. With *1-2-1* Private Tutoring, that student is you. Your instructor will tailor the course to your needs – greater focus on the subjects that cause you trouble, and less focus on the subjects that you're comfortable with. You can get all the instruction you need in less time than you would spend in a class.

Expert Tutors

Our outstanding tutoring staff is comprised of specially selected, rigorously trained instructors who have performed exceptionally in the classroom. They have scored in the top percentiles on standardized tests and received the highest student evaluations.

Schedules to Meet Your Needs

We know you are busy, and preparing for the test is perhaps the last thing you want to do in your "spare" time. The Princeton Review
1-2-1 Private Tutoring Program will work around your schedule.

Additional Online Lessons and Resources

The learning continues outside of your tutoring sessions. Within the Online Student Center*, you will have access to math, verbal, AWA, and general strategy lessons to supplement your private instruction. Best of all, they are accessible to you 24 hours a day,
7 days a week.

*Available for LSAT, GRE, and GMAT

www.PrincetonReview.com

The Princeton Review
Admissions Ser vices

At The Princeton Review, we care about your ability to get accepted to the best school for you. But, we all know getting accepting involves much more than just doing well on standardized tests. That's why, in addition to our test preparation services, we also offer free admissions services to students looking to enter college or graduate school. You can find these services on our website, *www.PrincetonReview.com*, the best online resource for researching, applying to, and learning how to pay for the right school for you.

No matter what type of program you're applying to—undergraduate, graduate, law, business, or medical—**PrincetonReview.com has the free tools, services, and advice you need to navigate the admissions process.** Read on to learn more about the services we offer.

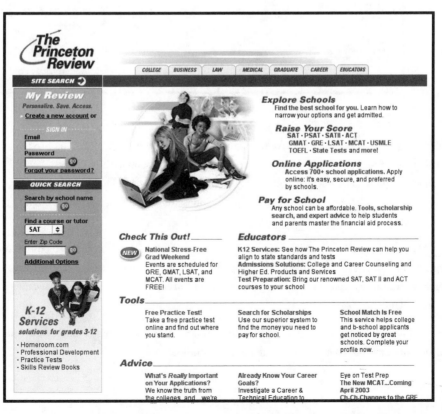

Research Schools
www.PrincetonReview.com/Research

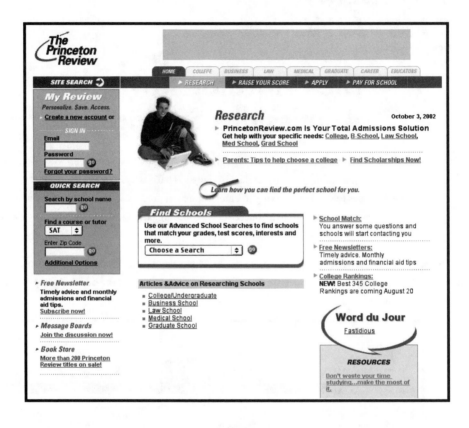

PrincetonReview.com features an interactive tool called **Counselor-O-Matic.** When you use this tool, you enter stats and information about yourself to find a list of your best match schools, reach schools, and safety schools. From there you can read statistical and editorial information about thousands of colleges and universities. In addition, you can find out what currently enrolled college students say about their schools. Once you complete Counselor-O-Matic make sure you opt in to School Match so that colleges can come to you.

Our **College Majors Search** is one of the most popular features we offer. Here you can read profiles on hundreds of majors to find information on curriculum, salaries, careers, and the appropriate high school preparation, as well as colleges that offer it. From the Majors Search, you can investigate corresponding Careers, read **Career Profiles**, and learn what career is the best match for you by taking our **Career Quiz**.

No matter what type of school or specialized program you are considering, **PrincetonReview.com has free articles and advice, in addition to our tools, to help you make the right choice.**

Apply to School
www.PrincetonReview.com/Apply

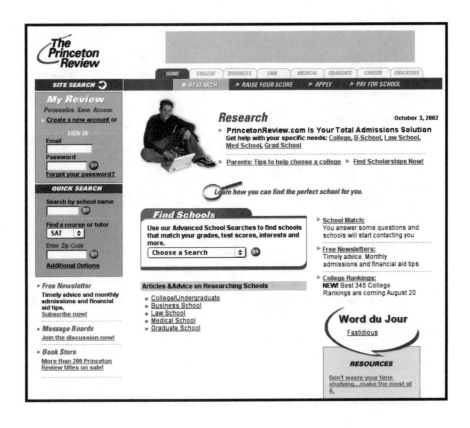

For most students, completing the school application is the most stressful part of the admissions process. PrincetonReview.com's powerful **Online School Application Engine** makes it easy to apply.

Paper applications are mostly a thing of the past. And, our hundreds of partner schools tell us they prefer to receive your applications online.

Using our online application service is simple:

- Enter information once and the common data automatically transfers onto each application.
- Save your applications and access them at any time to edit and perfect.
- Submit electronically or print and mail in.
- Pay your application fee online, using an e-check, or mail the school a check.

Our powerful application engine is built to accommodate all your needs.

Pay for School
www.PrincetonReview.com/Finance

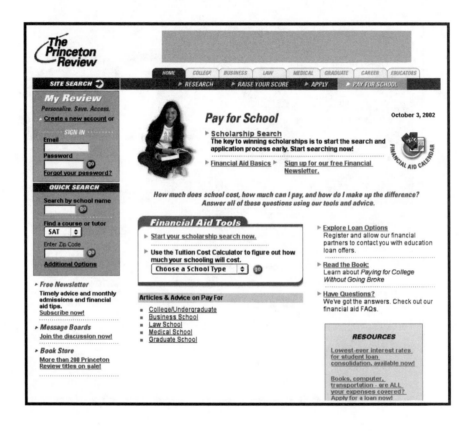

The financial aid process is confusing for everyone. But don't worry. Our free online tools, services, and advice can help you plan for the future and get the money you need to pay for school.

Our **Scholarship Search** engine will help you find free money, although often scholarships alone won't cover the cost of high tuitions. So, we offer other tools and resources to help you navigate the entire process.

Filling out the FAFSA and CSS PROFILE can be a daunting process, use our **Strategies for both forms** to make sure you answer the questions correctly the first time.

If scholarships and government aid aren't enough to swing the cost of tuition, we'll help you secure student loans. The Princeton Review has partnered with a select group of reputable financial institutions who will help **explore all your loans options**.

If you know how to work the financial aid process, you'll learn you don't have to **eliminate a school based on tuition.**

Be a Part of the PrincetonReview.com Community

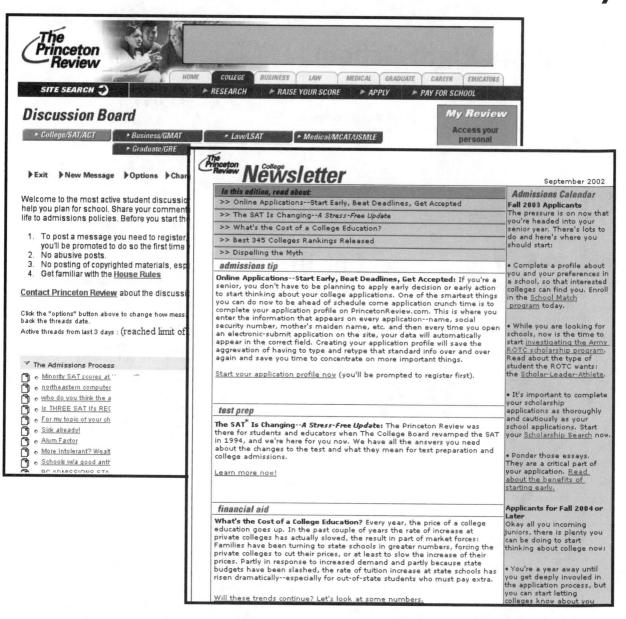

PrincetonReview.com's **Discussion Boards** and **Free Newsletters** are additional services to help you to get information about the admissions process from your peers and from The Princeton Review experts.

Find the Right School

BEST 357 COLLEGES
2005 EDITION
0-375-76405-4 • $21.95

COMPLETE BOOK OF COLLEGES
2005 EDITION
0-375-76406-2 • $26.95

AMERICA'S BEST VALUE COLLEGES
0-375-76373-2 • $15.95

VISITING COLLEGE CAMPUSES
7TH EDITION
0-375-76400-3 • $20.00

Get in

CRACKING THE NEW SAT
2005 EDITION
0-375-76428-3 • $19.95

CRACKING THE NEW SAT
WITH SAMPLE TESTS ON CD-ROM
2005 EDITION
0-375-76429-1 • $31.95

MATH WORKOUT FOR THE NEW SAT
0-375-76433-X • $14.95

VERBAL WORKOUT FOR THE NEW SAT
0-375-76431-3• $14.95

11 PRACTICE TESTS
FOR THE NEW SAT & PSAT
0-375-76434-8• $19.95

CRACKING THE ACT
2004 EDITION
0-375-76395-3 • $19.00

CRACKING THE ACT WITH
SAMPLE TESTS ON CD-ROM
2004 EDITION
0-375-76394-5 • $29.95

CRASH COURSE FOR THE ACT
2ND EDITION
The Last-Minute Guide to Scoring High
0-375-76364-3 • $9.95

CRASH COURSE FOR THE SAT
2ND EDITION
The Last-Minute Guide to Scoring High
0-375-76361-9 • $9.95

Get Help Paying for it

DOLLARS & SENSE FOR COLLEGE STUDENTS
How Not to Run Out of Money by Midterms
0-375-75206-4 • $10.95

PAYING FOR COLLEGE WITHOUT GOING BROKE
2005 EDITION
0-375-76421-6 • $20.00

THE SCHOLARSHIP ADVISOR
5TH EDITION
0-375-76210-8 • $26.00

Make the Grade with Study Guides for the AP and SAT II Exams

AP Exams

CRACKING THE AP BIOLOGY
2004-2005 EDITION
0-375-76393-7 • $18.00

CRACKING THE AP CALCULUS
AB & BC
2004-2005 EDITION
0-375-76381-3 • $19.00

CRACKING THE AP CHEMISTRY
2004-2005 EDITION
0-375-76382-1• $18.00

CRACKING THE AP COMPUTER SCIENCE
AB & BC
2004-2005 EDITION
0-375-76383-X• $19.00

CRACKING THE AP ECONOMICS
(MACRO & MICRO)
2004-2005 EDITION
0-375-76384-8 • $18.00

CRACKING THE AP ENGLISH
LITERATURE
2004-2005 EDITION
0-375-76385-6 • $18.00

CRACKING THE AP
EUROPEAN HISTORY
2004-2005 EDITION

0-375-76386-4 • $18.00

CRACKING THE AP PHYSICS B & C
2004-2005 EDITION
0-375-76387-2 • $19.00

CRACKING THE AP PSYCHOLOGY
2004-2005 EDITION
0-375-76388-0 • $18.00

CRACKING THE AP SPANISH
2004-2005 EDITION
0-375-76389-9 • $18.00

CRACKING THE AP STATISTICS
2004-2005 EDITION
0-375-76390-2 • $19.00

CRACKING THE AP U.S. GOVERNMENT
AND POLITICS
2004-2005 EDITION
0-375-76391-0 • $18.00

CRACKING THE AP U.S. HISTORY
2004-2005 EDITION
0-375-76392-9 • $18.00

CRACKING THE AP WORLD HISTORY
2004-2005 EDITION
0-375-76380-5 • $18.00

SAT II Exams

CRACKING THE SAT II: BIOLOGY
2003-2004 EDITION
0-375-76294-9 • $18.00

CRACKING THE SAT II: CHEMISTRY
2003-2004 EDITION
0-375-76296-5 • $17.00

CRACKING THE SAT II: FRENCH
2003-2004 EDITION
0-375-76295-7 • $17.00

CRACKING THE SAT II:
WRITING & LITERATURE
2003-2004 EDITION
0-375-76301-5 • $17.00

CRACKING THE SAT II: MATH
2003-2004 EDITION
0-375-76298-1 • $18.00

CRACKING THE SAT II: PHYSICS
2003-2004 EDITION
0-375-76299-X • $18.00

CRACKING THE SAT II: SPANISH
2003-2004 EDITION
0-375-76300-7 • $17.00

CRACKING THE SAT II:
U.S. & WORLD HISTORY
2003-2004 EDITION
0-375-76297-3 • $18.00

Available at Bookstores Everywhere.
www.PrincetonReview.com

Book Store
www.PrincetonReview.com/college/Bookstore.asp

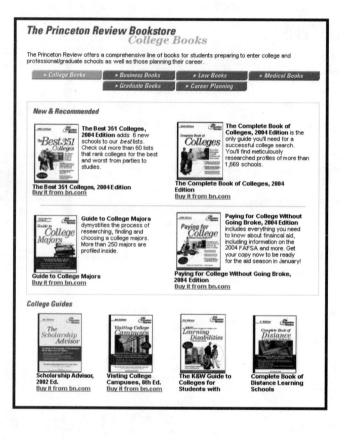

In addition to this book, we publish hundreds of other titles, including guidebooks that highlight life on campus, student opinion, and all the statistical data that you need to know about any school you are considering. Just a few of the titles that we offer are:

- Complete Book of Business Schools
- Complete Book of Law Schools
- Complete Book of Medical Schools
- The Best 351 Colleges
- The K&W Guide to Colleges for Students with Learning Disabilities or Attention Deficit Disorder
- Guide to College Majors
- Paying for College Without Going Broke

For a complete listing of all of our titles, visit our **online book store**:
www.princetonreview.com/college/bookstore.asp